HOLLYWOOD ASIAN

HYE SEUNG CHUNG

HOLLYWOOD
ASIAN

Philip Ahn and the Politics of
Cross-Ethnic Performance

TEMPLE UNIVERSITY PRESS
Philadelphia

Publication of this book was made possible by a generous grant from the Korea Foundation.

 Korea Foundation

한국국제교류재단

TEMPLE UNIVERSITY PRESS
1601 North Broad Street
Philadelphia PA 19122
www.temple.edu/tempress

Copyright © 2006 by Temple University
All rights reserved
Published 2006
Printed in the United States of America
Text design by Kate Nichols

Frontispiece photo: Philip Ahn, c. 1938. Photo credit, John Reed. Courtesy of the Ahn Family.

"Portrait of a Patriot's Son: Philip Ahn and Korean Diasporic Identities in Hollywood," previously appeared in *Cinema Journal*, Vol. 45, No. 2 (Winter 2006). Revised version reprinted in Chapter 1 by permission of University of Texas Press.

Portions of "Between Yellowphilia and Yellowphobia: Asian American Romance in Oriental Detective Films," previously appeared in *East Main Street: Asian American Popular Culture* (New York: New York University Press, 2005). Revised version reprinted in Chapter 3 by permission of the publisher.

Portions of "Hollywood Goes to Korea: War, Melodrama, and the Biopic Politics of Battle Hymn," previously appeared in *Historical Journal of Film, Radio and Television*, Vol. 25, No. 1 (March 2005). Revised version reprinted in Chapter 5 by permission of the editor.

♾ The paper used in this publication meets the requirements of the American National Standard for Information Sciences—Permanence of Paper for Printed Library Materials, ANSI Z39.48-1992

Library of Congress Cataloging-in-Publication Data

Chung, Hye Seung, 1971–
  Hollywood Asian : Philip Ahn and the politics of cross-ethnic performance
/ Hye Seung Chung.
    p. cm.
  Filmography:
  Includes bibliographical references and index.
  ISBN 1–59213–515–3 (hardcover : alk. paper) — ISBN 1–59213–516–1 (pbk. : alk. paper)
  1. Asians in motion pictures. 2. Asian Americans in motion pictures. 3. Motion pictures—United States—History. 4. Ahn, Philip, 1905–1978. I. Title.
  PN1995.9.A78C58 2006
  791.43'6529957—dc22   2006010401

2 4 6 8 9 7 5 3 1

To

all pioneering Asian American actors and actresses

whose struggles, spirits, and legacies have been

undeservingly forgotten

CONTENTS

ACKNOWLEDGMENTS

I WOULD LIKE TO BEGIN by expressing my gratitude to the many professors at the Univerity of California, Los Angeles, whom I have been fortunate to know, particularly my dissertation committee members—Chon A. Noriega, Nick Browne, Peter Wollen, and Shu-mei Shih—for inspiring me with their insights and encouragement. A special debt of gratitude goes to my advisor, Chon, who helped shape the structure of this project and provided me intelligent and timely feedback at the various stages of writing. Kathleen McHugh (UCLA) and Nancy Abelmann (University of Illinois) have both offered the kind of professional support and personal care so essential to the advancement of my academic career. I feel very privileged to have known them and hope to reciprocate their unflagging support in the near future.

Brian Taves at the Library of Congress read the entire manuscript, made innumerable helpful suggestions, inspired me with his knowledge and enthusiasm, and encouraged my writing with his generous praise. David Scott Diffrient, my colleague, husband, and best friend, painstakingly proofread every page of the manuscript, immensely improved it with many wonderful suggestions, and helped me through difficult times with his love and understanding. His intellectual and emotional support was indispensable not only to the completion of this project but also for my personal well-being.

Many people and institutions helped bring this book to fruition. Foremost among them are members of the Ahn family (Susan, Ralph, Flip, and Peter) who shared memories of Philip Ahn with me. Susan has been especially welcoming during my repeated research visits to her San Fernando Valley home. My book is greatly indebted to her preservation of the family archive and her openness in providing assistance to researchers. In the final stage of my writing, Ralph—with the help of his sister, Soorah—was very helpful in filling in many details about Philip's life that were otherwise unavailable to me. I am also grateful to all the archivists and librarians who helped with my research—those professionals at the Margaret Herrick Library, the UCLA Arts Library Special Collection, and the USC Korean Heritage Library (Los Angeles); the New York Public Library for Performing Arts and the Film Study Center of the Museum of Modern Art (New York City); the Library of Congress (Washington, D.C.); the National Archives and Records Administration (College Park, Maryland); the Center for the Study of the Korean War (Independence, Missouri); and the Library of National Assembly (Seoul, South Korea).

I wish to acknowledge the institutional support provided by the Department of Asian Languages and Cultures and the Korean Studies Program at the University of Michigan where I worked as a postdoctoral fellow for three academic years (2003–2006). In particular, I appreciate the support and friendship of my former colleagues Meredith Woo-Cumings, Kristy Demas, Henry Em, Sunyoung Park, and Yunah Sung.

This project was made possible by research grants and fellowships from the Freeman Foundation, the UCLA Institute of American Culture, and the Plitt Southern Theater Employees Trust. I especially want to thank the editors at Temple University Press for their faith in my book, and the Korea Foundation for a generous publication subsidy.

Last, but not least, I would like to thank my family members and friends in both Korea and the United States. In particular, I am grateful for the unwavering love and support of my parents, my sister Hye-Uk, and my parents-in-law Donna and Harry Diffrient.

INTRODUCTION

The Life and Death of a Hollywood Asian

G RACING THE COVER OF THIS BOOK is an image of a "Hollywood Asian" whose face may be familiar to many classic film fans but whose name may escape some of them. The performer in question is Philip Ahn (1905–1978), a prominent Korean American character actor of classical Hollywood cinema who portrayed a diverse cross-section of roles in over 200 films and television programs[1]—from the first Asian American romantic hero of the sound era in Paramount's *Daughter of Shanghai* (1937) to sadistic Japanese officers in World War II propaganda films; from a wronged Chinese merchant in an episode of NBC's *Bonanza* (1950–1973) to a superstitious South Korean farmer in an episode of CBS's M*A*S*H (1972–1983). Despite his reputation as one of the finest supporting actors in the history of American motion pictures and television, Ahn's career has largely been neglected in cinema studies, mentioned only in passing within the critical confines of World War II film studies and Anna May Wong biographies.

Nevertheless, Philip Ahn is posthumously enjoying a sort of cult stardom among film buffs, fans, and critics who have a vested interest in overlooked genres and early Asian American screen icons. Charlie Chan fans rhapsodize about the radical difference between Ahn's two roles in the series—the amiable yet nerdy son-in-law Wing Fu of Sidney Toler's Chan in 20th Century-Fox's *Charlie Chan in Honolulu* (1938) and the shrewd, sinister murder suspect Captain Kong in Monogram's *The Chinese Ring* (1947). Anna May Wong aficionados remember Ahn for playing opposite the Chinese American goddess, who was rumored to be his real-life romantic partner. For American war-film specialists, Philip Ahn is "the most sought-after villain of all, with his nasal, flat voice and his masklike face that looked as if it had been carved out of India rubber."[2] Fans of the ABC television series *Kung Fu* (1972–1975) remember him as Master Kan, who tests young Caine, the Eurasian protagonist, with a physical/philosophical mind game: "As quickly as you can...snatch the pebble from my hand.... When you can take the pebble from my hand, it will be time for you to leave." This celebrated scene from the pilot episode was habitually repeated in the credit sequence throughout the series' first-season run, making Ahn's phrase, "Snatch the pebble from my hand," one of the most frequently quoted lines of the 1970s.

Some readers might wonder why there should be a book-length treatment of an actor who, with few exceptions, played bit parts and secondary roles in classical Hollywood films and television programs. Let me first define the premise and purpose of this book to avoid any misunderstanding. Put bluntly, this is *not* a biography of Philip Ahn, although I do provide substantial details of his life and career. It is, rather, a discursive critical biography of a "Hollywood Asian," one that highlights Ahn's career as an anchoring case study while tracing the trajectory of Asian and Asian American representations from the 1930s to the 1970s within broader historical, industrial, and cultural contexts, as well as providing theoretical examinations of cross-ethnic performativity and bicultural spectatorship. The value of Ahn's career for this particular study is thus not measured by the size of his roles, the length of his screen time, or the extent of his stardom, but rather by its functionality as an indicator of what types of roles were allowed and disallowed for Asian American actors at given historical periods and how depictions of Asia in American film and television were transformed over the course of four decades.

In his entry on Asian Americans in *The Columbia Companion to American History on Film*, Terry Hong lists Philip Ahn along with Sessue Hayakawa and Anna May Wong as one of "three Asian American actors [who] managed to establish long-standing careers during the twentieth century," attesting to his canonical place in the history of Asian Americans in Hollywood.[3] Ahn remains a true pioneer, one of the few performers of Asian descent to survive the racist casting politics of studio-era filmmaking and make a successful transition to the Television Age. Although more iconic Asian American stars existed in the silent period (Tsuru Aoki and Hayakawa) and during the Cold War era (Nancy Kwan and James Shigeta), the longevity of Ahn's acting career (1935–1978) and the sheer diversity of his cross-ethnic roles qualify him as a uniquely emblematic yet distinct Hollywood "Oriental" deserving of close scrutiny. At various junctures in his career, Philip Ahn embodied all six faces of the Oriental as delineated by Robert G. Lee—the pollutant, the coolie, the deviant, the yellow peril, the model minority, and the gook.[4] In other words, his bottom-feeder status in the industry's racially stratified star system was determined by and reflective of the marginalization of Asian identities in American culture and society in general.

Ahn had landed his first movie parts and was most active during the studio system era of the 1930s and the 1940s. Before the consolidation of the studio system, the zenith of American Orientalism in the nascent consumer culture of the 1910s and 1920s was partly responsible for Japanese immigrant Sessue Hayakawa's transnational stardom in silent cinema.; after the studio era, the political and diplomatic necessity for egalitarian racial representations in Cold War-era neoliberal America made starring roles available for Hawaiian-born Japanese American actor James Shigeta during the 1950s and 1960s. In contrast, during the 1930s and 1940s, major Asian roles were played by Caucasian stars (such as Katharine Hepburn, Walter Huston, Boris Karloff, Peter Lorre, Paul Muni, Warner Oland, Luise Rainer, Edward G. Robinson, Myrna Loy, and Loretta Young) in yellowface, and only minor or character parts were available to real Asian American actors. Dozens of Asian American actors emerging from the studio era (including Philip Ahn, Benson Fong, Richard Loo, Keye Luke, and Victor Sen Yung) had to take on a large number of small or seemingly inconsequential roles because of systematized racial exclusion, not because of any lack of talent.

Ahn's pioneering status in Asian American screen culture is not the only reason why his career is worthy of special attention. As one of the first American citizens born to Korean parents and the eldest son of celebrated patriot An Ch'ang-ho (who led the Korean independence movement against Japanese colonial rule), Philip Ahn is a figure of paramount importance in Korean American history. Although other Korean American bit actors and extras (including Ahn's younger brother Philson, Methodist Minister Keye Chang, Hawaii-born night club dancer Suzanna Kim, and future California Senator Alfred H. Song)[5] occasionally appeared in studio-era films, and although talented Korean immigrant actors, such as Soon-Tek Oh and Johnny Yune, broke into the television industry during the 1970s and the 1980s, no other performer of Korean descent was able to match Philip Ahn's status as the "Number One Korean" in Hollywood.

As the first book-length treatment of a Korean presence in classical Hollywood cinema, this volume not only addresses Ahn's specific Korean roles and his displaced manifestations of diasporic identity in cross-ethnic performance but also charts out histories and genealogies of Korean representations dating back to World War II-era films. I also posit Philip Ahn as the object of a transnational study and highlight his lifelong struggle to bridge the American and Korean film industries through his political connections to his parental homeland. This book thus explores the complexity and richness of Ahn's hyphenated identity and border crossing legacy by framing it in the interstitial space of Korean diaspora and Asian America. This particular focus highlights the interdisciplinary nature of the project, which traverses the boundaries of film studies, Korean studies, Asian American studies, ethnic studies, and cultural studies.

Focusing my study of Hollywood's racial politics through the lens of the Korean American pioneer's career functions as a practical means to supplement two particular aspects lacking in scholarship in the field. Over the past three decades, only a handful of publications on the representation of Asians and Asian Americans have been published. Notable titles include Eugene Franklin Wong's *On Visual Media Racism* (1978), Gina Marchetti's *Romance and the "Yellow Peril"* (1993), Darrell Y. Hamamoto's *Monitored Peril: Asian Americans and the Politics of TV Representation* (1994), Jun Xing's *Asian America through the Lens: History, Representations and Identity* (1998), Hamamoto and Sandra Liu's anthology *Countervisions: Asian American Film Criticism* (2000), Robert G. Lee's *Orientals: Asian Americans in Popular Culture* (2000), and Peter X. Feng's *Identities in Motion: Asian American Film and Video* (2002) as well as his edited volume *Screening Asian Americans* (2002).

Although they collectively provide an excellent overview of historical contexts that shaped both mainstream and independent Asian images in American media, these studies tend to privilege two ethnicities, Chinese and Japanese, while unintentionally marginalizing other groups who lay equal claim to Asian American identity. With the exception of Hamamoto's brief analysis of M*A*S*H and *AfterMASH* (1983–1984),[6] Lee's discussion of the images of Korean shopkeepers in *Falling Down* (1993) and *Menace II Society* (1993),[7] and Helen Lee's essay on Korean American women's cinema reprinted in Feng's anthology,[8] Koreans remain virtually invisible in Asian American film criticism. Indeed, they have seldom been represented in Hollywood except in minor and supporting roles in Korean War films or, more recently, as stand-offish and money-hungry grocers in *Do the Right Thing* (1989) and other riot-related films. Although Korean roles remain scarce, a Korean

American face—that belonging to Philip Ahn—served as an ever-present screen icon of the Oriental (for mainstream audiences) and as a diasporic symbol (for Korean American audiences) from the mid-1930s to the late 1970s. By shifting the critical spotlight from more canonized Japanese American and Chinese American stars (such as Sessue Hayakawa and Anna May Wong) to a marginalized Korean American supporting performer, I hope to diversify the critical discourse of ethnic identities in both American film studies and Asian American media studies.

The second shortcoming of preexisting scholarship is its frequent recycling of a handful of canonized motion-picture texts, such as *The Cheat* (1915), *Broken Blossoms* (1919), *Sayonara* (1957), *Flower Drum Song* (1961), and *Year of the Dragon* (1985). In Hamamoto and Liu's anthology *Countervisions*, Rea Tajiri's accomplished thirty-two-minute documentary on the wartime Japanese internment, *History and Memory: For Akiko and Takashige* (1991), is habitually cited and analyzed. Although the aforementioned films have a level of thematic and stylistic significance deserving of meticulous scrutiny, their repeated reappearance in critical writings makes one wish that more academic attention had been paid to the excavation of lesser-known works. By largely limiting myself to the works comprising Philip Ahn's filmography, I was able to select a manageable cross-section of representative films and television series without recourse to bias or preexisting canons. This book seeks to contribute to the field's new, alternative canon formation by focusing on neglected yet significant films, such as *The General Died at Dawn* (1936), *Daughter of Shanghai* (1937), *King of Chinatown* (1939), *China Sky* (1945), and *Battle Hymn* (1957), as central case studies.

Overall, this project aims to shift the critical anchoring of ethnic identity from questions of *representation* (image as source of meaning) to those of *performance* (actor as enunciative agent) and Asian American *spectatorship*, while at the same time foregrounding the multi-valency of ethnic iconicity and addressing the deeper implications of screen performance within larger political, generic, and representational discourses in American film and television. Like the recently published anthology *East Main Street: Asian American Popular Culture*, edited by Shilpa Davé, LeiLani Nishime, and Tasha G. Oren, my work "eschew(s) the familiar representation-based models that emphasize victimization and alienation in favor of a multifaceted approach that highlights the intricacies and internal tensions"[9] in the construction and reception of mainstream images.

As Peter Feng correctly sums up, the consensus of Asian American media critics has been that "the dominant media industry denies subjectivity to Asians and Asian Americans, inviting them to participate in the American body politics at the expense of their agency and individuality."[10] It is true that Hollywood has excluded and marginalized performers of Asian extraction through the politics of role segregation (the prohibition against Asians playing whites while the reverse was accepted) and role stratification (in which leading roles are reserved for whites, leaving only character parts open to Asians).[11] In addition, the mainstream industry has continued to perpetuate such racial stereotypes as Fu Manchu, Madame Butterfly, and the "dragon lady" from the silent period onward. However, this does not necessarily amount to a total eradication of agency and subjectivity on the part of Asian American actors and spectators.

Lisa Lowe defines the title of her influential book, *Immigrant Acts*, as "the *agency* of Asian immigrants and Asian Americans: the *acts* of labor, resistance, memory, and survival, as well as the politicized cultural work that emerges from dislocation and disidentification."[12] Following her lead, I seek to recuperate Asian American agency involving performative and spectatorial *acts*. Rather than sustaining the reductionist binary between "bad" Hollywood (as the purveyor, if not the originator, of Oriental stereotypes) and "good" independent media (as the initiator of antiracist resistance), this book reinvestigates the complexities and contradictions of mainstream cinematic and television productions from the perspective of active agents, not passive victims—Asian American actors and spectators capable of negotiating, reinterpreting, or resisting misrepresentations and stereotypes of hegemonic texts without necessarily forgoing the benefits of employment (in the cast of actors) or dispensing with the pleasure of participation (in the case of audiences). I deploy the concept of cross-ethnic performativity as an overarching theoretical paradigm to address the subversive potential of these hermeneutic *acts*. Although ethnic differences between Philip Ahn and his contemporaries might have mattered little to mainstream (white) audiences who, by and large, readily accepted yellowface and interminority substitution as cultural norms, in this book I demonstrate how these crucial differences complicate and enrich Asian American performativity and spectatorship.

Philip Ahn's affiliation with a third East Asian ethnicity (neither Chinese nor Japanese) and his precarious position as an exilic/diasporic actor (both Korean and American) make this versatile cross-ethnic performer an ideal candidate for my study, which intervenes in ongoing critical debates regarding national cinema, identity performances (masquerade and passing), ethnic stardom, resistant spectatorship, and the political economy of representations. Ahn's existential and emotional distance from his screen ethnicities (primarily, Chinese and Japanese), as well as the actor's exceptional commitment to political causes for his homeland (namely, Korea's independence movement), differentiates his performance from those of other Asian American stars, such as Sessue Hayakawa and Anna May Wong. Ironically, Hayakawa's and Wong's personal frustration with Hollywood was greater than that of Ahn because of the ample opportunities afforded them by producers all too eager to cast them in unflattering and degrading roles of their own ethnicities. Ahn's well-publicized anticolonial pleasure of casting Japanese "heavies" in a negative light in World War II propaganda films contrasts sharply with his colleague Wong's repeatedly expressed displeasure in playing Chinese villainesses.

Likewise, Asian American spectators may also reinterpret stereotypes for the advancement of their groups' own political interests and can enter the narratives by experiencing ethnic solidarity with onscreen surrogates, whose performances may outshine their often caricatured roles and thus are things to celebrate rather than dismiss in anger or disgust. As Ella Shohat and Robert Stam point out in *Unthinking Eurocentrism,*

> [S]pectators themselves come equipped with a "sense of the real" rooted in their own experience, on the basis of which they can accept, question, or even subvert a film's representations. In this sense, the cultural preparation of a particular audience can generate counterpressure to a racist or prejudicial discourse.... [S]pectators may look beyond caricatural representations to see the oppressed performing self. African-Americans were not likely to take Step'n Fetchit as a typical, synecdochic sample of Black behavior or attitudes; Black audiences knew he was acting, and understood the circumstances that led him to play subservient roles.[13]

Jacqueline Stewart's recent study of early black spectatorship corroborates this account by pointing out urban black audiences' willingness to accept and celebrate the African American star/producer Noble M. Johnson's cross-racial roles (as Arabs, Mexicans, Native Americans, and Polynesians) in Hollywood films from the 1920s to 1940s "regardless of the race of his characters and despite the fact that he played villains in many...productions. For black audiences Johnson's star text undercut the classical diegetic world of mainstream films."[14] Stewart's formulation of "reconstructive spectatorship," a fluid, negotiated, polyvalent viewing position through which racialized subjects "reconstitute and assert themselves in relation to the classical cinema's racist social and textual operations,"[15] has been helpful in my own critical rethinking of Asian American spectatorship outside the assimilationist-versus-resistant dichotomy.

Although my work takes a discursive approach encompassing the interrelated questions of stardom, performance, spectatorship, and censorship, I find myself becoming inspired by an emerging trend in Asian American film criticism—one that provides an alternative, recuperative approach to mainstream ethnic images. In her article, "When Dragon Ladies Die, Do They Come Back as Butterflies? Re-Imagining Anna May Wong," Cynthia W. Liu distinguishes two modes of addressing Asian images in Hollywood: the "dismantling stereotypes" approach and the "refunctioning representation" approach.[16] Critiquing the former's problematic supposition of an essentialist, ethnic, and/or cultural "reality," Liu recasts the extradiegetic, cross-media discourse surrounding Anna May Wong's iconicity (the biographical details of her career and her importance to Asian American writers, such as David Henry Hwang, Jessica Hagedorn, and John Yau), which subverts screen stereotypes. Like Liu, I follow the path of "refunctioning representation" not only by critically resignifying Ahn's Koreanness (often masked behind Chinese and Japanese visage and costume) through a biographical narrative of his offscreen identity and agency but also by reclaiming his centrality in carving out a diasporic cultural space of transnational Korea in American popular media.

In his introduction to *Screening Asian Americans*, Peter Feng argues that "there is no such thing as a positive or negative representation, rather, there are representations that are mobilized positively or negatively depending on discursive context."[17] Sharing Feng's insightful thesis, this book concentrates on identifying various political and industrial contexts (i.e., American foreign and immigration policies, the Sino-Japanese War, World War II, the Korean War, state and industrial censorship, publicity discourse, etc.) that contributed to the erection of particular ethnic images for Chinese, Japanese, and, to a lesser extent, Koreans in American media throughout the studio era and in the Television Age. My study also interweaves a diverse selection of primary archival evidence derived from the Production Code Administration, the State Department, and the Office of War Information (OWI), with a view toward enriching our understanding of the institutional, diplomatic, and international maneuvering of ethnic images unique to given historical epochs. Complementing these public archival documents is a private collection of Philip Ahn's personal belongings (letters, photos, memorabilia, and newspaper clippings) that the Ahn family has generously made available to me. This exclusive access to the family archive in addition to my interviews with the late actor's family members were indispensable for the reconstruction of Philip Ahn's biographical history, which in many ways provides as much insight into broader social and cultural contexts as do public documents.

As mentioned earlier, this book is not a conventional biography, and its structure is admittedly unusual. It is divided into two parts followed by a stand-alone conclusion chapter. Part I concerns two central figures: the actor (Chapter 1) and the spectator (Chapter 2). The first chapter constitutes Philip Ahn's biography, focusing on his family history, Hollywood career, and close ties with his ancestral homeland. I make the argument that it is possible to reclaim his legacy in the lens of Korean cultural history by spotlighting his unrealized ambitions to participate in the South Korean film industry as a leader, actor, and producer, as well as his many manifestations of diasporic identities within Hollywood texts. While providing a biographical overview, this chapter also critically intervenes in questions of national cinema by recuperating Ahn's anti-Japanese roles in wartime Hollywood as expressions of the struggle for Korean independence and part of Korean diasporic cinema.

As a theoretical springboard for the entire project, Chapter 2 explores the relation between cross-ethnic performativity (masquerade and passing) and the differentiated viewing positions of bilingual and bicultural audiences. By applying psychoanalytic feminist theories of masquerade and gender performance to racial and ethnic discourses, we can conceivably expand the critical paradigms found in both the politically inclined sphere of race studies and the psychoanalytically informed sphere of feminist studies, thereby exposing the underlying intersections of these two often mutually exclusive hermeneutic paths. This chapter likewise broadens traditional theories of passing beyond the categories of race (nonwhite passing for white) and sexuality (gay passing for straight) by foregrounding forms of ethnic and linguistic passing in Philip Ahn's screen and television appearances. In the process, I posit the notion that a subversive, "accidental" kind of spectatorship exists among Asian American audiences and thus is indicative of an in-group literacy, one that enables them to see through and get past the Oriental masquerades and ethnic passings of Asian American stars.

Part II brings together three independent yet mutually enriching and chronologically presented case studies concerning classical Hollywood's Asian (sub)genres: the Oriental detective film, the "China film," and the Korean War film. Although the main subjects of my inquiry are motion picture productions from the 1930s to the 1950s, I also analyze several television episodes from the 1950s to 1970s that are relevant to the themes and genres in question. Chapter 3 addresses a plethora of contexts surrounding Oriental detective cycles of the 1930s and the 1940s (Charlie Chan, Mr. Moto, and Mr. Wong series) that offered non-yellow peril representations of "good" Orientals impersonated by white actors in yellowface. This chapter particularly emphasizes the political and ideological implications of the first self-representing

Asian American romantic couple (Anna May Wong and Philip Ahn) of sound-era Hollywood cinema in two Paramount B films—*Daughter of Shanghai* and *King of Chinatown*.

Chapter 4 investigates how the interaction between the industry and the U.S. government (specifically, the State Department and the OWI) as well as the ongoing pressure from Chinese officials to curtail backward images and promote a progressive, if propagandistic, vision of their nation influenced the production, distribution, and exhibition of Hollywood's "China films" of the 1930s and the 1940s (many of which featured Philip Ahn in various roles). Using a wide range of archival documents, this chapter provides a historical analysis of Hollywood's pivotal role in pre-Cold War American foreign relations with China. It culminates with an in-depth case study of *China Sky*, in which Ahn's role changed from Chinese to Korean in light of the federal government's wartime prohibition of negative images of Chinese allies.

Chapter 5 fills a significant gap in the study of American war films by putting a fresh spin on the overlooked Korean War film genre and focusing on Douglas Sirk's *Battle Hymn*, a work that offers the most substantial representation of Korea in classical Hollywood cinema. Ahn's onscreen mutability—his fluctuations between South Korean ally and North Korean enemy—in this particular genre is yet another indication of his versatile and vacillating identity. Finally, the Conclusion returns to Philip Ahn's family history by exploring the connection between the actor's paternal screen persona and his relationship to his own famous father. Palimpsestic traces of the actor's real-life father can be found in his many parts, culminating with his most-remembered role as Master Kan of *Kung Fu*. The latter part of the final chapter concludes with thoughts on Ahn's life and career in the context of Asian American history and identity politics.

Although this book uses Philip Ahn's career trajectory and cross-ethnic performativity as an anchoring device, extensive portions of the text are devoted to historical and theoretical overviews not directly related to the actor. To use a casting metaphor, after foregrounding Ahn as a kind of "lead actor" in the first chapter, I strategically position him in supporting, minor, and bit parts throughout the rest of the text in order to put his career in a macro-perspective lens and extend my critical inquiries beyond the boundaries of a star biography. The experience of reading this book may very well be akin to that of viewing one of Philip Ahn's many films. As a researcher-spectator, I grew accustomed to sitting and sifting through numerous classic films and television programs, patiently waiting for Ahn's frequently fleeting appearances, which sometimes lasted no more than a few minutes. This cumulative act of spotting (Philip Ahn) and decentering (texts/narratives) gave me a peculiar pleasure and insight, which I hope to share with readers by re-creating the macro-textual system in which the actor functions as a rhizomic phenomenon. His brief yet continual reemergence in film narratives—across genres and decades—triggers inquiries about the interrelationship among textual systems, typecasting politics, ideological positions, and historical circumstances, which all contributed to the erection of the Oriental other. Seen literally from the margins of the screen—a hermeneutic hinterlands populated by often neglected or underappreciated Asian American character actors—this book attempts nothing less than a rewriting of American film history and star studies.

When closely examined, Philip Ahn's filmography and television credits constitute an incredibly diverse cross-section of roles, which are often unfairly lumped together under a convenient category: the Oriental stereotype. In light of the historical and cultural circumstances of segregated America that oppressed nonwhite subjects, it is imperative that we devise an alternative, nondismissive critical discourse sensitive to the industrial and professional limitations imposed on early Asian American performers in order to recuperate their acting careers outside the sphere of stereotype theories. John Flaus is one of the few critics to have commented on the quality of Ahn's acting in a semi-theoretical fashion. He singles out Ahn—along with other distinguished character actors Morris Ankrum, Cliff Clark, Joseph Crehan, Clarence Kolb, Connie Gilchrist, and Katherine Warren—as a screen performer endowed with so-called *lamprotes* (a Greek term meaning splendor or brilliance). As a condition contrary to Walter Benjamin's notion of "aura," the patina-like radiance of Ahn's myriad screen roles outshines any one particular performance—a quality that can be better appreciated with cumulative and repeated viewing (what Flaus calls "buffing"). As Flaus puts it,

> No matter how clichéd the characters they play and the dialogue they must say, they give enough of themselves to transcend, however briefly, mere professionalism. It is a joy to see them again; I feel a sense of welcome. For the short time they are on the screen their performance qualifies the narrative, rather than vice versa. These, and others, are hard-nosed, time-worn professionals who can become endeared to us just for "doing their job," as they merge into our personal map of the American industry.[18]

The lamprotic qualities of Ahn and his equally significant cronies (such as Richard Loo and Keye Luke) should be reevaluated before dismissing wholesale any racial stereotypes (e.g., the coolie, the servant, the yellow peril, the kung-fu master) apparent in the parts available to them.

The title of this Introduction, *"The Life and Death of a Hollywood Asian,"* pays homage to both French-émigré filmmaker Robert Florey's *The Life and Death of 9413—A Hollywood Extra,*[19] and Korean writer Ahn Junghyo (An Chŏng-hyo)'s novel *The Life and Death of the Hollywood Kid (Hŏlliudŭ k'idŭ ŭi saengae,* 1992), the story of a movie buff who dedicates his life to pursuing the fantasies on display in classical Hollywood films.[20] Whereas Florey's groundbreaking avant-garde film is a tribute to the industry's neglected minor players who remain anonymous behind sinister-looking, archetypal masks, Ahn Junghyo's autobiographical novel is a collective portrait of cinephilic Koreans who managed to endure postwar poverty and hardship in the therapeutic glow of the movie screen. Thus, this book borrows both tropes—the life and death not only of an actor but also of a spectator. I, too, was a "Hollywood Kid," a star-struck classic film aficionado, who throughout adolescence and early adulthood was passively sutured into a cross-racial set of identificatory gazes and thus was often oblivious to the ideological transparency normalizing the implicit white, male subject position. This book marks the death of my former self (an innocent, passive Hollywoodphile) and the birth of a film scholar who still harbors genuine affection for classical Hollywood cinema, but is critical of its ideological pitfalls. This study is the result of my own diasporic journey from one nation to another, which enabled me to discover Ahn and other Hollywood Asians while articulating a differentiated spectatorial position vis-à-vis the very "Dream factory" products that brought me such intense pleasure.

The death of Asian villains and victims has been a recurrent theme of American motion pictures and popular culture for the past century. Anna May Wong once complained about her Hollywood career: "I died so often. I was killed in virtually every picture in which I appeared. Pathetic dying seemed to be the best thing I did."[21] In *Marginal Sights: Staging the Chinese in America,* James S. Moy likewise acknowledges this cultural phenomenon, stating that "both Fu Manchu and dragon-lady characters...would live on to die and die again, forever reinscribing the dangers of the Orient and miscegenation while spiraling through seemingly endless cycles of death."[22] Apart from their oft-repeated "reel" deaths and notwithstanding their inevitable encounter with "real" death, early Asian American actors (with the exception of Sessue Hayakawa and Anna May Wong) could be said to have "died" critically because of a lack of scholarship in the field. Dedicating this study to all pioneering Asian American performers whose struggles and legacies have been unjustly forgotten, I anxiously await future scholarship that will shed light on the careers of many other deserving actors.

PART I

Asian American Acts:
Performance and Spectatorship

1

PORTRAIT OF A PATRIOT'S SON

Philip Ahn and Korean Diasporic
Identities in Hollywood

OVER THE PAST DECADE, Korean faces have become ever more conspicuous in American mass media and popular culture. For example, veteran film comedian Pak Chung-hun played Yi Il-sang, an ex-soldier of fortune in the Bosnian War in Jonathan Demme's *The Truth about Charlie* (2002).[1] Originally conceived as Japanese, this substantial supporting role was rewritten as Korean at the request of Pak, whom Demme had grown fond of after seeing him in director Yi Myŏng-se's *Nowhere to Hide* (*Injŏng sajŏng pŏlgŏt ŏpda*, 1999), a stylistic police thriller that had become a Sundance Festival sleeper. Two Korean American actors, Rick Yune and Will Yun Lee, were cast as sinister North Korean villains in the twentieth installment of the James Bond series, *Die Another Day* (2002) — roles that had been turned down by several South Korean stars, including Ch'a In-p'yo, Ch'oe Min-su, Song Kang-ho, and Ch'oe Min-sik. Although criticized by South Korean boycotters for collaborating in Hollywood's representation of North Korea as an "Axis of Evil,"[2] Yune, in particular, made a strong impression on international Bondophiles for his iconic incarnation of a classic Bond nemesis. Margaret Cho, another high-profile Korean American player, has made a successful comeback with a series of independently produced concert films — *I'm the One That I Want* (2000), *Notorious C.H.O.* (2002), *CHO Revolution* (2004), and *Margaret Cho.*

Assassin (2005)—after her ABC sitcom *All-American Girl* (1994–1995) was unceremoniously canceled after its first season. With candid, innuendo-sprinkled humor and biting yet witty criticism of institutional racism, Cho has established herself as a leading Asian American standup comedian. More recently, John Cho joined the club of Korean American stars when he played Harold, one of the two leads in New Line Cinema's unconventional buddy film, *Harold and Kumar Go to White Castle* (2004), establishing a new role model for up-and-coming Asian American actors. Korean Canadian actress Sandra Oh has likewise gained mainstream exposure with two popular roles—as the sultry winery worker Stephanie in Alexander Payne's *Sideways* (2004) and as the sassy surgical intern Cristina Yang in ABC's hit hospital drama *Grey's Anatomy* (2005–). In 2004, the producers of another ABC show, *Lost*, created a fully developed, three-dimensional Korean character specifically for bilingual actress Kim Yun-jin, who had earlier starred in the popular Korean blockbuster *Shiri* (Swiri, 1999).

But despite this recent emergence of Koreans and Korean Americans in Hollywood and network television, few younger audiences today know their precursor, Philip Ahn, the first actor of Korean descent to become a Hollywood "star." I put the word *star* in quotations, since mainstream audiences were more likely to label Ahn a supporting or character actor. He was certainly no Gary Cooper, Gregory Peck, Humphrey Bogart, or John Wayne, although he shared screen time with these and many other Hollywood stars. Despite being promoted as an ethnic star at various points in his career (especially during his early years at Paramount Studios), Philip Ahn never achieved the status of a top-billed star, which was a "whites only" club in classical Hollywood cinema. In this chapter, I hope to critically recuperate his unsung stardom in relation not only to the pioneering roles he played in both the U.S. and South Korean film industries but also to his familial role as the heir of an indisputable celebrity in modern Korean modern history: Tosan An Ch'ang-ho.

As the first and most historically significant Korean American actor to work in the film industry, Philip Ahn has been undeservingly neglected in film and media studies. The discipline of Korean studies has been equally negligent in exploring the intersecting legacies of Tosan and his son Philip Ahn in the formation of Korean American nationalism. Tosan's name is a hagiographic fixture in the annals of Korea's tumultuous twentieth-century history, yet many scholars in the field are oblivious to the fact that his son was once called an "Oriental Clark Gable" in Hollywood,[3] where he played lead roles opposite Anna May Wong, and was a distinguished character actor until his death in 1978.

I argue that Ahn's career can and should be recuperated as part of Korean film and cultural history on two grounds: First, evidence from his personal papers demonstrates that he made efforts time and again to enter the South Korean film industry as a leader, actor, and producer, although many opportunities were regretfully lost because of political and economic conditions in postcolonial Korea. Second, Philip Ahn's direct and indirect manifestations of Korean diasporic identities in American film and television deserve critical attention in the broader context of transnational Korean media. By foregrounding his critical biography, which intersects at two different national and film histories, I hope to demonstrate not only the interdisciplinary scope of this project but also the intricate relationship between diasporic screen identities and the homeland (both real and imaginary).

HOW THE "ORIENTAL CLARK GABLE"
BECAME A "YELLOW MONSTER"

The legacy of Philip Ahn should be remembered in Korean and Korean American studies not only because he was the first Korean to "make it" in Hollywood and pursue his acting career for forty years but also because he was the eldest son of celebrated national leader An Ch'ang-ho. Reverently referred to by his followers as Teacher "Tosan" (a pen name meaning "island mountain"), An Ch'ang-ho was not only an anticolonial revolutionary, statesman, reformer, educator, and writer but also a pioneering leader of the first wave of Korean immigrants to hit the American shores.[4] In 1902, at the age of twenty-three, An Ch'ang-ho and his eighteen-year-old bride, Yi Hae-ryŏn (Helen Lee), sailed for America, becoming the first married couple from Korea to enter the United States. Soon after arriving in San Francisco, Tosan became the first organizer and reformer of the nascent Korean immigrant community. Ushering in reforms that would improve the living conditions of Korean laborers, Tosan motivated his fellow countrymen to become model citizens so that they could show the world the Korean capacity for independence. In 1903, he established the Friendship Society (Ch'inmokhŏi), the first Korean diaspora association on American soil, which evolved into the United Korean Association (Kongniphyŏphŏi) two years later to serve the wider population of compatriots in California, Hawaii, Washington, DC, Mexico, Cuba, Manchuria, and Siberia. After moving to a farming community in Riverside, California, Tosan continued his efforts to better the lives of immigrants through his inter-city community network based in San Francisco.

In 1907, An Ch'ang-ho returned to Korea, then under Japanese protectorate rule, and created the New People's Society (Sinminhŏi), a revolutionary organization. He also founded and served as the principal of Taesŏng School in P'yŏngyang. Exiled for his political activities from his homeland in 1910 immediately before Japan's annexation of Korea, Tosan returned to the United States in 1911 via China, Russia, and Europe. The next year, he unified many Korean associations throughout the United States into the Korean National Association ([KNA]: Kungminhŏi). The KNA performed diplomatic functions for overseas Koreans and provided education for the children of immigrants.[5] In 1913, An Ch'ang-ho established the Young Korean Academy (Hŭngsadan), a globally networked Korean leadership training organization that still remains in operation today.[6] In 1919, five years after he and his family moved to Los Angeles, Tosan went to Shanghai to serve as the interim prime minister and minister of labor for the exiled Korean Provisional Government (KPG). Arrested by Japanese forces in Shanghai and forcefully repatriated in 1932, the unbending patriot spent many of his final years in different prisons and under house arrest in Korea until he died in 1938 from illness stemming from torture and imprisonment.

Tosan had five children—Philip, Philson, Susan, Soorah, and Ralph—all of whom were born and raised in America. Born in a mission in Los Angeles on March 29, 1905, Philip was one of the first Korean Americans born in the continental United States.[7] Like his father, Philip became a leader of the Korean American community, although he focused on the second-generation community based in Southern California. He organized the first Korean American youth group (Ip'al, or Two-Eight Club) and supervised assimilation and social activities of immigrant children during the 1920s.[8] As the eldest son of a poor immigrant family, Philip shouldered the responsibility of aiding his mother, who worked as a cleaning lady, a cook, and a seamstress, as well as supporting younger siblings while his father was absent. He began selling newspapers at the age of nine and, to support his family, subsequently took various menial jobs, such as dishwashing, cleaning, truck driving, and delivering vegetables. In 1925, two years after graduating from high school, Ahn took over a fruit stand at a Tower Grocery Market where he had been delivering fresh produce. The family-run small business prospered for years and facilitated the Ahns' move to a spacious two-story house near the University of Southern California (USC) campus shortly after Philip's admission to the university in 1933.

In 1926, Philip Ahn helped Hŭngsadan members start a rice farm in Colusa County, California. As the Alien Land Law of 1913 prohibited immigrant Asians from owning or leasing land, Ahn's American citizenship was

FIGURE 1.1 *A family portrait, 1918* (from left to right: Philson, Tosan with baby Soorah in his arms, Philip, Susan, and Helen Lee). Courtesy of the Ahn Family.

required to establish this agricultural joint venture, which was partly aimed at raising funds for Korean resistance activities. In addition to signing a land lease on behalf of the patriotic farmers, Tosan's son personally assisted them in hauling crops to Los Angeles. Unfortunately, to Ahn's dismay, the rice farm soon faced bankruptcy and left him with unexpected debts, which took him years to settle. The young Korean American also operated elevators at the

FIGURE 1.2 *Philip Ahn as a young man, prior to entering the film industry.* Courtesy of the Ahn Family.

Talmadge and the Bayson, luxurious residential hotels where he gained an appreciation for fine furnishings, which would come in handy during the war years when he turned his attention to producing antique-style lamps, furniture, and ceramicware as a part-time business.

Despite his early exposure to the world of commerce, Philip's true passion lay elsewhere. As a teenager, Ahn began to show his talent in drama and public speaking, gifts that he inherited from Tosan, a bell-toned orator who gave many emotive, patriotic speeches in Korea, the United States, Mexico, Manchuria, and China. Young Ahn honed his acting chops in school and church plays, developing dramatic skills and learning to harness a charismatic voice, perhaps his greatest natural asset.

It was Philip's childhood friend and neighbor, Anna May Wong, who first introduced him to the world of professional acting. In the 1920s, Philip's family lived one block away from Anna May's house in downtown Los Angeles. Anna May and Philip went to the same junior high school, Central Junior High, where they became close friends and confidants. While still in high school, Ahn was spotted by silent screen legend Douglas Fairbanks, Sr. when he accompanied Anna May to the set of *The Thief of Baghdad* (1924), a film in which the Chinese American actress played a Mongolian slave girl. Fairbanks Sr. gave Ahn a screen test and offered him a minor role.

Flushed with pride, Philip hurried home to deliver the good news, only to encounter the fierce disapproval of his mother, who said, "No son of mine is going to get mixed up with those awful people." As an immigrant woman from a Confucian society, Yi Hae-ryŏn held a low opinion of actors, who were thought to occupy the lowest stratum of Korea's traditional caste system. Family friends and community elders likewise strongly denounced film actors, labeling them with the derogatory term *kwangdae* (clown). However, when Tosan returned home for the last time in 1925, the visionary leader— known for thinking outside of the box—gave permission to his son to pursue an acting career, stating, "Film is also an art; all I ask is that if you want to become an actor, be the best that you possibly can."[9]

Not until 1935, three years before his father's death, did Philip Ahn get another lucky break. As a sophomore majoring in foreign commerce at USC, Ahn applied for a part-time position at Paramount Studios, where many USC athletes and students worked as extras in college football pictures. But instead of being offered an extra's job, Philip was given a chance to audition for director Lewis Milestone, who was searching for a Chinese comedian to appear in a Bing Crosby musical entitled *Anything Goes* (1936). The American-born Korean's English was so perfect, however, that Milestone turned him down, saying he was looking for someone who spoke pidgin English. On his way out, Philip had a flash of inspiration. He sauntered back to Milestone's desk. "You like...aligh," he said. "You no likee me...aligh. Me no care. Hip sabee? Me go school...aligh." The director broke into laughter and said, "Okay...the part's yours!"

In 1936 alone, Philip Ahn appeared in five films, playing supporting roles opposite Hollywood's top stars, such as Gary Cooper, Mae West, and Shirley Temple. Now best remembered as the wizened guru Master Kan in *Kung Fu* (1972–1975) or any one of the interchangeably hideous Japanese "heavies" in World War II films, Ahn's early career was in fact peppered with dynamic supporting roles. He played the loyal aide, "Oxford," to Akim Tamiroff's titular general in Paramount's Oriental epic, *The General Died at Dawn* (1936); the endearing Chinese guardian Sun Lo who passes fortune-cookie wisdom down to Shirley Temple's moppet in 20th Century-Fox's musical, *Stowaway* (1936); and Chinese secret agent "Hong Kong Cholly" who poses as the pidgin English-speaking sidekick of Larry "Buster" Crabbe's police detective in Universal's serial *Red Barry* (1938). His prewar heyday culminated with two roles as a romantic lead opposite Anna May Wong in the Paramount B pictures, *Daughter of Shanghai* (1937) and *King of Chinatown* (1939).

Concurrent with Ahn's debut as an actor, Anna May Wong returned from a year-long trip to China and signed a new contract with Paramount, which provided her sympathetic roles (departing from her "dragon lady" persona) in a series of B detective and crime pictures, including *Daughter of Shanghai* (1937), *Dangerous to Know* (1938), *King of Chinatown* (1939), and *Island of Lost Men* (1939). Because the Production Code prohibited portraying interracial couples, Wong's portrayal of an active romantic heroine in the first of these films necessitated the introduction of a new Asian American romantic hero. Ahn thus landed his first leading role opposite his childhood friend. In *Daughter of Shanghai*, Ahn and Wong dismantled Oriental stereotypes by playing, respectively, an FBI agent and a quasi detective who jointly solve a murder case and emerge as a romantic couple in the final scene. The screen duo reunited in *King of Chinatown*, a gangster film set in San Francisco's Chinatown. Ahn plays a lawyer who romantically pursues Wong's character, who is a medical doctor.

During Ahn's prewar career at Paramount, the studio promoted him as a Chinese actor. Thus, Ahn's exceptional Korean heritage was masked to facilitate a comfortable, homogeneous "Chinese" coupling that allayed any anxieties mainstream audiences' might have had concerning any ethnic or racial mixing—a blending that might evoke, however remotely, the threat of "white-yellow" miscegenation. Fan magazine discourse further solidified the myth of this idealized Hollywood Oriental couple by promoting an offscreen romantic union between the two Asian American performers. Wong's response to this rumor was that the romance "would be like marrying my brother."[10] Ahn's younger siblings, Susan and Ralph, assert that the two felt a kind of puppy love for one another as adolescents, but that their relationship in adulthood was one of close friends and confidants. Peter Ahn, a Korean immigrant who maintained a surrogate father–son relationship with the actor, remembers Philip Ahn mentioning that he had tried to marry the Chinese American actress, but was talked out of it by his mother, Yi Hae-ryŏn, who opposed an interethnic marriage.[11] However, his brother Ralph contends that Philip accepted and respected the Korean American community's mores against intermarriage and would not have wed a non-Korean woman for that reason.[12] In any case, one can conclude that marriage was not simply a matter of personal choice for Philip Ahn, who felt pressure both to fulfill his parents' wish and to satisfy the community's need to witness their leader Tosan's legacy being carried out through his heir's in-group marriage. Neither Ahn nor Wong ever married and both were rumored to be gay; however, Korean newspapers often interpreted Ahn's bachelorhood as the result of his taking on responsibility for his younger siblings as well as his Korean-style piety to his mother, with whom he lived until her death in 1969—only nine years before he succumbed to a fatal bout with lung cancer.[13]

FIGURE 1.3 *As alumni of the Central Junior High School in Los Angeles, Philip Ahn and Anna May Wong remained close friends throughout their professional careers.* Courtesy of the Ahn Family.

Daughter of Shanghai and *King of Chinatown* represent the only romantic leads Ahn played among some hundred titles in his filmography. Although studios once promoted him as the "Oriental Clark Gable," this chance to rise above the level of bit player was short-lived because of institutionalized racism, which relegated him to minor roles supporting white protagonists or Asian leads played by Caucasian actors in yellowface. As Hollywood realigned its modes of representation with the public consensus of the "yellow peril" in the wake of Pearl Harbor and the subsequent U.S. involvement in World War II, Philip Ahn increasingly played Japanese impersonator characters (replacing Japanese American actors, many of whom faced internment during the war years). He earned such appellations as "the man we love to hate" or "leering yellow monster" while appearing in a number of anti-Rising Sun propaganda and war films, including *Behind the Rising Sun* (1943), *The Purple Heart* (1944), *Back to Bataan* (1945), and *Blood on the Sun* (1945).

During the war, the studios and media capitalized on Ahn's Korean American identity by actively promoting his father's involvement in anti-Japanese struggles and underscoring his own double commitment to America's war efforts against Japan both as an American citizen and the son of a renowned Korean nationalist leader. Later, one of the questions interviewers often asked Ahn was whether the death of his father at the hands of the Japanese affected his portrayal of Japanese characters during the war years. In a 1978 television interview, Ahn responded,

> In those days, the Japanese were the enemies of the United States, and they were more viciously the enemy, at that time, of the Koreans. And of course, being of Korean ancestry...I had tremendous, shall we say, hatred for the Japanese.... So when I get a Japanese role that calls for me to be vicious...I played it to the hilt. I had fun doing it.[14]

In fact, the patriot's son considered his "to-the-hilt" impersonation of Japanese enemies to be a way of carrying on his late father's legacy in the independence movement of Korea. In another interview, Ahn acknowledged his pride in contributing to anti-Japanese propaganda: "True, I hated the Japanese," he said, "but I told myself that if I was going to play the enemy, I was going to play him as viciously as I could. In *Back to Bataan* I slapped little children and went so far as to hang a teacher from an American flagpole. I took pride in being the most evil man alive."[15]

Although many commentators and historians point out the contradiction between his real identity as the son of Korea's foremost patriot and his screen persona as a Japanese bad guy,[16] even his most villainous roles as enemy officers and spies indirectly served as an extension of his familial heritage. He was instrumental in giving Japan bad publicity around the world through the hegemonic distribution network of Hollywood films. American studies scholar Thomas Doherty notes that Philip Ahn "sacrificed ethnic pride to contribute to the war effort as moral-enhancing Japanese villains."[17] In reality, Ahn's self-esteem as a Korean patriot's son was further solidified the more his roles called for him to play "wicked" Japanese characters. To quote Ahn, "I felt that the more vicious I portrayed [the Japanese], the more I was accomplishing."[18] However, any pleasure Ahn derived from his imaginary revenge was undermined by hate mail and threats on his life by enraged movie fans who confused his onscreen evil persona with the real Ahn. In February 1945, the patriotic actor finally joined the U. S. Army after getting deferments because producers wanted him to appear in their films.[19] Although his short-lived military career and temporary dissociation with Hollywood effectively halted the spate of hate mail, Ahn became permanently branded as a "bad guy" because of the many villainous roles he had played in World War II propaganda films.

The South Korean Reception of a Diasporic Actor

In South Korea, Philip Ahn's prewar film roles and wartime career are little known among even the savviest, most encyclopedic film scholars and historians. As the relationship between Japan and America began to deteriorate during Ahn's early years in Hollywood, exhibition of American films in colonial Korea gradually dwindled until they were completely banned during World War II. During the postwar occupation of the southern half of liberated Korea by the American military government (1945–1948), a branch of the Central Motion Picture Exchange (an overseas arm of the New York-based Motion Picture Export Association of America) was established. The importation of Hollywood films rapidly resumed, increasing by 1949 to account for 90 percent of all films on South Korean screens.[20] Interrupted by the Korean War, the influx of Hollywood action-adventures, melodramas, musicals, and westerns regained momentum in 1953. Accordingly, several titles in Philip Ahn's filmography were released in South Korea in the 1950s, including *Fair Wind to Java* (1953), *Love Is a Many-Splendored Thing* (1955), and *Battle Hymn* (1957).

But by the time Koreans had become cognizant of Ahn as an actor, his role in Hollywood had changed. All of his personal favorite films, those in which he played substantial and positive roles, such as *Daughter of Shanghai, China* (1943), and *The Story of Dr. Wassell* (1944), had been produced before or during World War II. When he returned to Hollywood from army service in September 1946, Ahn was no longer "a much-in-demand actor for wartime oriental roles" (as a Paramount press kit describes him in 1943)[21] who could alternately impersonate "evil" Japanese enemies and "friendly" Chinese allies. Lavish epics based on Pearl S. Buck's novels, such as MGM's *The Good Earth* (1937) and *Dragon Seed* (1944) and Pacific War and espionage pictures were things of the past. After appearing in fifty-six films between 1936 and 1945, Ahn only had forty-one screen roles between 1946 and 1960 and sixteen between 1961 and 1978. He made up for this precipitous decline by taking bit parts in television series. He made more than eighty TV appearances between 1955 and 1978 and played the regular part of *Kung Fu*'s Master Kan for three years (1973–1975). However, with the exception of *Kung Fu* and

M*A*S*H (1972–1983), his television appearances failed to reach audiences in South Korea where the belated Television Age did not begin until the 1970s.

In the 1992 novel *The Life and Death of the Hollywood Kid* (*Hŏlliudŭ k'idŭ ŭi saengae*), by renowned journalist–author Ahn Junghyo (An Chŏng-hyo), the narrator describes Philip Ahn as follows:

> Having regarded textbook heroes such as Yi Sun-sin and King Sejong as imaginary rather than real-life figures, I could not comprehend how Tosan An Ch'ang-ho's son Philip Ahn was living in Hollywood, had a American-style name, and worked as an actor. Although Philip Ahn surely played a Korean in *Battle Hymn*, he was cast as a Javanese in *Fair Wind to Java*; a Chinese uncle in *Love Is a Many-Splendored Thing...*; a Japanese in *The Teahouse of the August Moon...*; and again as a Chinese mentor in the recent television series *Kung Fu....* As an actor who monopolized Oriental supporting and bit roles during the 1950s and 1960s, Philip Ahn was a person who could not at all be connected to our reality of the time, notwithstanding his Korean face.[22]

In this nostalgic, semi-autobiographical novel about the author's postwar adolescent obsession with classical Hollywood films as a momentary escape from the harsh realities of poverty during the 1950s and 1960s, Philip Ahn is remembered as both an enigmatic and crystalline figure—someone who simultaneously resists and facilitates categorization. The narrator confesses his difficulties in understanding the father–son relationship between Hollywood's "Oriental" actor Philip Ahn and Tosan—a national hero comparable to King Sejong (a much-admired fifteenth-century monarch who oversaw many scientific and scholarly inventions including *hangŭl*, the Korean alphabet) and Admiral Yi Sun-sin (a sixteenth-century naval hero who defended the country from Japanese invasion). Instead of being proud or pleased to see a Korean face sharing the frame with such popular American idols as Rock Hudson, William Holden, and Jennifer Jones, Ahn Junghyo's cinephilic narrator identifies Tosan's son as an unfamiliar and contradictory individual who bears no relation to the people of his generation.

This lack of identification with Ahn stems from the discontinuities in the histories of Korea and Korean America. Although Tosan's achievements in Korea and the KPG in Shanghai have been lionized in history textbooks, his leadership among early Korean immigrants in the United States and the success of his American-born children have flown under the cognitive radar of the majority of South Koreans. Although older-generation film buffs (such as

Ahn Junghyo, who was born in 1941) still remember the fact that Tosan's son appeared in popular films of their youth, such as *Love Is a Many-Splendored Thing* and *Battle Hymn*, many younger South Koreans have likely never heard of him. Even members of Ahn Junghyo's generation have no memory or knowledge of Philip Ahn's prewar and wartime career and thus pigeonhole him in the roles he played in the 1950s and 1960s.

Philip Ahn visited his ancestral homeland for the first time in March 1959. The *Chosun Daily* (*Chosŏn Ilbo*) introduced Philip Ahn as a Hollywood actor "whose name is familiar to us for the role of an old man in *Chŏnsongga* [*Battle Hymn*], released two years ago."[23] In his interview with Philip Ahn in *International Film* (*Kukje yŏnghwa*), a monthly film magazine, Korean director Yi Pyŏng-il likewise told him, "In South Korea, you are known as the son of great patriot Tosan and your performance in *Chŏnsongga* is well publicized; nevertheless we do not know much about you."[24] Although *Battle Hymn* was undoubtedly the most famous of Philip Ahn's films in South Korea, most viewers had probably noticed his name and face first in *Love Is a Many-Splendored Thing* (*Mojŏng*) in 1956, a year before *Battle Hymn*'s release.

In addition to the presence of glamorous Hollywood stars and high production values, these two films had special appeal to South Korean audiences because they foregrounded the Korean War. In *Love Is a Many-Splendored Thing*, Ahn plays Third Uncle, a disempowered Chinese patriarch who reluctantly surrenders his Eurasian niece, Han Suyin (Jennifer Jones), a curiously superstitious medical doctor, to an American suitor named Mark Elliot (William Holden). Burdened by racially tinged gossip percolating through a white community in Hong Kong, as well as Mark's inability to obtain a divorce from his estranged wife, the interracial couple's romance ends tragically when Mark, working as a war correspondent, is killed in Korea. Retitled *Mojŏng* ("Affectionate Love"), this sentimental melodrama was enormously popular among South Korean audiences, who most likely sympathized enough with the cruel fate imposed on the young lovers by the war to ignore the inauthenticity of having an all-American girl in the role of a Eurasian.

Because of its unprecedented treatment of Korean themes and settings, *Battle Hymn*, a biopic depicting the story of the so-called Father of Korean Orphans, Colonel Dean E. Hess, likewise enjoyed great popularity in South Korea. Ahn plays an old ivory carver from Pusan named, Lu Wan, a converted Christian who not only assists Rock Hudson's Hess with the orphans but also inspires him with religious wisdom. But despite his spiritual maturity, Lu Wan represents an enfeebled Korean masculinity lacking the technical proficiency and physical potency of the American hero, who assumes the role of savior for South Korean women and children. Although Philip Ahn was only fifty-one years old during *Battle Hymn*'s production, he played a man in his seventies, a figure of Old Korea who habitually wears traditional garments of Chosŏn Dynasty vintage. The actor's younger brother Ralph Ahn recalls that Philip was enraged when Universal Studios dubbed his voice in the release print because they felt that it was too sonorous for his screen age.[25] Philip Ahn's emasculated, traditional characters in *Love Is a Many-Splendored Thing* and *Battle Hymn* pale in comparison with his more dynamic and modern roles in *Daughter of Shanghai* (federal investigator), *King of Chinatown* (attorney), *The Story of Dr. Wassell* (medical assistant), and *Shock Corridor* (1963; psychiatrist). These films were never theatrically released in South Korea.

The South Korean press has nevertheless emphasized the importance of Ahn's role as a Korean in *Battle Hymn*. In the interviews in both *Chosŏn Ilbo* and *Kukje yŏnghwa*, Philip Ahn and the interviewers identify that role as his most memorable and important, as well as his role in *The Story of Dr. Wassell* (a World War II biopic in which he plays the young Chinese assistant to Wassell, a naval hero played by Gary Cooper). In American interviews, however, Ahn never said *Battle Hymn* was his favorite work. Rather, he cited *The Story of Dr. Wassell* and his amiable working relationship with director Cecil B. DeMille.

Another focus of South Korean publicity was Philip Ahn's heartwarming reunion with twenty-five children at the Orphan's Home of Korea (Han'gukboyukwŏn), who were sent to Hollywood to appear in Hess's biopic three years earlier. According to an article in the *Hankook Daily* (*Han'guk Ilbo*) dated March 16, 1959, the children ardently welcomed Ahn, calling him "Grandpa," and performed traditional music and dance for him as they did for Rock Hudson onscreen.

But despite efforts by the South Korean media to bridge the gap between Ahn and his parental homeland, his Hollywood career was not fully appreciated because of the historical and cultural disconnection that barred American B movies and wartime anti-Japanese films from Korean viewers. Further, the press about the films Ahn made in the 1950s appears to have been filled with misinformation. For example, accompanying the aforementioned article in *Kukje yŏnghwa* was a still from *Love Is a Many Splendored Thing* in which Richard Loo was mistakenly identified as Philip Ahn. In fact, the Hawaiian-born Chinese American actor Loo was habitually cast as Japanese villains, appearing in many films alongside Ahn—the two ethnically separate thespians creating a double or mirror image of one another.

Subsequently, in an obituary for Loo in the French journal *Cine Revue* dated December 15, 1983, a picture of Ahn in *Kung Fu* was used instead of the late Loo's image.[26] This confusion speaks to the interchangeability of Asian actors, regardless of nationality and ethnicity, which was fostered by an industry insensitive to the diversities and differences within the same racial group.

As evidenced in the above-quoted passage of *The Life and Death of the Hollywood Kid*, South Korean movie fans had only a vague impression of Philip Ahn despite his father's lofty status in history. Although the narrator in Ahn Junghyo's novel grumbled about Ahn's Americanized name, the Korean American actor's first name in fact had a double meaning, standing for P'il-ip ("inevitable independence") in Sino-Korean. Like his name itself, Philip Ahn (An P'il-ip) attempted to traverse the boundaries of Korean and American cultures throughout his life. In this respect, his career can and should be recuperated as part of Korean cultural history.

Lost Projects and Forgotten Histories of Transnational Korean Cinema

One might wonder how the career of Philip Ahn, an actor who never appeared in a film made outside of America or Europe, could be contextualized in the history of Korean cinema. The foremost justification would be his concerted and abiding efforts to take part in the Korean film industry from the late 1940s onward. On February 28, 1949, the first president of the Republic of Korea (ROK), Syngman Rhee (Yi Sŭng-man), replied to a letter that Ahn had sent him on that subject:

> Sometime ago I read your good letter with deep interest. I do appreciate your desire to come to Korea and use your education and ability in the service to your own country and I am sure you have the right idea that it will be a great help to us. It is my sincere advice to you to come and help develop the motion picture industry in Korea. There are a number of organizations that are engaged in its development, but like everything else, it must have an experienced leader to direct it properly. I have no idea what I can do to help you but I assure you I will do anything in my power. In fact, you do not need much of anyone's help. If you only manage to come they will all be glad to get your help and direction and will be glad to assist you. I would not tie up with any one particular organization. You can see what we have and choose the one you think best.[27]

Considering that the reconstruction of South Korea's film industry only began in 1946 (with the revision of propaganda-oriented Japanese censorship laws) and that fewer than fifty domestic films were made between 1946 and 1949, the leadership role proposed by President Rhee could have been Ahn's ticket to prominence in South Korean film history. Regretfully, the opportunity was lost.

Rhee's second letter to Ahn, dated December 8, 1949, contains passages that might explain why Ahn did not or could not accept this invitation to go to South Korea.

> I have received your letter and am glad that you have decided to help in the film industry. It is a noble idea and I appreciate your spirit. Of all of the Koreans at home and abroad you are the logical one to undertake this enterprise since you have spent so many years in preparing yourself for bigger things for our nation.... However, my advice to you is not to scrap everything there in order to build up something here at the beginning. The living conditions, money exchange difficulties, lack of housing, etc. combine to make the situation somewhat impractical for anyone who has lived in America for so many years. Some of our people who have come from Hawaii and the United States to spend the rest of their lives have packed up and gone back because of these difficult living conditions. I would advise you, therefore, not to make final arrangements until after you have been here and seen the situation.[28]

In spite of Tosan's wish for his five children to return to and work for the betterment of Korea, none of them were able to realize their father's dream. Philip made the most diligent effort to this end, but the difficulties of adjustment, as suggested in Rhee's letter, as well as the ensuing civil war, seem to have discouraged him from going to South Korea.

One might also question the sincerity and commitment of Rhee's invitation in light of his political rivalry with An Ch'ang-ho in the KPG and the Korean American community, as well as his authoritarian disposition. He brooked no challenges to his power, engaging in the ruthless elimination of his opponents and fraudulent elections, until his regime was eventually toppled by a student revolution on April 19, 1960. As John Cha, biographer of Philip's sister Susan Ahn Cuddy, notes, "After the Japanese retreated from Korea, Syngman Rhee's political machinery also kept Tosan in obscurity.... It was no secret that Rhee's people (Tongjihŏi) and Tosan's people were antagonistic towards each other from way back when, even though Tosan himself had always supported Rhee."[29] According to Ralph Ahn, when his brother Philip visited South Korea in 1959 he was monitored by the secret police, although Syngman Rhee on one occasion confided to the actor, "If your father was alive, Korea would not be divided today"—a tribute to Tosan's diplomatic skills as a mediator.[30]

After Rhee was forced to step down from the presidency, Philip Ahn was offered another opportunity to enter the Korean film industry—this time as an actor. Famous screenwriter Ch'oe Kŭm-dong wrote to him on May 6, 1960:

> As you may know, the great upheaval has ensued...and everything is going to be renovated now.... At this opportunity, I have renewed my resolution to film the life of "Ahn Tosan," one of the greatest patriots in our recent history. As I wrote to you last year, there were many difficulties in the way of realizing our aims to film this patriot's life. But now things have changed and we may be free to make this movie without any hesitation.... I sincerely wish you will play your father's part in the film. This will meet the enthusiastic welcome from our people. You said you are not good at your mother tongue, Korean. But I think this will not matter. We will locate the scenes in Korea first and then we, you and our location team, will go over to America to [scout locations] there.... Production will begin in September this year and I will begin to write the scenario now.[31]

Although many anti-Japanese films were made in postliberation South Korea under the rule of Syngman Rhee (a former independence movement leader himself), only the lives of selected patriots were allowed to be adapted for the screen, including *King Kojong and An Chung-gŭn* (*Kojong hwangje wa ŭsa An Chung-gŭn*, 1959), about a prominent revolutionary who assassinated Ito Hirobumi, the first Japanese resident-general in Korea, at Harbin station, in 1909; *Yu Kwan-sun* (1959), about the "Jeanne d'arc of Korea," who was martyred for her leadership in the March First Movement of 1919; and *Independence Society and Young Syngman Rhee* (*Tongnip hyŏphŏi wa ch'ŏnyŏn Yi Sŭngman*, 1959). As Ch'oe Kŭm-dong insinuated in his letter, Rhee probably would not have allowed cinematic tribute to be paid to Tosan, as doing so might undermine his own authority.

In the wake of the April 19 Revolution and Rhee's departure for exile in Hawaii, film censorship was relaxed in the democratized political climate, which led to the advent of socially conscious masterpieces including *Mr. Pak* (*Pak sŏbang*, 1960), *Housemaid* (*Hanyŏ*, 1960), *The Stray Bullet* (*Obalt'an*, 1961), and *Third Rate Manager* (*Samdŭng kwajang*, 1961) during a very short transitional period before Park Chung Hee (Pak Chŏng-hŭi) seized power in a May 16, 1961 military coup. Among the films released in 1960 was *Ah! Teacher Paekbŏm Kim Ku* (*A! Paekbŏm Kim Ku sŏnsaeng*), a biopic centering on the charismatic anticolonial leader Kim Ku (who admired Tosan and worked closely with him), written by none other than Ch'oe Kŭm-dong. Despite Ch'oe's specific production plans, his proposed project on Tosan An Ch'ang-ho never materialized for reasons that remain unclear today. Perhaps it was because of a lack of financing, the lack of popularity of nationalistic biopics, or the discouragement of anti Japanese themes by the Park Chung Hee regime, which eventually normalized diplomacy with Japan in 1965. This lost project nevertheless remained Philip's lifelong dream.; just a few days before suffering complications resulting from a biopsy for lung cancer (which led to his death on February 28, 1978), Ahn confided to his friends and relatives that he was torn between whether to produce a documentary or a commercial feature film about his father's life.

As Ch'oe's letter reveals, Ahn seems to have regarded his deficiency in his ancestral language as an obstacle to his potential career as an actor in the South Korean film industry. For an American-born second-generation Korean American, Ahn could speak Korean reasonably well, as he communicated with his parents in the language while they were alive. Since Tosan was habitually absent from home, Ahn and his siblings learned Korean primarily from their mother, who came to the United States in 1902 as a young bride and only returned to Korea once, in 1963, when she was invited by Park Chung Hee to receive the Korean National Medal of Honor on Tosan's behalf. Yi Hae-ryŏn's Korean was understandably old-fashioned, and she spoke with a thick North Korean accent. There is a trace of a similar North Korean accent, as well as awkward, grammatically incorrect expressions when Ahn occasionally utters Korean dialogue in films and television shows, such as *Charlie Chan in Honolulu* (1938), *I Spy* ("An American Empress," December 25, 1967), and *M*A*S*H* ("Hawkeye," January 13, 1976). In the 1959 interview with *Kukje yŏnghwa*, Ahn asked the interviewer, director Yi Pyŏng-il, if his Korean sounded strange. Yi politely answered, "Yes, your accent is a little unusual...but for a person born and raised in America, you speak fluently."[32] Ahn even told Yi that if he could get a good part in a Korean film, he would practice the language every night. Ahn's lack of confidence in speaking Korean probably contributed to his subsequent pursuit of U.S.-ROK coproductions as a producer (rather than an actor), following his 1959 trip across the Pacific.

Yi Pyŏng-il seems to have given the green light to the idea of a coproduction when he mentioned the South Korean film industry's increased interest in pursuing foreign co-producers and his personal desire to collaborate with Hollywood studios. Coincidentally or not, Ahn had his own plans for such a co-production, and, on his trip back to America, he stopped by the Tokyo branch of Columbia Pictures International to discuss the possibility of a joint partnership with the studio. Walter Briggs of the *New York Herald Tribune* was present at the meeting as a prospective writer. In a newspaper article entitled "Actor Is a Villain at Home, a Hero in Korea," Briggs announced Ahn's plans:

> Mr. Ahn discovered considerable interest among Korean movie producers for a co-production with an American film company. "I would like to do one suitable for the international market," he states enthusiastically, "that would mirror Korean traditions yet capitalize on the drama inherent in the 'static war' between Communism and the Free World that exists across the Thirty-eighth Parallel." Mr. Ahn visualizes joining two or three American stars with Korean talent in a picture that would be shot entirely in Korea.... "I want to produce a good picture," Mr. Ahn says. "The Americans would help give it pace, something that most Oriental films lack. It would be a true picture of life in that troubled land."[33]

Philip Ahn apparently nurtured the ambitious plan of making a Hollywood motion picture entirely on location in Korea, a project that had never been undertaken before.

In the mid-1950s to the early 1960s, films set in Asia were shot primarily on back lots and location shots were inserted, as in *Soldier of Fortune* (1955), *Love Is a Many-Splendored Thing* (1955), *The Teahouse of the August Moon* (1956), and *The World of Suzie Wong* (1960). *Battle Hymn*, for example, was shot entirely in studios and in Arizona, the rocky terrain of the American Southwest doubling for war-torn Korea. As noted by Korean War film historian Paul M. Edwards, "Few films, or parts of films, were ever filmed in Korea."[34] One of the two first Korean War films, Samuel Fuller's *The Steel Helmet* (1951), was shot in Griffith Park in southern California, as well as on artificial sets (filled with Chinese and Indian props) standing in for a Korean temple. Such inauthentic images of Korea were perpetuated in American media as late as the 1970s and 1980s, particularly in Robert Altman's *M*A*S*H* (1970) and on the television series spawned by the film (1972–1983). Korea was depicted as a nondescript, mountainous rural backdrop occasionally peopled with pidgin English-speaking farmers, orphans, profiteers, and "business girls" adorned in Vietnamese hats and Chinese garb.

Philip Ahn was eager to rectify the Western media's misrepresentations of Korea. On April 6, 1959, several weeks after his return from Seoul, Ahn wrote to Syngman Rhee, notifying him of a preliminary plan to join with Columbia Pictures, as well as making a strong argument about the imperative need for and benefits of a co-production:

> Since seeing you in Seoul, I have been thinking over our discussion on developing the Korean motion picture industry. To be perfectly frank, at the present time I think we can most constructively envisage this as a problem in presenting to the Western World an accurate portrayal of the multi-faceted Korean life and culture, rather than attempting to further "push" our own films.... Columbia is the most active motion picture studio from the point of view of foreign co-production.... They are interested in reaching the same contractual basis in Korea as the Governments of, for example, England, Japan and Italy have previously agreed to.... Unfortunately, up until now, most movies dealing with Korea have shown it during the War and we are hopeful that this [co-production] will prove to Westerners that there is more to our country than foxholes and mud.... The profits can be plowed back into the embryo Korean film industry, enabling further technical development which will eventually result in world release of our better Korean films.[35]

The transfer of power from Rhee to Park Chung Hee did not deter Ahn's resolve to bring the first U.S.-South Korean co-production to fruition. On November 6, 1962, Philip Ahn took a giant leap toward realizing his dream by entering into a co-production contract with Shin Films—the first Korean film company remotely resembling a Hollywood studio—and run by legendary director Shin Sang-ok, (Sin Sang-ok), who was personally favored and supported by Park Chung Hee. The project was provisionally entitled *A Long Way from Home* and was to be an adaptation of a Korean War novel by Vern Sneider about the intercultural bonding that develops between young South Korean siblings and five American GIs who save them. According to the contract, Shin Films was to supply financing of $350,000, whereas Philip Ahn Productions was to provide the story, the script, the male lead and other American acting personnel, the American technical crew, the director, and partial mechanical, technical, and photographic equipment. The net profits were to be shared at a 70 percent (Shin) to 30 percent (Ahn) ratio. Ahn first invited his mentor and friend Lewis Milestone to be director. Ahn had made four films with Milestone, including *Anything Goes, The General Died at*

Dawn, *The Purple Heart*, and *Halls of Montezuma* (1950). Although he was not interested in directing the film, Milestone agreed to review the scripts and serve as an advisor. In his place, Milestone recommended Tay Garnett, who accepted the offer to be the film's director. The main candidates for the male lead were, Jeffrey Hunter and Audie Murphy (the latter being a less favored choice by Shin Films because of his low marquee value in South Korea) were main candidates.

Despite the difference in opinions between Ahn and Shin about financial liabilities and executive details, the project was developed smoothly until the South Korean government withheld its approval of Shin's application for overseas financing. In a letter dated February 18, 1963, Hong Man-kil, representing the Foreign Department of Shin Films, notified Philip Ahn of the indefinite deferment of their co-production on the grounds that the ROK government had begun taking stronger measures to "prevent the consumption of scarce dollars" in light of a foreign funds shortage and the weak economy.[36] Although Hong suggested the possibility of resuming the joint project as soon as the economic situation improved, Yi Chae-myŏng, president of Asia Motion Pictures, who had met with Shin Sang-ok to discuss the status of the co-production on Philip Ahn's behalf, confirmed a virtual breakup of the project when he wrote in a letter to Ahn dated February 21, 1963 that the project had been halted:

> The ROK Ministry of Finance decided that the contract signed between you and Shin fails to show the project is a mutual contract of common interest between the parties, with Shin producing the planned film single-handedly. In this case, the government cannot provide Shin with foreign exchange, which means the impossibility of the program.... It is my conclusion that nothing indicates any possibility of the film's materialization in the foreseeable future.[37]

The Park Chung Hee regime's strict regulation of foreign exchange and prioritization of domestic economic interests in heavy industries effectively aborted the birth of the first co-production between American and South Korean film industries.

Overcoming bitter disappointment about this failed project, Philip Ahn continuously sought to build bridges between the United States and South Korea in political, diplomatic, and cultural spheres. In May 1962, in recognition of his civic activism, Ahn was installed as honorary mayor of Panorama City (a post he kept until his death) in the San Fernando Valley, northeast of Los Angeles. There he had helped his sister Soorah open an upscale

Cantonese restaurant in 1954, which would prosper over the next three decades as the famous "Phil Ahn's Moongate." Between his dual career as a movie and television actor and a successful restaurateur, Ahn actively worked as a spokesman of the Korean American community and a mediator between Korean politicians, diplomats, and businessmen and their American counterparts.

Philip Ahn Cuddy describes his uncle's distinguished leadership in the community as follows:

> The pioneer Korean American community was centered on the Ahn family's residence in the early 1900s. And, many of the Koreans coming from Korea in the 1960s and early 1970s came to Philip and his mother for advice and assistance. Once, an entire crew from a Korean navy ship docked in Long Beach came for dinner. Korean businessmen and politicians came to Philip's home for support and introductions. American politicians sought Philip's fame to enhance their campaigns and raise funds. American businessmen sought his endorsements of their products and contacts in Korea.[38]

In addition, in 1969 when Los Angeles was under the governance of his friend Mayor Sam Yorty, Ahn made a significant contribution to the establishment of the Los Angeles-Pusan sister city affiliation, a program for which he served as chairman.

Although his co-production plans with South Korean film companies misfired, the Tosan Memorial Committee headed by Ahn and his South Korean counterparts gained strong support from Park Chung Hee and the city of Seoul. As a result of the committee's work, Tosan Memorial Park, an eight-acre burial and commemoration site for Tosan and his wife, opened in Kangnam, a newly developed district south of the Han River, on November 10, 1973. The dedication ceremony was attended by thousands of citizens and high officials, including Prime Minister Kim Chong-p'il, as well as Ahn family members Philip, Susan and her two children Flip (Philip Ahn Cuddy) and Christine.

Ahn's personal correspondence file is filled with letters from South Korea seeking his assistance or thanking him for his hospitality. In a letter dated September 8, 1949, An Chŏl-yŏng of the Seoul Motion Picture Company asked the actor to procure a price list of Monogram and Eagle-Lion films for possible exportation to South Korea. Hwang On-sun, the director of the Orphan's Home of Korea, with whom Philip Ahn became acquainted during the filming of *Battle Hymn*, wrote him requesting that he introduce the

FIGURE 1.4 *Philip Ahn, an unofficial Korean cultural ambassador in Hollywood, meets South Korean President Park Chung Hee on June 3, 1971.* Courtesy of the Ahn Family.

Korean actress, Kim Yu-mi to American film companies. President Park Chung Hee sent him a thank-you letter dated June 9, 1965, expressing his gratitude for Ahn's reception at the airport on the occasion of his recent visit to Los Angeles. On June 14, 1968, Yi Sŭng-yŏp of Dong Yang Motion Pictures sent a synopsis of his company's new film, *Unfinished Desire (Han)*, to the actor, soliciting his advice regarding its marketability in the international film festival circuit. Likewise, in August 1976, Sin Il-yong, a Korean martial artists under contract with Hong Kong's Golden Harvest studio, sought Ahn's advice with regard to his potential career opportunities in Hollywood.[39] These and other correspondences clearly illustrate that Ahn served as a bridge between the two nations and their film industries, providing a role model for younger South Korean actors and actresses dreaming of making films in Hollywood.

Philip Ahn never gave up his dream of producing a film about Korea. In the final years of his life, he purchased the rights to Pearl S. Buck's *The New Year* (1968), with a view to adapting the story for the big screen. This novel tells the story of Christopher Winters, a Harvard-educated lawyer and

FIGURE 1.5 *Philip Ahn's star on the Hollywood Walk of Fame, dedicated on November 14, 1984. Following Sessue Hayakawa, Sabu, and Anna May Wong, who received their stars when the Walk was inaugurated in 1960, Philip Ahn's honor was the fourth one for an Asian American actor.* Courtesy of the Ahn Family.

politician who reconnects with his half-Korean son, whom he abandoned as a soldier during the Korean War. In a January 1970 issue of *San Fernando Valley and Que Magazine*, John Ringo Graham reported that Philip Ahn was "actively working on a project that is certain to bring recognition to him as a Korean." Noting that the source of the project was Buck's novel, Graham added, "When this happens, it will fulfill a life-long ambition."[40] Sadly, this project was never completed.

As a token of esteem for this otherwise overlooked figure, the city of Los Angeles, under Mayor Tom Bradley, proclaimed November 14, 1984 Philip Ahn Day or Korean Day and posthumously honored the actor with a star on the Hollywood Walk of Fame. Amid festive Korean dancing and music, the dedication ceremony of Ahn's star was attended by 400 members of the film industry and Korean communities. This lone Korean star on the Walk of Fame (at 6211 Hollywood Boulevard) sadly goes unnoticed by hundreds of Korean tourists and immigrants passing by each day. Among Ahn's contemporary actors of Asian descent, only Anna May Wong and Keye Luke have received stars.

THE MANY DISPLACED IDENTITIES OF
THE FIRST KOREAN IN HOLLYWOOD

Let us return to my previous proposition that Philip Ahn's career should be recognized as part of Korean film history. First, evidence from his personal papers demonstrates that time and time again he made efforts to enter the South Korean film industry as a leader, actor, and producer, although he lost many opportunities because of political and economic reasons. Second, Ahn's direct and indirect manifestations of Korean diasporic identities in American film and television deserve critical attention in the broader context of transnational Korean cinema. Rather than employing the notion of national cinema as a geographically confined concept, we need to acknowledge a deterritorized, diasporic space pertaining to Korean history and culture both *inside* and *around* Hollywood texts, at the center of which is the often-peripheralized Philip Ahn. It has become difficult to separate his images in anti-Japanese propaganda films from the ideological impetus of the Great Korea Independence Spirit *(Taehan tongnip chŏngsin)*, symbolized by Tosan An Ch'ang-ho, who was himself a kind of liminal figure.

The recuperation of Ahn's legacy in the context of transnational Korean cinema should not be misconstrued as an act of romanticization or hagiographic elevation. There is a solid historical basis for a diasporic national cinema, apart from Philip Ahn's efforts to infiltrate the South Korean industry. Between 1941 and 1945, no films except for pro-Japanese propaganda (in the Japanese language) could be produced and distributed in colonial Korea, and the producers who refused to be involved in this propaganda effort were subject to persecution at the hands of colonial authorities.[41] In light of this total suppression of national cinema in his homeland, Ahn's displaced expressions of the struggle for Korean independence in Hollywood's anti-Japanese propaganda films during World War II can be reclaimed from the perspective of a Korean colonial diaspora, which does not always coincide with the politics of Asian America.

Philip Ahn's Hollywood career parallels that of Kim Yŏm (known as Jin Yan in China), the so-called Emperor of 1930s Shanghai Movies. As one of Korea's first surgeons, Kim P'il-sun, the actor's father, was an ardent supporter and financier of the Korean independence movement. In 1912, when he was two years old, Kim Yŏm migrated to the northern part of Manchuria with his family. Determined to become an actor, Kim Yŏm went to Shanghai at age seventeen , where he debuted in a silent film in 1929. A matinee idol during the 1930s, he played leads opposite such famous actresses as Ruan Ling-yu and Chen Yan-yan. Like Philip Ahn, Kim Yŏm expressed the anti-colonial spirit inherited from his father in his performances in resistance films, such as *The Big Road* (*Da Lu*, 1935). Not only were both Ahn and Kim sons of patriots and emblems of colonial diaspora but they also explored and widened alternative avenues for expressing the anti-Japanese sentiment of the Korean people, whose freedom of speech, native language, and historical traditions had been either lost or forbidden during the years of occupation. In this transnational relocation of the spirit of independence, both actors had to displace and disguise their ethnic identities: Chinese for Kim Yŏm, and both Chinese and Japanese for Philip Ahn.

Ahn's wartime career in Hollywood—his onscreen oscillation between Chinese allies and Japanese enemies—not only registers the imperative of cross-ethnic masquerade as a means of survival for a minority actor working in a mainstream industry oblivious to ethnic differences among racial others but also reflects the theme of displacement in that era's Korean and Korean American identity politics. In the collective consciousness of Koreans (domestic or overseas), the Sino-Japanese War (1937–1945) and World War II functioned as surrogates for a war for independence. When Koreans in America first heard the news of the Pearl Harbor attack, they exploded, *"Taehan tongnip manse!"* (Long Live Korean Independence!), and cried for joy.[42] For them, American involvement in the war against Japan and the Allies' victory meant much more than the protection of the world from fascists; it signified the long-dreamed-of independence of their homeland. Just as Shanghai and Chungking provided bases for exiled KPG leaders, and just as Manchuria became a battleground for Korean guerrillas, Hollywood offered Philip Ahn an imaginary national space where he could carry on his father's legacy by participating in anti-Japanese propaganda. What was forbidden and repressed in colonial Chosŏn (Korean) films under the strict censorship of the Japanese government could be freely expressed in Hollywood, as well as in Shanghai before the city fell to Japanese occupation in 1937.

In *China Girl* (1942), for example, Philip Ahn embodies the very image of Tosan in his portrayal of Dr. Young, a dignified Chinese educator who unwaveringly gives lessons in patriotism to a classroom full of orphans, despite the threat to his life posed by Japanese bombs. In *China*, Ahn plays the valiant Chinese guerrilla leader Lin Cho, a cross-ethnic personification of a member of the Korean Independence Army (Kwangbokgun) who fought against Japanese troops in China, Burma, and India.[43] Later the paternalistic role of Kan, Senior Reverend and Grand Master of Martial Arts of the Shaolin Temple, in *Kung Fu* afforded Philip Ahn the last chance to play his father in an imaginary, displaced form. In a 1973 interview, he admits to his feeling a strong identification with Tosan's philosophy while acting in the series: "So much of what *Kung Fu* says is what my father taught me. He preached brotherhood and peace in Korea.... His inspiration [has] been of enormous help to me in my being able to project the essence of oriental philosophy in the *Kung Fu* series."[44]

Unlike Kim Yŏm, a popular star of the 1930s Shanghai film industry who played no ethnicity besides Chinese, Philip Ahn occasionally played Koreans. Two of his most significant Korean roles, Dr. Kim in *China Sky* (1945) and Lu Wan in *Battle Hymn*, are discussed in detail in Chapter 4 and Chapter 5, respectively. He also appeared as several minor Korean characters, such as a South Korean assistant for American troops in *Battle Zone* (1952), a North Korean prisoner of war in a MASH unit in *Battle Circus* (1953), and a South Korean army captain in *The Great Impostor* (1960). Several television programs likewise accentuated his ethnic identity. One of his earliest television appearances was the titular role of Korean interpreter Pak Chang in the "Mister Pak Takes Over" episode of *TV Reader's Digest* (June 13, 1955). Although initially mistrusted because of his World War II service in the Japanese army and previous residence north of the thirty-eighth parallel, Pak proves his loyalty and earns respect (thereby becoming "*Mister* Pak") when he intercepts an enemy radio transmission and confuses the Chinese troops with false military orders, decisively contributing to an American victory. In addition to this role and to other characters in Korean War dramas, Ahn played a Korean consul stationed in the United States in several programs, including *The Eve Arden Show* ("Liz Meets Young Korea," March 4, 1958) and *Mannix* ("Shadow of a Man," January 25, 1968). This televisual image of Philip Ahn as an ROK diplomat is symbolic of his unofficial role as Korea's cultural ambassador in Hollywood where no other actors of Korean descent have ever come close to the length and breadth of his career.

Like Pak Chung-hun, who persuaded Jonathan Demme to change the ethnicity of his role in *The Truth about Charlie*, Philip Ahn seems to have influenced director Robert Florey to emphasize the Korean background in the "Lady Godiva" episode of ABC's *Hong Kong* (February 8, 1961). In this crime drama, he plays a Korean journalist-turned-killer, C.Y. Hyung. Not only is Ahn's Korean role meaty but also the episode refers to Korea several times as a nostalgic place of romance between the protagonist Glen Evans (Rod Taylor), an American correspondent in Hong Kong, and his ex-lover, Helen "Lady Godiva" Randolph (Dina Merrill), another reporter, who encounter each other ten years after their initial separation. What is amazing about the episode is that there is no mention of the Korean War, which was virtually the only reason why Korea had been referenced in contemporaneous American films and television programs. Instead, the closing scene shows the reunited romantic couple fondly reminiscing about their "good old days" in Seoul, thus capsizing the conventional wisdom of Korea as a mountainous, rural war zone with few signs of modernity or comfort. Helen affectionately recalls, "You know...I miss it. Those days in Seoul when we used to eat chocolate bars for breakfast, drink beer in those funny little places." Thus, the shared memory of Seoul functions as a catalyst for rekindling a romance between the two Americans, just as Paris serves as the inspiration behind the mutual longings of Rick Blaine (Humphrey Bogart) and Ilsa Laszlo (Ingrid Bergman) in *Casablanca* (1942). It is hard to imagine the writers and producers voluntarily coming up with this novel idea of a "romantic Seoul" without Ahn's persuasion. Ahn must have used his friendly relationship with Florey (a director with whom he collaborated on a number of films and television programs beginning with *Daughter of Shanghai*) to adjust the script to accommodate such unusual references to Korea.

Although Philip Ahn actively sought to express his diasporic identities at every possible opportunity in whatever limited capacity he could, these efforts likely meant little to the majority of mainstream audiences who did not distinguish differences among Asian ethnicities, histories, and cultures. Perhaps the peculiarities and complexities of Ahn's stardom can best be understood by an "ideal spectator," one who is armed with the combined knowledge of American B movie culture, the Ahn family's history, and his cultural liminality (which bridges different national cinemas and film industries). In a way, this chapter constitutes a critical reinscription of Ahn's stardom, which remained unconsummated in his lifetime due to institutional, economic, and cultural constraints of both the American and South Korean film industries.

MIN, CHIN, OR A POSITION IN BETWEEN?

On October 1, 2003, I presented an early version of this chapter at a Korean cinema symposium held at Yonsei University in Seoul. Following my talk, *Daughter of Shanghai* was screened as a one-film Philip Ahn "retrospective." This hard-to-find B film had never been released in South Korea. My talk and the screening were greeted with enthusiasm by Korean film scholars, who encouraged my further research on Ahn's legacy in the context of transnational Korean cinema. I was particularly touched when a lecturer told me that he was deeply moved seeing Tosan's son onscreen. I suddenly realized that Philip Ahn had not been *forgotten* in South Korea. Rather, his career was never properly promoted because of the lack of scholarship and the limitation of video and DVD markets. After the conference, one professor asked me, "Philip Ahn was a star, wasn't he? He was famous but we just don't know him in Korea." I was hesitant to answer. Was he a star? Americans have called him everything but a star: an Oriental actor, a character actor, a supporting actor, a sidekick, a third wheel. I was then reminded of something David Jung, a former Chinatown resident, said about Anna May Wong: "The Chinese people accepted second best.... They accepted her saying, 'Well, somebody made it.' Anna May Wong was actually a star; outside of the Chinese community, she was just an actress but she was a star in our community."[45] Philip Ahn was accepted in a similar way in the Korean American community.

Ahn's correspondence file includes a letter, dated September 20, 1974, from a twenty-year-old college student named Lisa Min. Min introduces herself as "an insatiable movie and television buff" and confides her ambition to become an actress. Soliciting Ahn's advice about her career, she writes, "You are the only actor [by whom] I have ever felt empowered to write. I have always felt a kinship to you when watching you in *Kung Fu* or one of your past movies, because, like myself, you are Korean."[46]

The same performance that produced in Min a sense of ethnic solidarity and empowerment provoked the exact opposite reaction from other Asian American audiences. For example, Frank Chin, a Chinese American playwright, vehemently attacked the racial politics behind and in the popular ABC series *Kung Fu* in a 1974 *New York Times* article. He cynically compares the evolution of apes with that of Chinese images in mainstream media:

> In 40 years, apes went from a naked, hairy King Kong, gigantic with nitwit sex fantasies about little human women, to a talking chimpanzee leading his fellow apes in a battle to take over the planet. We've progressed from Fu Manchu, the male Dragon Lady of silent movies, to Charlie Chan and then to *Kung Fu* on TV. We've made no progress at all. We've still made out to be the likes of Keye Luke, Benson Fong, Philip Ahn and Victor Sen Yung at our worst and middling, and David Carradine—talking like he's in a trance—at our best.[47]

Accompanying the piece is a close-up publicity shot of a bald, wizened Philip Ahn in Master Kan makeup, epitomizing the very image of an anachronistic Oriental fiercely denounced in Chin's article.

Min's and Chin's contending interpretations of Ahn's legacy represent the dilemmas and difficulties that scholars of early Asian American performers inevitably face. On the one hand, these pioneers were inspirational role models for younger Asian American actors and drama students. Their ubiquitous presence throughout the studio era and the Television Age sustained the visibility of Asian Americans in popular media, who otherwise would have been completely absent except in yellowface. On the other hand, the careers of these performers comprise a composite of Oriental stereotypes retrospectively condemned by post-civil rights Asian American activists who have benefited from increased political agency and institutional access to independent filmmaking (which enabled corrective self-imaging). As a critical strategy to see beyond textual stereotypes and structured racism, I have thus far employed a transnational paradigm to reclaim Philip Ahn's legacy outside the confinement of U.S. racial politics and to underscore the diasporic hermeneutics of Asian American representations.

Now let us turn our attention from the diasporic actor to the bilingual, bicultural spectator, a hypothetical yet highly plausible figure capable of gleaning differentiated meanings from cross-ethnic performance. Yin Kim, Ahn's friend, casually commented, "I always *laughed* when I saw Philip play mean Japanese villains. He was Korean and one of the sweetest guys I ever knew."[48] Here we find a perfect example of the subversive spectatorial pleasure articulated by Ella Shohat and Robert Stam: "In a kind of double consciousness, spectators may enjoy what they know to be misrepresentations."[49] This pleasure of ethnic recognition is a subject I explore in the next chapter.

2

THE AUDIENCE WHO KNEW
TOO MUCH

Oriental Masquerade and Ethnic Recognition
among Asian Americans

O NE OF THE BIGGEST CHALLENGES that I have faced in my reading of Philip Ahn's career has been to see beyond my own cultural position and accommodate hermeneutic strategies outside the domain of Korean identity politics. As a scholar born and raised in South Korea who then immigrated to the United States in my late twenties, I am necessarily caught up in the process of developing a hyphenated, bicultural identity. Despite conscious efforts to immerse myself in America's diverse cultural traditions and to become a "Korean American," the educational pursuits, social values, and personal memories of my formative years in South Korea continue to affect my intellectual life significantly. Beginning with my elementary school years, I grew up learning about the patriot Tosan An Ch'ang-ho. In Seoul, I lived only twenty minutes away from Tosan Memorial Park and traveled down a boulevard named after him (Tosan daero) every day. Just as South Korean audiences lack the cultural memories of U.S.-born cinephiles and television addicts weaned on the Orientalist imagery of Charlie Chan, Anna May Wong, and *Kung Fu* (1972–1975), Americans (including second-generation Korean Americans) can hardly be expected to identify with the reverence Koreans feel for this national hero.

As discussed in Chapter 1, it is almost impossible for audiences with ontological ties to Korea to separate Philip Ahn's archetypal screen roles

(Japanese villain, Chinese educator, etc.) from his offscreen identity as the son of an icon in the pantheon of Korean nationalists. This knowledge generates additional meanings about his characters and the texts themselves—meanings that are part of a transnational, cross-cultural reading position that further enriches an understanding of the complexities and contradictions underlying the formulaic façade of American films from the studio era.

The scope of my book, however, is not limited to the Korean viewpoint. In this chapter, I mobilize Philip Ahn as a cross-ethnic signifier whose multivalent performativity provides an opportunity to theorize Asian American spectatorship. My main task is to explore the relationship between the cross-ethnic performer and the bilingual, bicultural spectator. Although this spectatorship is based on my own viewing position as a native speaker of Korean, it can encompass variegated ethnicities and language affiliations (Korean American, Chinese American, Japanese American, South Korean, mainland Chinese, Hong Kong Chinese, Taiwanese, Japanese, etc.), depending on the specific texts and scenes in question.

This chapter thus makes a contribution to both gender and ethnic studies by expanding feminist theories of masquerade and race/queer theories of passing to address Asian American performativity and spectatorship. Psychoanalytic theory and Asian American studies have traditionally been considered incompatible or mutually exclusive because of the latter discipline's predilection for "[talking] about racial subjects as 'real' subjects" through materially based paradigms, such as sociology, anthropology, and history.[1] However, as David L. Eng points out, "This unorthodox pairing...yields a more comprehensive understanding of the historical intersection of race, gender, and sexuality that produce a dominant image of the Asian American male subject in the U.S. cultural imaginary" by recuperating the immaterial, unquantifiable, and psychological elements of racial subjectivity and "reality."[2] Whereas Eng mobilizes psychoanalysis in his study of Asian American masculinity to account for the significance of sexuality and sexual difference in racial formation, I am interested in applying masquerade and passing theories to highlight ethnic and linguistic differences among Asian American performers and spectators.

Asian American spectatorship is a severely understudied subject. Peter X. Feng's essay, "Recuperating Suzie Wong: A Fan's Nancy Kwan-dary," is a rare contribution to the topic. Feng argues that Asian American spectatorial pleasure in a racially retrograde Hollywood feature like *The World of Suzie Wong* (1960) depends upon a "strategy of selectively re-narrativizing elements of a star's performance." A resistant spectator, according to Feng, mentally traces over a racist narrative and recasts stereotyped characters "from scavenged bits and pieces of a film" in a way similar to the strategies employed in Helen Lee's experimental short film *Sally's Beauty Spot* (1990), which manipulates and reedits Nancy Kwan's images from *Suzie Wong* for the pleasure of the Asian American spectator.[3]

Although a "resistant spectator" is an oft-recycled formation in the discourse of black spectatorship, Feng nevertheless puts a fresh spin on the text/star/spectator triad by foregrounding the ethnic star image as a site of resignification, a critical strategy that my own study shares. Feng builds up his conceptualization of Asian American spectatorship from Stuart Hall's tripartite model, first postulated in his influential 1980 essay, "Encoding/ Decoding." In this essay, Hall proposes three positions of reading or decoding media texts: *dominant*, *negotiated*, and *oppositional*. When the viewer decodes connotative meanings of the text in a way preferred and intended by the encoder, he or she is operating inside the sphere of *dominant* ideology. When the viewer acknowledges dominant definitions but adapts or retrofits them to his or her "local conditions" and rules, the spectator is engaging in *negotiated* reading. When the viewer resists intended or preferred meanings and reinterprets the text for the sake of his or her group interest, that spectator is following a path that runs in *opposition* to dominant ideology.[4]

Hall's theory of oppositional or resistant readings was subsequently adopted by Manthia Diawara and bell hooks to account for African American spectatorship in relation to Hollywood cinema. Although Diawara and hooks speak from different gender positions, both theorists see black spectatorship as a mode of resistance. Diawara in particular puts emphasis on the "ambiguous experience" that black spectators (regardless of gender and sexuality) encounter when the narrative pleasures of hegemonic texts serve the white male heterosexual spectator at the expense of their own subject position. According to him, resistant spectatorship lies in anti-identification or an act of disavowal of racist representations of blacks. Quoting Frantz Fanon's famous line, "every spectator is a coward or traitor," he calls for the spectator who transforms "the problem of passive identification into active criticism which both informs and interrelates with contemporary oppositional film-making."[5]

Hooks redeploys Diawara's formation of resistant spectatorship from a black feminist perspective. For her, African American female spectators actively refuse to identify not only with the white male subject (the perpetrator) but also with the white female object of the phallocentric gaze (the victim). Locating the "oppositional gaze" in black female spectatorship, hooks elaborates:

We do more than resist. We create alternative texts, ones that are born not solely in reaction against. As critical spectators, Black women participate in a broad range of looking relations, contest, resist, revise, interrogate, and invent on multiple levels.[6]

Unlike Diawara's and hooks's conceptualizations, Feng's notion of resistant spectatorship is not confrontationally aligned against a "racist text." His concept of the text as the object of both critical inquiry and potential fetishization is more amorphous and fluid, taking into consideration those "star texts" that transcend the logic of narrative closure. Instead of denouncing the pleasures of dominant texts born out of white supremacist and/or sexist desires, Feng recuperates the differentiated pleasures that Asian American spectators derive from the imaginary renarrativization and recontextualization of ethnic star images.

Feng admirably expands resistant spectatorship theory by contributing an Asian American standpoint, as well as a focus on star discourse. However, his construction of a monolithic "Asian American" spectatorship is problematic precisely because linguistic and cultural differences, as well as interethnic political conflicts—especially the imperial domination of Japan over several nations during the first half of the twentieth century—divide Asian and Asian American identities into heterogeneous units. As Feng puts it elsewhere, "The label 'Asian' is not used in Asia—it is only used in the West."[7] The historical and cultural ruptures among different ethnic groups point to the difficulty of applying a race-based concept of resistant or oppositional spectatorship to the particular case of Asian American viewing positions. Whereas Sidney Poitier, Eddie Murphy, and Whoopi Goldberg are all African Americans,[8] James Shigeta, Lucy Liu, John Cho, and Dante Basco are, respectively, Japanese American, Chinese American, Korean American, and Filipino American— men and women whose different ancestral languages, cultures, and family immigration histories formed their screen personalities and testify to the heterogeneity that often gets lost in Hollywood's continuous reinvention and reinterpretation of the Oriental other.

Since the U.S. government abolished national origins quotas with the Immigration and Nationality Act of 1965, the heterogeneity of the Asian American population has increased dramatically. As Lisa Lowe points out, "[T]he majority of Asian Americans are at present Asian-born rather than multiple-generation, and new immigrant groups from South Vietnam, South Korea, Cambodia, Laos, Thailand, the Philippines, Malaysia, India, and Pakistan have diversified the already existing Asian American group of largely Chinese, Japanese, Korean, and Filipino descent."[9] The growing diversity and linguistic differences within the group further complicate Asian American spectatorship.

Although black spectatorship likewise inhabits a diverse range of categorical modalities in terms of gender, class, sexuality, and even color (light-skinned vs. dark-skinned African Americans), Asian American spectatorship engages a wider array of potentially disruptive ethnic and linguistic schisms. The history of Japanese colonialism in Asia further problematizes the dichotomy between the white colonizer and the nonwhite colonized, which dominates the discourse of postcolonial and ethnic studies. During World War II, the demeaning representation of the Japanese in American media no doubt enraged Japanese American audiences, but at the same time may have pleased many patriotic Asian immigrants from Korea, China, and the Philippines whose homelands were under Japanese colonial or occupational rule. For the latter group, the resistant or oppositional reading does not necessarily contest the "yellow peril" stereotypes, but rather reinterprets them according to the anticolonial interests of their own groups. Any attempt to theorize Asian American spectatorship should first acknowledge this historical and political chasm separating diverse ethnic groups.

Although the colonial/postcolonial dimension is particularly important in my case study of Philip Ahn (who was himself a descendant of the colonial diaspora), in this chapter I primarily focus on the impact of cross-ethnic masquerade and Asian American "passers" on bilingual and bicultural spectators. I have opted to replace the phrase "Asian American spectator" with the phrase "bilingual and bicultural spectator" to make it clear that I acknowledge that there are many Asian American audience members who are incapable of speaking their ancestral languages. Here, I am not trying to privilege Asian-born immigrants who speak dual languages over multi-generation Asian Americans who have assimilated into the mainstream. Rather, I am merely acknowledging multiple levels of cultural differences within Asian American groups despite my exclusive focus on a hypothetical spectatorial position that hinges on bilingual and bicultural capability. It should furthermore be understood that I have no intention of providing hard evidence of actual historical test subjects through an anthropological and sociological study of real audiences.

Although my observations are based partly on my own experience of viewing Philip Ahn's films and television shows, I am primarily interested in theorizing the textual construction of differentiated spectators. In lieu of the much-recycled model of resistant spectatorship, I use the theory of masquerade as a springboard for my discussion. Some readers might wonder how a theory heavily entrenched in psychoanalysis and feminism can be useful in

addressing the identity politics of Asian Americans. In an effort to substanti-
ate my claims, I would first like to offer the following brief survey of this theory's genealogy before discussing its applicability to Asian American
performance and spectatorship.

THEORIES OF MASQUERADE AND PASSING

Many feminist theorists have adopted the notion of masquerade to destabilize
the phallocentric discourse of Freudian psychoanalysis and to explore a subversive alternative to the conventional gender hierarchy by claiming femininity as a mask or an artificial construct. The English Kleinian analyst, Joan
Riviere, became the progenitor of masquerade theory when she published the
now-canonized essay, "Womanliness as Masquerade," in the *International
Journal of Psychoanalysis* in 1929. Influencing such poststructuralist theorists as Jacques Lacan, Luce Irigaray, Michele Montrelay, and Stephen
Heath, this pioneering work has sparked an intellectual interest in masquerade as a theoretical concept that articulates the complexity and contradiction of femininity.

In a much-quoted passage, Riviere argues the following:

> Womanliness therefore could be assumed and worn as a mask, both
> to hide the possession of masculinity and to avert the reprisals
> expected if she was found to possess it—much as a thief will turn out
> his pockets and ask to be searched to prove that he has not the stolen
> goods. The reader may now ask how I define womanliness or where I
> draw the line between genuine womanliness and the "masquerade."
> My suggestion is not, however, that there is any such difference;
> whether radical or superficial, they are the same thing.[10]

Riviere derives her theory from the behaviors of her female patients who,
despite being in intellectual professions (such as a "propagandist" and a university lecturer), feigned excessively feminine attributes or joked defensively
and became flippant after delivering successful public performances.
Interestingly, Riviere observes that the intended audiences of this feminine
masquerade were almost always father-figures and male co-workers whom
these women desperately sought to please and placate as a reaction-formation
to downplay their professional rivalry with these men. In Riviere's words,
"[the] woman's mask, though transparent to other women, was successful
with men, and served its purpose very well."[11]

Feminist film theorist Mary Ann Doane applied and expanded Riviere's work in her seminal 1982 essay, "Film and the Masquerade: Theorizing the Female Spectator." Doane mobilizes masquerade theory for two purposes: first, to consider the filmic image of women looking and performing a masquerade, and second, to theorize differentiated female spectatorship vis-à-vis classical narrative cinema. For Doane, although "the woman as subject of the gaze is clearly an impossible sign"[12] in mainstream texts, the image of the masquerading woman (aligned with an excess of femininity typical of such seductive manifestations as the femme fatale) does destabilize the hegemonic structure of the male gaze by defamiliarizing female iconography. Doane furthermore suggests the emancipatory possibility of masquerade in providing a different viewing position for female spectators caught between "the masochism of over-identification or the narcissism entailed in becoming one's own object of desire, in assuming the image in the most radical way."[13] She goes on to say, "The effectivity of masquerade lies precisely in its potential to manufacture a distance from the image, to generate a problematic within which the image is manipulable, producible, and readable by the woman."[14]

Subsequent works by Judith Butler, Valerie Smith, and Michael Rogin have highlighted the cross-performativity of gender, race, ethnicity, class, and sexuality as radical alternatives to prescribed, normative identities. Couching the term "masquerade" in different forms—"drag" for Butler, "passing" for Smith, and "cross-dressing" for Rogin—these theorists collectively emphasize the potentially subversive yet ambivalent implications of assuming identities of alterity through performance. Applying masquerade theory to the question of sexuality, Butler sees gender as "the repeated stylization of the body, a set of repeated acts within a highly rigid regulatory frame that congeal over time to produce the appearance of substance, of a natural sort of being."[15] In other words, gender is not an essence (being) but a socially constructed performance (doing) that naturalizes and reproduces heterosexual norms. Drawing on gay cultural practices, Butler privileges drag as a subversive form of performed parody that calls attention to the constructedness of heterosexual identities. She elaborates as follows:

> As much as drag creates a unified picture of "woman" (what its critics often oppose), it also reveals the distinctness of those aspects of gendered experience which are falsely naturalized as a unity through the regulatory fiction of heterosexual coherence. *In imitating gender, drag implicitly reveals the imitative structure of gender itself—as well as its contingency.*[16]

Making similar inquiries about the potential subversion of identity, Valerie Smith turns her attention from drag (cross-sexual performance) to passing (cross-racial performance). In her article, "Reading the Intersection of Race and Gender in Narratives of Passing," she examines the masquerade of light-skinned black characters in passing narratives by juxtaposing a classic example, John Stahl's *Imitation of Life* (1934), against its more modern counterparts, such as Julie Dash's *Illusions* (1982) and Charles Lane's *True Identity* (1991). Although *Imitation of Life*'s narrative condemns passing by punishing a light-skinned daughter for her abandonment of dark-skinned kin and their communities, the more contemporary counterparts suggest the potential of passing as a subversive act to uplift the race. For example, in *Illusions*, Mignon Dupree, a black female Hollywood executive working in the 1940s, passes with the intention of bringing the suppressed histories of her people to the screen. Unlike the black daughter in *Imitation of Life*, Mignon maintains connections to the community through her close relationship with her black lover and mother, as well as her bonding with black female singer Esther Jeeter, who is hired to dub the voice of a white star. As Smith points out, Dash's film stresses the "significance of masquerade in the production of cinematic illusion as well as racial and gender identity."[17]

In his book-length study of blackface as a form of racial cross-dressing for early Jewish entertainers, Rogin states, "Admiration and ridicule, appropriation and homage, transience and permanence, pathos and play, deception and self-deception, stereotyped and newly invented, passing up and passing down, class, sex, and race—all these elements in contradictory combination can play their role in masquerade."[18] Although Rogin acknowledges the postmodernist celebration of racial and ethnic masquerade as a subversive strategy to denaturalize the binary opposition of constructed identities, he balances his discussion with sensitive attention to the long history of segregation that excluded actual African American performers from theatrical and filmic productions centering on blackface.

The works of Butler, Smith, and Rogin are just a few of the many examples that demonstrate how the theory of masquerade can be modified and rearticulated according to different emphases: sexuality, (racial) passing, and blackface. Although black-white, cross-racial masquerade has received ample critical attention in the past two decades, cross-ethnic masquerade within the same racial group or between minority groups remains greatly understudied. Indeed, "Oriental masquerade" and "ethnic passing"—two prerequisites for the survival of early Asian American actors in Hollywood—need to be addressed within the overlapping lenses of film history and cultural studies. Although this chapter, which takes up this challenge to expand masquerade and passing theories, is exclusively confined to the career and filmography of Philip Ahn, its applicability across a broad range of disciplines rests on its ability to gesture toward the many other actors and ethnicities that, however peripheral to mainstream cinema, prove to be just as vital to the understanding of representation, stardom, and spectatorship.

Oriental Masks and Pidgin Performances

Like other pioneering Asian American players such as Richard Loo and Anna May Wong, Philip Ahn was born and raised in the United States. He did not visit his ancestral homeland until 1959, despite his father's lofty status in modern Korean history. As mentioned in Chapter 1, Ahn almost missed his Hollywood debut when director Lewis Milestone initially turned him down for a minor Chinese role in the Bing Crosby musical *Anything Goes* (1936) because of his perfect command of English. After the screen test, Milestone told the native Californian, "You're the type we're looking for, but you don't speak the kind of English we want. We want that laundry man-pidgin-English."[19] It was not until Ahn faked pidgin English on the spot that the director changed his mind and offered him the role. This much-quoted episode in Ahn's life attests to the fact that Oriental masquerade was a strategy that the actor was compelled to employ from his very first job hunt in Hollywood. Indeed, masquerade is a recurring diegetic motif throughout Ahn's career and performances.

In several films, he plays the role of a masquerader. The Universal serial *Red Barry* (1938) textually inscribes the concept of Orientalness-as-masquerade in a literal sense. In this breakneck, thirteen-chapter serial, Ahn's character, "Hong Kong Cholly," oscillates between two identities—the pidgin-English speaking sidekick of the white detective hero, Red Barry (Larry "Buster" Crabbe), and the undercover foreign agent (working for a nationalist Chinese general) who can speak perfect English; this wavering within a liminal state reflects Ahn's own screen career of Oriental charades.

Indeed, Ahn's first screen role in the low-budget Lon Chaney, Jr. vehicle, *A Scream in the Night* (1935),[20] similarly registers the double identities of Chinese undercover detective Wu Ting, a clean-cut, elegant English speaker who poses as a shabby, foreign peddler to infiltrate an unsavory Singapore waterfront club serving as a criminal hideout. In marked contrast to his earlier appearance in a dandy Western suit at a hotel café with two American detectives (Inspector Green and Detective Jack Wilson, the latter played by Chaney), Wu Ting reappears later in the movie, this time wearing a Vietnamese hat, faux mustache, and dark makeup encircling his eyes—embodying the classic image of a deceptive, sinister Oriental. Disguised as a pathetic pidgin-English speaker, Wu Ting approaches Butch Curtain (also played by Chaney), the notorious one-eyed bar owner and henchman for the film's chief villain, Johnny Fly (Manuel Lopez). The Oriental masquerader's gestures, mannerisms, and speech patterns ("me very solley, excuse please...me just want link [drink]...me come boat yesterday") are all grossly yet self-knowingly exaggerated. Philip Ahn's intentionally hyperbolic acting calls attention not only to the fact that his character Wu Ting is putting on an act for his secret investigative operation but also to the artificial construct of Oriental otherness itself. Wu Ting's camouflage foreshadows the hero Jack Wilson's masquerade as his look-alike Butch Curtain in the narrative, stressing the film's overarching themes of doubling, duplicity, and deception.

Likewise, *Something to Sing About* (1937), a low-budget musical produced at the "Poverty Row" studio Grand National, contains a self-reflexive moment that deconstructs the phoniness of Oriental masquerade. Philip Ahn appears as a studio houseboy, Ito, attending to Terry Rooney (James Cagney)—a New York bandleader who is making his debut in a Hollywood picture. Subservient and obsequious to the extreme, Ito speaks over-embellished pidgin English, habitually repeating stock phrases, such as "honorable master," "humble servant," and "ssanku, please." Discouraged by the exhausting wardrobe fittings, beauty sessions, and diction lessons, not to mention the manipulative schemes of studio executives and publicists, one evening Rooney confides the following to Ito:

ROONEY: You're the only one around this studio who will even deign to talk to me, and all you can say is "yes-a, sir."
ITO: (with flawless elocution) Would you rather that I spoke ordinary English, sir?
ROONEY: (surprised) Was that you?
ITO: (smiling) Yes, sir. My former employers felt that the accent lent a certain dignity.
ROONEY: Now look here, you're not going to stand there in all of this heat and tell me this Japanese lingo was an *act*.
ITO: Very much so!
ROONEY: Pull up a chair, sit down. I want to hear about this. Tell me about yourself.
ITO: I came here aspiring to be an actor.
ROONEY: Uh-huh. And they couldn't mold you, huh?
ITO: They didn't even try.

ROONEY: Well tell me, how do you like being a gentleman's
   gentleman?
ITO: Oh, very much. As an actor it was a long time between meals

Although Ito immediately regresses to his usual lingo and mannerisms, this
brief exchange of dialogue not only self-reflexively plays on the industry's
racist tendencies but also exposes how Oriental otherness is very much a mask
that can be worn and removed, just like femininity.

Reminiscent of the MGM musical, *Singin' in the Rain* (1952), *Something
to Sing About* playfully exposes the "behind the scenes" constructs of
Hollywood filmmaking and stardom. As soon as Rooney arrives in Los
Angeles and disembarks from the train, the studio publicist Hank Meyers
(William Frawley) orders him to pose with four swimsuited models for publicity shots. As Bennet O. Regan (Gene Lockhart), an executive at the fictional Galor Studios, opines, "In Hollywood, we create not only pictures but
actors and actresses as well. We mold them." Rooney's physical appearance
and voice are indeed molded into star-like shape during a two-week intensive
makeover program. The profit-driven studio even keeps his runaway marriage
confidential and spreads a false rumor of romance between Rooney and his
onscreen leading lady.

However, although both Rooney and Ito engage in a form of role-playing to
fit Hollywood's prescribed identities, race plays a determining factor for the
assignment of each role (marquee stardom for the white hoofer and that of personal assistant for the Asian would-be actor). Ito performs a verbal masquerade
to mimic the ideal of an Oriental servant—a social act of passing that reflects
both racial and class differences. The Japanese immigrant's performative down-
grading of his class through language-based ethnic masquerade reflects Ahn's
own marginal standing and survival tactics in the vertically stratified star system.

What is remarkable about the abovementioned scene is that it is couched
in a film that, although made only two years after Philip Ahn's Hollywood
debut, prophesied his career path as a marginalized Asian character actor.
Like Ito, Ahn at that time was an aspiring actor who had just debuted with
small roles. Although Paramount cast him as a romantic lead opposite childhood friend Anna May Wong in the mystery thriller *Daughter of Shanghai*
the same year (1937), the studios soon stopped fostering him as an ethnic star.
Instead, they frequently typecast him as a hideous Japanese villain or a
friendly Chinese sidekick in a series of propaganda and war films made during World War II. Discounting his exceptional roles as upwardly mobile Asian
American professionals in *Daughter of Shanghai* (federal agent), *King of*

Chinatown (1939; attorney), *The Big Hangover* (1950; medical doctor), *Shock Corridor* (1963; psychiatrist), and *Diamond Head* (1963; public prosecutor), Ahn's persona is primarily codified according to Oriental stereotypes—whether the monstrous "yellow peril" enemy on view in such films as *Back to Bataan* (1945), *Betrayal from the East* (1945), and *Halls of Montezuma* (1950) or the mystical martial arts guru, Master Kan of *Kung Fu*.

One of the physical features often singled out to describe Ahn is his mask-like face. In hindsight, the strong impression of his blank face (comparable to a *tabula rasa*) attests to the versatility required to impersonate diverse Oriental characters of different ages, personalities, and ethnicities in back-to-back roles. For example, in 1948, the forty-three-year-old actor played a geriatric Chinese restaurant owner named Ming Gow (in radical aging makeup) in *The Miracle of the Bells*; in that role he generously serves a hearty dinner as a gift to the main white couple (Fred McMurray's Hollywood press agent Bill Dunnigan and Alida Valli's actress-hopeful Olga Trocki) on Christmas Eve. Six years later, in *The Shanghai Story* (1954), Ahn seemed to have stumbled upon the proverbial Fountain of Youth for his role as the lecherous Ling Wu, a young Chinese army major who attempts to rape a married white woman, one of the thirty-seven unfortunate Westerners forcefully interned in Shanghai after the communist takeover. In 1952, he appeared as the lame, traditionally costumed septuagenarian Eitaro Shimizu in *Japanese War Bride*. Marie Windsor, the actress who played the xenophobic American sister-in-law of Shimizu's granddaughter (the titular war bride), reunited with Philip Ahn two years later in Republic's noir mystery, *Hell's Half Acre* (1954); however, in that film Windsor's character (a femme fatale named Rose) has an adulterous, interracial love affair with Ahn's villainous Roger Kong.

Hell's Half Acre features an intriguing, self-reflective moment when Donna, the female protagonist played by Evelyn Keyes, is interrogated by the Honolulu police chief (Keye Luke) and asked to identify Ahn's character—a murder suspect—after spotting him at the crime site:

> CHIEF DAN: Can you describe this man? Was he Chinese?
> DONNA: Well...Oriental...It's difficult for me...
> CHIEF DAN: What you're trying to say is that, to you, all Orientals look the same.
> DONNA: I could have been wrong about that. He might be of a mixed nationality.

The diegetic identification of Philip Ahn as an "Oriental" or of a "mixed nationality" is indeed indicative of mainstream audiences' confusion about his ethnicity. This confusion stemmed from discrepancies perpetuated by studio publicity, the wide range of screen roles he played, and Korea's low profile in the United States, particularly during the period when the Korean American actor was most active. As a result, Ahn's face was imprinted on the collective American psyche (or, at least, on the collective imagination of filmgoers) as something quintessentially Oriental: a composite of multiple Asian ethnicities.

Along with the use of aging makeup and traditional costumes, his accent—the stress and inflection placed on particular syllables and sounds—played a pivotal role in orientalizing Philip Ahn. Like those of Ito in *Something to Sing About*, Ahn's employers (producers and directors) apparently "felt that the accent lent a certain dignity" to his screen persona. In many films, Ahn faked foreign accents, hiding his true identity as an American-born Asian. The actor's younger brother, Ralph Ahn (who himself worked occasionally as an extra or minor actor in Hollywood film and television for several decades)[21] recollects, "The only thing Philip had qualms about was that demeaning Oriental accent and he tried to avoid [using it]. Sometimes he interviewed for a part, put on an accent to get the part, then, when it came time to shoot, didn't use it."[22] This interview clearly indicates that Philip Ahn's Oriental masquerade was not voluntary but compulsory—a necessary if sometimes negotiable means of surviving the racist casting and representational politics of the mainstream film industry.

As Ito says, for most Asian American actors in Hollywood, "it was a long time between meals." The so-called Big Three Asian male actors to emerge during Hollywood's classical period of the 1930s to 1950s—Philip Ahn, Keye Luke, and Richard Loo—took secondary jobs to ensure a steady income: Ahn made furniture and ceramicware and then became a restaurateur, Luke was a graphic artist and then a voice actor, and Loo was in the printing business. Typically playing three to nine supporting roles a year, these actors were largely at the mercy of Hollywood producers and directors, who often (if not always) mobilized them as Oriental archetypes, rather than fully developed characters. Given this historical marginalization of Asian American performers, we might ask if there is anything subversive about their Oriental masquerades, anything that might restore a sense of ethnic self-esteem.

RETURNING THE RACIAL JOKE AND EMPOWERING ASIAN AMERICAN SPECTATORSHIP

To address this question, it behooves us to shift the focus of our discussion from image and representation to spectatorship and reception. Both Joan Riviere and Mary Ann Doane suggest that masquerade hinges upon the presence of audiences. Riviere's study reveals that target audiences of feminine masquerade are men with authority and power to whom masqueraders pose an intellectual or professional threat. It is noteworthy that Riviere observes that the woman's mask is transparent to other women, whereas it works successfully with men. According to this logic, the audience of masquerade is divided into two categories: a dupe (one who cannot see through it and thus takes it at "face value") and a clairvoyant (one who sees through it and discerns its artificiality).

If womanly masquerade hides the possession of masculinity (phallic power), as Riviere puts it, what precisely does Oriental masquerade work to conceal in the context of Hollywood cinema? Simply put, it is the possession of Americanness. As an actor of Asian extraction, Philip Ahn could pass as an Oriental (of diverse ethnicities, from Japanese and Chinese to Indian, Vietnamese, Burmese, and Eskimo) in appearance but not in speech: because of his flawless command of English as a native speaker, he had to put on a verbal act.

I therefore differentiate my conceptualization of masquerade from Riviere's and Doane's by shifting the emphasis from the visible to the audible. It is true that in his impersonation of Oriental characters Ahn incorporated many visual components and tactics, such as makeup, blank expressions, and hyperbolic or flamboyant gestures. However, aural or linguistic masquerade takes precedence as a determinant of differentiated spectatorial positions vis-à-vis his cross-ethnic performance, which I hereafter refer to as ethnic passing. Not only was Philip Ahn frequently cast in a wide range of roles, requiring him to substitute for other ethnicities throughout a prolific career that lasted four decades (of his more than 100 big screen appearances, he played a Korean character only five times) he also occasionally spoke Korean onscreen in place of other languages. For example, Ahn speaks his ancestral language while playing Chinese roles in *Charlie Chan in Honolulu* (1938), *The Rebel* ("Blind Marriage," April 17, 1960), *The Wild Wild West* ("The Night the Dragon Screamed," January 14, 1966), and *I Spy* ("Carry Me Back to Old Tsing Tao," September 29, 1965; "An American Empress," December 25, 1967). The inappropriate incorporation of the Korean language in place of Mandarin or Cantonese clearly indicates the textual normalization of the dupe position based on the assumption that American audiences would not be able to distinguish the differences between these languages and cultures. Despite the exclusion of bilingual or bicultural audiences as target consumers in the sphere of production, ironically embedded in these texts with is an unintended and accidental spectatorial position—the ethnic clairvoyant—for whom masquerade is all too evident or transparent.

FIGURE 2.1 *In one of the many Oriental masquerades during his prolific career, Philip Ahn plays a Vietnamese guerrilla leader in* Rouges' Regiment *(Universal, 1952). Note that the wall behind him shows Korean graffiti (including the phonetic inscription of director Robert Florey's last name), likely scribbled by the actor himself.* Courtesy of Brian Taves and the Estate of Robert Florey.

Before moving to specific textual examples that illustrate my argument, I now examine the paradigm of passing laid out by Amy Robinson in her article, "It Takes One to Know One: Passing and Communities of Common Interests." According to Robinson, passing is a "triangular theater of identity" that requires three major participants: the passer, the dupe, and the in-group clairvoyant. She elaborates as follows:

> The moment of passing in drag is always a moment of collaboration. It is precisely the silence of the third term (the literate member of the in-group) that establishes the conditions for the successful pass. The perverse pleasure of duping the dupe, which transforms a painful scenario of collaboration into an occasion to make and remake community, is always and already a qualified pleasure.[23]

Robinson's triangular formulation corrects the shortcomings of Riviere's and Doane's bilateral configuration revolving around the masquerader and the spectator. Although both Riviere and Doane imply different spectatorial positions assumed by male and female audiences, they fail to fully convey the comprehensive mechanism of masquerade, which involves three parties, rather than two. Even though Robinson's theory specifically relates to racial and sexual passing, it is applicable to our discussion of ethnic passing among Asian Americans.

Similar to Robinson's triad, Philip Ahn's ethnic passing calls for three players: the passer/masquerader (the Korean American actor passing as non-Korean), the dupe (the mainstream audience who does not recognize his passing), and the in-group clairvoyant (the bilingual, bicultural spectator who spots the incongruity between the actor's role-playing and his true ethnic identity). I argue that this in-group recognition displayed by the third member of the triad hinges upon not only the foreknowledge of the actor's off-screen identities but also a familiarity with linguistic difference.

One of the early examples of Ahn's linguistic masquerade punctuates the final scene of *Charlie Chan in Honolulu*. In the film, Ahn plays an endearing yet nerdy son-in-law of the titular Chinese detective (played by white actor Sidney Toler in yellowface).

Two minutes into the film, Ahn's character, named Wing Fu, visits the Chan home to inform his "honorable" parents-in-law that his wife, Ling, is about to give birth. Thrilled by the news, Chan, his wife, and nine of their children rush to the maternity ward of the hospital. Jimmy (Number Two Son: Victor Sen Yung) and Tommy (Number Three Son: Layne Tom Jr.) dally behind and receive a message from the Homicide Bureau requesting that their father immediately report to the freighter *Susan B. Jennings* where a murder has been committed. Would-be detective Jimmy sees this as his opportunity to prove his ratiocination skills and decides to take the case himself. When he arrives at the boat, he is mistaken for his father and awkwardly embarks on an investigation. Chan belatedly learns about the summons to the freighter and hurries to the ship where he divulges both his son's mistaken identity as well as the identity of the murderer. After the case is solved, Chan receives a phone call from Wing Fu:

> WING FU: 아버지예요? 아이 이제 들어왔는데 참 그와요.
> [Is that you, father? The baby came out and he is fine-looking.]
> CHAN: Please, exercise self-control.
> WING FU: 링과 같이 생겼어요. [He looks like Ling.]

TOMMY: (snatching the phone away from Wing Fu) It's a boy, Pop!

CHAN: (to Jimmy standing besides him) It's a boy!

RANDOLPH: Who's he talking to?

HOGAN: I get it. He is having a baby.

TOMMY: (pulling the handset closer to the crying baby) Can you hear it, Pop?

HOGAN: (hearing the baby cry from the receiver) Congratulations, Mr. Chan.

CHAN: Contradiction, please. In present case, I am only innocent bystander.

Three white characters are present in the scene, eavesdropping on Chan's phone conversation: the ship's chief officer George Randolph (John King), the animal custodian Al Hogan (Eddie Collins), and the legal secretary Judy Hayes (Phyllis Brooks). In their collective confusion, they seem to represent the mainstream American audience's position as the dupe. They mistakenly assume that the baby in question is Chan's son and are bewildered when Chan tells them that he is "only innocent bystander." These characters are indeed bystanders from whom the information about the baby's true identity (Charlie Chan's grandson) is withheld. On both sides of the phone-line are Chinese American characters linked by familial and ethnic solidarity: Wing Fu and Tommy in the hospital and Charlie Chan and Jimmy in the ship cabin. Although mainstream audiences would undoubtedly serve as in-group clairvoyants with regard to Missouri-born actor Sidney Toler's cross-racial masquerade as a Chinese detective, few would question the authenticity of Wing Fu's lines as a foreign language. They would most likely accept both Philip Ahn's ethnicity and dialogue as Chinese. By comparison, Korean-speaking audiences representing the in-group can derive not only subversive laughter but also establish an extratextual, cultural bonding with the diasporic actor through the mechanism of ethnic recognition. Chinese-speaking audiences are likewise in-group clairvoyants who know that the dialogue is not Chinese and that the actor is passing.

Ahn even spoke Korean while playing a Japanese military figure in MGM's *They Met in Bombay* (1941), an exotic adventure film set in India and starring Clark Gable and Rosalind Russell as rival jewelry thieves. Ahn's linguistic masquerade in this film created an international political scandal after being detected and disclosed by culturally informed audiences. In a 1941 article entitled "International Incidents," *New York Times* reports the following:

> Philip Ahn...appeared as a Japanese general in the recent *They Met in Bombay* for Metro. When the studio got word the picture had been banned in Japan they couldn't understand it. Investigation revealed that Ahn had explained at the start that he knew no Japanese, that he is a Korean. He was told to go ahead and read the lines in his native tongue because nobody would know the difference anyway. When the film got to the Orient it was discovered that his Korean remarks were considered as highly uncomplimentary to the Japanese and the film was barred.[34]

It is indeed significant that Ahn managed to inject an anticolonial message in the Korean langauge while playing a Japanese character in pre-Pearl Harbor Hollywood. Regretfully, this scene was subsequently deleted (presumably because of the controversy it generated and the problems it posed for a studio interested in the Japanese market) and is currently unavailable for viewing. Judging from the Japanese government's disapproval reported above, one can only imagine the conversely positive reaction it generated among Korean expatriates in Japan—colonized members of the in-group—who had been lucky enough to spot Ahn's masquerade before the film was banned.

As such, despite the lack of Korean roles in Hollywood, Ahn was occasionally capable of encoding his diasporic identity through his inappropriate utterances of Korean lines, which could be decoded only by bilingual and bicultural spectators. I do not want to propose that this resistant or subversive spectatorship is uniform because there exist multiple reading positions, depending on the degree of audience members' knowledge of the Korean language and culture, as well as of the history of the Ahn family. Although there are many Korean American audiences who cannot speak Korean fluently and thus are unable to glean meanings from Ahn's delivery of the language, South Korean ears are likely attuned to awkward, grammatically incorrect expressions, as well as a heavy North Korean accent—distinct markers of the speaker's identity as a second-generation Korean American who learned the language from his parents, who were natives of South Pyŏngan Province (north of the thirty-eighth parallel). Chinese- and Japanese-speaking audiences may discern the fact that Ahn is speaking Korean in lieu of their native tongues, owing to their basic familiarity with distinct sonic qualities of different East Asian languages sharing Sino characters. Thus, heterogeneity within the in-group leaves room for further theoretical development of the triangular structure of passing proposed by Robinson.

Another textual example of ethnic passing complicates this triangular paradigm. Ahn's substitution of Korean for another language mostly occurs in television programs made with lower budgets and less attention to cultural authenticity. Among several TV shows in which the actor speaks Korean in place of Chinese, an episode of NBC's *I Spy* (1965–1968) entitled "An American Empress" stands out not only for the duration of time allotted for speaking of the language but also for its narrative pretext, involving translation between faux Chinese and English. Originally broadcast on December 25, 1967, this episode is set in San Francisco's Chinatown, a perennial setting of the "Home Orient" in many television westerns, crime dramas, and adventures.

After a series of touristic establishing shots of San Francisco (from the Coit Tower and the Bay to the ubiquitous cable car and Fisherman's Wharf) come images of a Chinatown distinctively marked by exotic architecture and a sign in the foreground that reads "Lotus Ball Chinese Food," as well as a generic Oriental tune on the soundtrack. The camera cuts to the interior of a souvenir shop where the espionage series' main characters—Kelly Robinson (Robert Culp) and Alexander Scott (Bill Cosby)—are shopping for a child's toy box, a gift for Scott's nephew. In their vicinity, a beautiful Asian girl (Frances Nuyen) in cheongsam dress is trying on a pair of sunglasses, which she likes but cannot afford. Noticing this, Robinson pays for the sunglasses and has the clerk give them to her as a gift. The mysterious girl (who later introduces herself as Mei Lin) thanks Robinson and reciprocates his act of generosity by presenting him with her ring. Robinson and Scott offer to give her a tour of San Francisco. To their surprise, Mei Lin (who claims to have lived in San Francisco most of her life) has never seen any of the city's landmarks, including Alcatraz and the Golden Gate Bridge. At the end of their itinerary, a couple of Chinese bodyguards attack Robinson and Scott in a zoo and forcefully take Mei Lin away.

Suspicious of Mei Lin's identity, the duo meets with a museum's curator of antiques and discovers that Mei Lin's ruby ring is a part of a Chinese royal jewelry collection, many items of which now belong to a local collector named Tu Po (Philip Ahn). Robinson and Scott visit the Tu Po residence to return the ring to its owner. A Chinese servant takes the American guests down to the cellar where the old master appears in traditional garb:

TU PO: 이 손님들하고 변변치 못한데 와서들 반갑다고 말해줘.
    [Tell the guests that I am glad to see them in this humble place.]
SERVANT: My master, Tu Po, he says welcome to poor house.
TU PO: 이 손님네하고 영어하지 못해서 미안하다고 말해줘. [Tell
    the guests that I am sorry that I cannot speak English.]
SERVANT: My master say sorry, English too bad for speaking to honored guests.

SCOTT: I speak Chinese.

SERVANT: (in Mandarin) Ke dong zhong wen ne. [He understands Chinese.]

TU PO: (to the servant) 아 그럴것 같으면 너 가라. [Well then, you can go.]

(to Scott) 아주 시간 맞춰왔어. [You came at the right time.]

SCOTT: (to Robinson) We've come just in time.

TU PO:(pointing to the two bodyguards tied to the wall, then handing a pair of bamboo sticks to Scott and Robinson) 이 놈들 맬디 잇빈 치라우. 열다섯번. 쌍놈들. [Hit these guys fifteen times! Fifteen! These sons of bitches!]

SCOTT: Oh, yes, yes. These are the two guys who assaulted us, you see. So he wants us to kind of be good drummers and beat on the skins.

ROBINSON: A little Buddy Rich?

SCOTT: A little bit of Gene Krupa, one time!

ROBINSON: (referring to the bamboo they've been given) It breaks up. I don't like this. These are not right. No good.

TU PO: 어, 그럼 다른 것 가져와요. [Then, bring another one.]

SCOTT: He says he's got another one. He'll give ya another one.

ROBINSON: I'm out of the mood now. No mood. No good.

SCOTT: (to Tu Po) No sengga.

TU PO: 그럴 것 같으면 언제든지 생각나는 대로... [If so, when-ever you are reminded of...]

SCOTT: He says anytime you want to, you can come on back.

TU PO: 당신네 가기 전에 꼭 중국여왕을 만나보고 가셔야 겠습니다. [Before you go, you must see the Empress of China.]

SCOTT: He says before we leave, he wants to introduce us to the Empress of China.

The Empress of China turns out to be none other than Mei Lin, who has been exiled in the United States under the custody of Tu Po. In the following scene, Scott continues to translate what Tu Po says to Mei Lin for Robinson. Later Tu Po is murdered by the traitorous General Chang (Benson Fong), a communist who attempts to forcefully repatriate Mei Lin to Red China. Scott and Robinson save the day and rescue the empress, who then is transformed into an American college girl by the end of the episode.

In the above-quoted scene, Bill Cosby's character, Alexander Scott, acts as a bilingual translator facilitating communication between Tu Po and Robinson. *I Spy* was the first dramatic series on network television to star an African American male as a leading character. Originally, the role of Scott

FIGURE 2.2 *Alexander Scott (Bill Cosby) acts as a cultural translator between the duped white American Kelly Robinson (Robert Culp) and the masquerading Oriental Tu Po (Philip Ahn) in the "American Empress" episode of* I Spy *(NBC, 1965–1968).*

was to have been that of a bodyguard for Robert Culp's character, Kelly Robinson, an American espionage agent disguised as a professional tennis player. The role was upgraded to an equal (buddy agent/trainer) after the casting of Cosby.[25] In many episodes, Cosby's knowledge and linguistic talents outshine Culp's physical and sexual prowess, capsizing the stereotypes of black and white masculinity (black-body-sports vs. white-mind-intellect). As a graduate of Temple University and a Rhodes Scholar, Scott is fluent in eleven languages—a talent that proves handy during the duo's global espionage operations. This deliberate *interpellation*,[26] or hailing, of an African American character as a mediator between white America and the rest of the world—someone who translates racial, ethnic, national, and linguistic differences—is significant in the context of the Cold War. As Mary Beth Haralovich points out, *I Spy* represents "an official response to the U.S. Cold War predicament of the 1950s" when racial discrimination gave American democracy a bad name.[27] The black-white integrated partnership in the series flaunts not only the improved race relations of civil rights-era America but also the egalitarian citizenship of the "Free World." As a sort of living billboard, a pre-Benetton advertisement for racial tolerance, Cosby's Scott communicates to the world (in different languages) that people of color have equal access to democracy, freedom, and mobility in the United States.

Earlier in the aforementioned episode, Cosby's ability to comprehend Chinese saves Culp and himself from being arrested when the Chinese curator (James Hong) calls the police to report the duo as suspects in the jewelry theft—Cosby intercepts a phone call in Chinese that he is able to translate. Unlike the authentic utterances of the veteran Chinese American actor James Hong, Philip Ahn speaks Korean (with many grammatical glitches and awkward enunciation) in the given scene, opening up multilayered positions of identity. Culp's Robinson is undoubtedly positioned as the dupe, a diegetic representation of the dominant mainstream spectator with little understanding of other languages and cultures. Ahn is the passer who impersonates a Chinese character through cross-ethnic and cross-lingual masquerade. The Chinese servant (Allen Jung), the only actual Mandarin speaker in the scene, allegorizes the in-group clairvoyant, the bicultural spectator whose knowledge and complicity are indispensable for the successful pass. The presence of a fourth character, Cosby's Scott, complicates the otherwise comfortable triadic configuration. Cosby functions as an intercultural facilitator and ventriloquist who translates the language of Oriental others for the dupe (the mainstream audience/Culp). Cosby quickly takes the place of the servant, the in-group literate. However, he too is another passer/masquerader who only pretends to be a cultural insider and simply recites his English lines. Bilingual spectators with a knowledge of Chinese and Korean recognize his inadequacy as the translator, thus exposing the constructedness of his interpellated identity as the assimilated, upwardly mobile, middle-class black position unique to the civil rights era.

Herman Gray defines the "civil rights subject" as:

> black, largely middle-class benefactors who gained the most visibility as well as material and status rewards from the struggles and opportunities generated by the civil rights movement. This cultural figure embodies complex codes of behavior and propriety that make it an exemplar of citizenship and responsibility—success, mobility, hard work, sacrifice, individualism.[28]

Cosby/Scott's assimilation in mainstream America is maintained through an exclusion and juxtaposition of the feudal Oriental whose inability to speak English, exotic costumes, and primitive means of discipline accentuate the black subject's identity as a modern, mobile American.[29] The civil rights subject (the model black citizen) is thus situated as the mediator between the white character/audience and racial/cultural others whose alterity cancels out Cosby's own minority position and empowers his status. As Rogin points out in his study of Jewish entertainers' blackface performances, "the inclusion of some people is predicated on the violent exclusion of others."[30]

There are many reasons to feel ambiguous about the subversive potential of masquerade. Postmodernist celebration of masquerade and passing as identity subversion might direct one's attention away from the actual historical and social conditions that gave rise to the discrimination and exclusion that compel marginalized subjects to wear masks in the first place. However, we should not downplay the significance of the empowering pleasure (however qualified it may be) that the in-group spectator derives from the recognition of masquerade. These subversive moments of rupture establish imagined communities between masquerading actors and ethnic spectators through a shared knowledge of languages and cultures, as well as self-conscious distancing from the hegemonic narratives that distort and misrepresent their identities.

The parodic sketch comedy *The Kentucky Fried Movie* (1977) provides a good example of this self-conscious distancing. In the episode "A Fistful of Yen," Loo (Evan C. Kim)—a wonky-toothed, Bruce Lee-impersonating Hong Kong martial artist—is hired by the British Intelligence Agency to rescue a Chinese nuclear scientist (oddly named Ada Gronick, played by Ingrid Wang) who has been abducted by Dr. Klahn, head of a notorious criminal syndicate based in a remote mountain region of Central Asia. Flanked by bodyguards and concubines at the doorsteps of his ancient Chinese palace, Dr. Klahn (played by Hapkido master Bong Soo Han [Han Pong-su]) makes a majestic entrance. As the camera cuts between close-ups of Loo and Gronick exchanging winks, Dr. Klahn's offscreen speech in an untranslated foreign language fills the soundtrack.

The Dr. Klahn character is a flat-out parody of the classic Bond villain Dr. No, a half-Chinese who similarly hides a steel hand under a black glove. Although Dr. Klahn is Chinese, the language spoken in the scene is Korean:

한국말로 무조건 말하라니 한심하군. 우리 한국사람이 들으면 정신나갔다고 말할게 아니야. 아무튼 하라니 할 수 밖에. 결과는 어쨌든 간에 말이야. 이런 미국에서 영화생활 하려니 한심하군 그래. 한심한 처지가 한두번이 아니야. 아무튼 한국 팬들에게 실례가 되겠습니다.

[How pitiful it is that (the filmmakers) make me speak Korean! If Koreans hear this, they will think I am out of my mind. Anyway, I must do as I am told whatever the result may be. Oh, the many pathetic things I have to endure to make movies in America! Not just once or twice, either. Please excuse me, Korean fans.]

What the independent production *The Kentucky Fried Movie* parodies in this episode are not just big-budget Bond movies[31] and the martial arts genre (in particular, *Enter the Dragon* [1973]) but also the very mechanisms through which Oriental masquerade and ethnic passing are perpetuated in mainstream cinema. Actor Bong Soo Han speaks for Philip Ahn and other Asian American actors who underwent similar "pathetic" and "pitiful" experiences throughout their careers. He also directly addresses in-group audiences who can understand what he is saying, creating an invisible community. Although mainstream viewers may enjoy the scene's visual gags, stemming from Loo and Gronick's flirtatious gestures, the bigger audio joke of the scene is inaccessible to them because of their lack of ethnic "reading" competency. As the film's producers and writers testify in the DVD commentary, *The Kentucky Fried Movie* was a big hit in South Korea primarily because this scene provided extra pleasure and comedy to in-group audiences.

The pleasure inherent in joke-telling lies partly in the duping of in-group illiterates. Throughout the history of the American motion picture and television industries, Oriental characters and their linguistic or cultural difference have often been objects of ridicule, playing comic figures who facilitate the bonding among white characters. Examples run the gamut from the early sound western *The Virginian* (1929), which features a Chinese cook named Hong (Willie Fung) whose nonstop, untranslated babble bewilders the cowboys and serves as comic relief, to *Chinatown* (1974), a neo-noir in which Jake Gittes (Jack Nicholson) tells a classic "Chinaman joke" to his colleague. Viewers of the television classic *M*A*S*H* (1972–1983) might recall episodes in which the silly manners and antiquated customs of grossly caricatured, unconventionally named Korean farmers, peddlers, and "business girls" (played by Chinese, Japanese, and Southeast Asian extras) are gently (or, in the case of the bigoted Major Burns, vociferously) ridiculed by the doctors and nurses of the 4077th.

The latent subversiveness of masquerade and passing manifests at the moment when Asian or Asian American audiences *return the joke* and celebrate their accidental spectatorship. As an audience who "knows too much," their in-group literacy encompasses not only the cultural ability to discern the diegetic rupture and contradiction created by ethnic passing but also the critical distance necessary to laugh back at (as opposed to laughing with) those hegemonic cultural texts that have in their own way contributed to the institutionalization of masquerade, misrepresentation, and countless stereotypes.

PART II

Oriental Genres
1930s to 1950s

3

BETWEEN YELLOWPHILIA
AND YELLOWPHOBIA

Asian American Romance in
Oriental Detective Films

ART II RESETS OUR CRITICAL FOCUS by subsuming questions of performance and spectatorship within the larger contexts of Hollywood's Oriental genres, which were popular from the 1930s to the 1950s. With the possible exception of the war film, no other genre has received more critical attention than romance in contemporary scholarship on cinematic representations of Asians and Asian Americans (as the title of Gina Marchetti's influential book, *Romance and the "Yellow Peril,"* attests).

Throughout the 1990s, media scholars writing on the topic have privileged a handful of now-canonized silent films, such as *The Cheat* (1915), *Madame Butterfly* (1915), and *Broken Blossoms* (1919), which are continuously recycled in critical discourse.[1] Each of these texts—like their latter-day permutations, including *The Bitter Tea of General Yen* (1933), *Love is a Many-Splendored Thing* (1955), *Sayonara* (1957), and *The World of Suzie Wong* (1960)—shares the theme of interracial romance (or sexual contract) entrenched in the Orientalist imaginary of racialized and gendered others. However, discounting the few exceptional silent films starring Sessue Hayakawa and his wife Tsuru Aoki, as well as *The Good Earth* (1937), *Dragon Seed* (1944), and *Flower Drum Song* (1960), classical Hollywood films seldom foreground Asian romantic coupling as the central plot element. Furthermore, the blossoming of romance between two "Orientals" in the latter sound-era films is either mediated through the inscription of white actors in yellowface or facilitated through a kind of casting apartheid—an all-Asian counterpart to segregationist African American musicals like *Hallelujah* (1929), *Stormy Weather* (1943), and *Cabin in the Sky* (1944).

Capsizing this representational schemata and casting politics, two obscure, critically overlooked Paramount B films—*Daughter of Shanghai* (1937) and *King of Chinatown* (1939)—not only proffer nonstereotyped, upwardly mobile, middle class Asian Americans as active protagonists but also culminate with the constitution of an Asian romantic duo (self-represented by two Asian American actors, Anna May Wong and Philip Ahn) in place of the traditional Caucasian coupling. This chapter situates the positive representation of Asian Americans and the formation of the Wong–Ahn couple in these films in the context of the Oriental detective genre of the 1930s to the 1940s (the Charlie Chan, Mr. Moto, and Mr. Wong series), which popularized the images of "good" Orientals as a counterpoint to established "yellow peril" stereotypes, such as Fu Manchu and the "dragon lady." The emergence of otherwise anomalous Chinese American romantic leads at this particular historical juncture reflects various sociopolitical and industrial factors, such as the Immigration Act of 1924 (which put an end to Asian immigration), the Sino-Japanese War (1937–1945), the double bill system and B filmmaking, the dictates of the Production Code, and strategies of ethnic star marketing. Paramount's promotion of Philip Ahn as a new Chinese star and the creation of an ideal Oriental couple in both filmic narratives and the publicity discourse reflect a complicated set of contradictory attitudes of a prewar American public shuttling between yellowphilia (expressed through philanthropy and paternalism for China) and yellowphobia (vexations and fears of miscegenation).

BAD ORIENTALS, GOOD ORIENTALS: COOLIES GO HOME! BUT LET'S SAVE CHINA

Daughter of Shanghai is a thriller revolving around the exploits of Lan Ying Quan (Anna May Wong), the daughter of a San Francisco-based Chinese art dealer, Quan Lin (Ching Wah Lee), who has been secretly gathering evidence about an alien smuggling ring. Quan Lin is shot and killed after he refuses to cooperate with the smugglers' demands that he employ illegal Chinese laborers. On the night of her father's murder, Lan Ying is introduced to detective Kim Lee (Philip Ahn)—a federal agent assigned to the case—through family friend and patron Mrs. Hunt (Cecil Cunningham). Unbeknownst to Lan Ying and Lee, the benevolent, wealthy art collector is actually the mastermind of the smuggling ring, which has ties to Central America. Resolved to bringing justice to the murderers on her own, Lan Ying travels alone to an exotic Port O' Juan saloon run by Otto Hartman (Charles Bickford), Mrs. Hunt's overseas underling, where she masquerades as a dancer in hopes of gathering clues about the smuggling operation. At Port O' Juan, Lee reappears incognito, wearing the clothes of a sailor, and is quickly hired as an interpreter by the captain of the smuggler's ship. After a series of perilous pitfalls and last-minute rescues that demonstrate Lee's intelligence in outwitting the villains, the couple manages to expose Mrs. Hunt and her cohorts, who are then handed over to the police. The dénouement of the film not only brings the mystery to the satisfying resolution that audiences have come to expect in classical Hollywood storytelling. It also slyly undercuts this horizon of expectations and reconfigures the racial norm by showing, in the penultimate shot, the triumphant Lee proposing marriage to Lan Ying in the backseat of a car. The iconic space of the automobile's backseat, which is typically reserved for a final, romantic fade-out, leads to another car's backseat—that of the police's paddy wagon—as the arrested white villain, Mrs. Hunt, is whisked away to jail in handcuffs.

Garnett Weston's original story, *The Honor Bright*, from which the film's screenplay evolved, is loosely based on a *Los Angeles Times* article (dated June 4, 1934) about the arrest of a ring responsible for smuggling thousands of Chinese citizens into the United States. An extract from the newspaper article, which accompanies Weston's story draft, reports that the syndicate ruthlessly murdered aliens by jettisoning them overboard from contraband ships when detection became imminent.[2] *Daughter of Shanghai* opens with a montage of newspaper headlines, such as "Foreign Horde Floods U.S.," "Human Cargo Payoff Totals Millions!," and "Uncover Coast Smuggling Ring." The following scene shows a smuggler's plane being chased by state patrol aircraft. In a fashion similar to that recounted in the *Times* article, the smugglers open the trapdoor of a secret compartment, discharging human cargo into the ocean just before the anticipated seizure. The film continues to condemn the illegal immigration by inserting menacing statistics in the form of newspaper reports—into the diegesis: "Fifty thousand aliens make illegal entry into this country each year." In addition to the narrative's negative portrayal of illegal entrants and of their smugglers, one of the publicity posters for *Daughter of Shanghai* explicitly attempts to arouse anti-alien sentiment by directly addressing the audience with a series of didactic questions:

FIGURE 3.1 *Philip Ahn and Anna May Wong as the sound era's first self-representing Asian American romantic couple in* Daughter of Shanghai *(Paramount, 1937)*. Courtesy of the Academy of Motion Picture Arts and Sciences.

> Did you know that thousands of aliens are smuggled annually into the U.S.A? Did you know that blackmailers bleed them to the tune of $1,000,000 a year? Did you know that 100,000 of these illegal entrants are subjects for Relief? Did you know that 3,500,000 more have taken the jobs of American citizens?[3]

Ironically, in the film, this critique of ignorance of illegal immigrants issues from the mouth of Quan Lin (a Chinese immigrant himself), who tells his daughter that racketeers are importing

> misguided human beings. Among them men of my own blood.... They find the victims from all parts of the world—the ignorant, the helpless, who have heard of America. And when these people are finally landed here, they are sold like slaves.

In an earlier version of the script, entitled *Anna May Wong Story* and dated September 8, 1937, the upper-middle-class entrepreneur Quan Lin utters a harsher expression than "misguided human beings." He instead uses the term, "misguided coolies," thereby stigmatizing underclass illegal laborers of his own ethnicity.[4] By situating Chinese American males—Quan Lin and Kim Lee—on the side of immigration authorities,[5] *Daughter of Shanghai* not only effectively evades any potentially racist, anti-Sinitic allegations concerning its portrayal of "misguided coolies"[6] but also erects a distinct demarcation between the "good" Oriental (the assimilated American citizen) and the "bad" Oriental (the illegal immigrant).

In his trail-blazing treatise, *On Visual Media Racism: Asians in the American Motion Pictures*, Eugene Franklin Wong argues that the passing of the 1924 Immigration Act (or National Origins Act)—which denied admission to all aliens ineligible for citizenship, thus practically excluding all Asians except Filipinos—and "the subsequent social relief accompanying the end to the Asian immigration problem, gradually provided a psychological incentive and social climate given to the acceptance of an image of a non-villainous Asian."[7] Even before passage of the 1924 Act, which was specifically intended to exclude the Japanese (the only Asian community besides Filipinos whose immigration had been permitted, although restrictively, under the terms of the Gentlemen's Agreement of 1907 between the United States and Japan), Chinese immigrants had been barred from American shores through the 1882 Chinese Exclusion Act.[8] Originally welcomed to the United States as cheap laborers mobilized en masse to excavate California's gold mines and build the transcontinental railroads, the Chinese quickly became perceived as "yellow peril" coolies who were usurping the jobs of European immigrants. This anti-Chinese xenophobia was translated, throughout the following decades, into abhorrent cinematic images of emasculated, opium-addicted coolie laborers or derivatives of the archetypal enemy to the white race, Dr. Fu Manchu.

The popularization of the Charlie Chan series beginning with *Charlie Chan Carries On* (1931), however, marked a turning point in Hollywood's sinophobic representations. Despite white actors' yellowface impersonations of Charlie Chan's exaggerated, yet stoic, pseudo-Confucian mannerisms, the Chinese detective hero, as Norman K. Denzin points out, "neutralized previous negative images of the Asian-American, and offered to Asian-Americans (and Americans) a particular Americanized version of who they were and who they should be."[9] Likewise, *Daughter of Shanghai* provides an Althusserian interpellation (hailing) of an American-born, acculturated, middle-class

Chinese identity that is completely distinct from the subaltern class of illegal coolie laborers. The film thus captures the rebound of yellowphilia's predilection for good, likable Orientals against the backboard of a yellow-phobia erected against illegal immigrants. Eugene Wong evaluates the film positively, albeit with minor hesitations: "While failing to explain that given anti-Asian legislation the only way in which Chinese could enter America was through illegal means, *Daughter* was a favorable treatment of Chinese.... The combination of Ahn and Wong provided an extraordinarily interesting filmic attempt to develop Asian American characters."[10]

In addition to domestic immigration policies, the Sino-Japanese conflict in the East Asian political theater began to influence the representation of the Chinese and Japanese in American films. Although U.S. government edicts before Pearl Harbor maintained an isolation policy toward Japan's imperial expansion in East Asia (its annexation of Korea in 1910 and of Manchuria in 1931 and its subsequent full-scale military aggression against China leading to the outbreak of the Sino-Japanese War in 1937) in order to avoid a direct military conflict with Japan, the American public increasingly sympathized with the Chinese people suffering under the heels of the Japanese. A public opinion poll from August 1937 shows 59 percent of American respondents expressing sympathy for China as opposed to 1 percent who supported Japan. In February 1940, 76 percent sided with China in contrast to only 2 percent with Japan.[11] Warren I. Cohen defines the period stretching from 1900 to 1950 as an "era of paternalism" in Sino-American relations.[12] Fostered by American missionaries, journalists, and writers in China, America assumed the fatherly self-image of protector for the peace-loving, defenseless Chinese violated by belligerent Japanese imperialists.

The myth of the American protector permeates pro-Chinese Hollywood films made throughout the duration of the Sino-Japanese War, including *China Girl* (1942), *China* (1943), *The Story of Dr. Wassell* (1944), and *China Sky* (1945). In these films white American journalists, merchants, doctors, and officers heroically support, protect, or save their Chinese subordinates. Produced only months after the outbreak of the Sino-Japanese War and released concurrently with the Rape of Nanking (the Japanese military's bru-tal massacre of hundreds of thousands of Chinese civilians in the capital city),[13] *Daughter of Shanghai* indeed manifests, however obliquely, the pater-nalistic pro-Chinese sentiments percolating among the American populace — without making any direct reference or allusion to the war.

Less than two years after the release of *Daughter of Shanghai*, Paramount unveiled another Anna May Wong vehicle, *King of Chinatown*, a gangster film with all the trappings of the genre, yet one that couches a subtextual discourse concerning the relief of wartime China. Not unlike her role in *Daughter of Shanghai* as a wealthy heiress-turned-female detective, Wong again plays a nonstereotypical character. In *King of Chinatown*, she is Dr. Mary Ann Ling,[14] a surgeon who saves the life of Frank Baturn (Akim Tamiroff), the film's titular underworld racketeer who has been wounded in a shoot-out. Baturn falls in love with Mary, despite her engagement to attorney Bob Li (Philip Ahn), and gradually reforms under her care. Mary and Bob are involved in fundraising activities to establish an ambulance unit in war-ravaged China. Baturn is eventually double-crossed and assassinated by his right-hand man, the "Professor" (J. Carrol Naish), who has taken control of his rackets during his absence. In a philanthropic gesture before dying, Baturn endows an honestly earned portion of his fortune to Mary for her Red Cross operations. The final scene shows Bob and Mary, recent newlyweds, on a plane to China.

Thus, in *King of Chinatown*, the China relief program is fueled by white money, mirroring America's $25 million aid package to China in the form of purchase credits in February 1939, given one month before the release of the film.[15] The penultimate scene of the film vocally conveys the paternalistic countenance of America patronizing a weaker nation with relief funds in Baturn's emphatic last words to Mary: "I want you to buy the finest ambulance and equipment you can get.... Hurry! Hurry! They need you there. I'll be with you! Hurry! Hurry!"

Although white humanitarian assistance to China is emphasized through the reformed Baturn's altruistic last will and testament, a politically conscious speech directly referring to the war in China was included in an earlier version but dropped from the final script. In that earlier version, dated June 6, 1938, Mary's Chinese father states the following in his New Year's speech: "Unfortunately, friend, there can be no Happy New Year tonight in our homeland—our people are at war, invaded by an enemy nation. There are those who say that this war marks the end of ancient China—they don't know China—that is only the beginning of a new and greater China." In a second draft, dated August 1, 1938, his speech is less concrete about China's plight: "The old year has brought all the ingredients of good life to us and our people here in this country.... But in the land of my ancestors, no laughter rises above the groans of the sick, the suffering and the oppressed." In the final script, Mary delivers the toast speech, and it lacks any allusion to the political situation in China: "And may the New Year bring peace to our people and the whole world!"[16]

This change clearly reflects the U.S. government's reluctance to intervene in East Asian conflicts prior to the Japanese attack at Pearl Harbor in December 1941, as well as Hollywood's avoidance of sensitive subjects that might disturb the State Department or upset overseas markets. As further evidence of this ideological disinclination, Paramount changed the title of another Anna May Wong film from *Guns for China* to *Island of Lost Men* (1939) in light of the exhortation by the studio's Foreign Department not to evoke any reference or allusion to the Sino-Japanese War.[17]

The Oriental Detective Cycle and Ethnic Star-Making

As discussed earlier in this chapter, Fox's profitable cycle of Charlie Chan mysteries inaugurated an Oriental detective craze whose longevity attests to an ongoing fascination with "good" Orientals in the B movie market. However, before discussing the popularity of the Oriental detective genre, let us consider the particularities of B movie production. Although many American film historians have investigated the economic and industrial practices central to the profitable management of the studio system (notably, Douglas Gomery, Robert Sklar, Thomas Schatz, David Bordwell, Kristine Thompson, and Janet Staiger), the B movie production of the period remains an understudied area. Brian Taves's essay, "The B Film: Hollywood's Other Half," is a rare and valuable contribution to this subject. Taves recuperates the significant role of B movies during the studio era, contending that "to concentrate upon the A would emphasize the art of a few films and elide the basis of production, the underlying commercial and artistic means by which the industry survived—as well as the vast quantity and range of films offered to the spectators."[18]

B film production should be understood in the context of the double bill, which allowed moviegoers to see two features for the price of one. The double bill was implemented by Hollywood as it began to lose its audiences as a result of the Depression in the early 1930s.[19] By 1935, 85 percent of all U.S. theaters showed double bills[20] consisting of an "A" picture and a "B," or "program," picture, as well as short subjects (cartoons and live action shorts) and newsreels, offering more than three hours of entertainment for the price of one admission. The demarcation between the A feature and the B feature is neither clear nor consistent. Roughly speaking, an A feature, planned for the top half of a double bill, consists of seven reels or more, has an average budget of $350,000 or more, and features stars with broad audience appeal.[21] In contrast, a B feature is generally characterized as a cheap, quickly shot, hour-long genre film with no big name stars. This "two-for-the-price-of-one" system lasted as a predominant exhibition practice throughout the 1930s and the 1940s until the studios ceased B film production in the wake of the Supreme Court's 1948 Paramount Decree, which forced the divestiture of their exhibition branches.[22] The 1930s marked the zenith of low-budget B film productions, which accounted for nearly 75 percent of the entire movie output of the decade.[23]

The studios' interest in B films was superficial at best, as the whole concept of the double feature was introduced as an audience incentive, rather than as a profit maker. While A films were rented to exhibitors on a percentage basis, B films were rented at a fixed rate of $100 or $200.[24] Thus the studios had very little to lose or gain in the production of B features. By the early 1930s, a dozen small "Poverty Row" studios (such as Republic Pictures, Grand National Films, and Monogram Productions) came into being to supply 300 "quickies" annually.[25] The "Big Five" studios (MGM, Paramount, Warner Bros., 20th Century-Fox, and RKO) also began operating their own B units, and two minors, Columbia and Universal, even downgraded some of their A projects to meet the increasing demand for B features. Some of the major studios' B features proved to be enormously popular, as illustrated by 20th Century-Fox's Charlie Chan and Sherlock Holmes series or MGM's Andy Hardy and Thin Man series.

One of the most undeservingly neglected B film auteurs is French émigré director, Robert Florey (1900–1979). Best known as the creator of the early American avant-garde masterpiece, *The Life and Death of 9413—A Hollywood Extra* (1927), and as the director of *Murders in the Rue Morgue* (1932), one of Universal's early horror classics shot by legendary cinematographer Karl Freund, Florey made an average of seven pictures per year from 1933 to 1942, working in the B division of Warner Bros. and Paramount.[26] At Paramount, Florey made two B films with Anna May Wong: *Daughter of Shanghai* and *Dangerous to Know* (1938).[27] He and Reginald Owen also wrote an original version of *A Study in Scarlet* (1933) as a Sherlock Homes film to co-star Wong as a mysterious Chinese widow. As a visionary stylist whose predilection for German expressionist and avant-garde techniques makes him an unheralded forerunner of film noir aesthetics, Florey consistently experimented with his directorial signature—combining fast, sometimes schizophrenic rhythms, subjective points of view, bizarre (often oblique) camera angles, chiaroscuro lighting, and catty-cornered compositions—in a bevy of quickly shot thrillers, the genre with which he is most associated.[28] Despite his frustration as a minor contract director with little recognition and no control over story selection and editing, Florey confesses to having enjoyed a certain degree of creative freedom in the flexible B unit: "As long as I remained on schedule, I could shoot all the angles and set-ups I wanted, and move the camera whenever and wherever I wanted to, in the limited time I had."[29] In addition to unusual visual flourishes, less conventional subject matter and characterizations could pass relatively unscathed in low-budget B pictures, perhaps none more so than in the Oriental detective films theatrically released in the 1930s and 1940s.

The progenitor of this genre is the Charlie Chan series. Although the first two Chan films (a ten-chapter Pathé serial entitled *The House without a Key* [1925] and Universal's *The Chinese Parrot* [1927]) used Asian actors of Japanese descent (George Kuwa and Kamiyama Sojin) as the Chinese sleuth, it was not until the 1931 Fox production, *Charlie Chan Carries On*, with the Swedish immigrant actor Warner Oland in the lead role, that the series began to gather steam and succeed at the box office.[30] Oland played Charlie Chan sixteen times for Fox until his death in 1938. Missouri-born actor Sidney Toler replaced Oland, beginning with *Charlie Chan in Honolulu* (1938). Subsequently, Toler performed in twenty-two Charlie Chan films, eleven at 20th Century-Fox and another eleven at Monogram. Upon Toler's death in 1947, Roland Winters inherited the role, appearing in the last six Charlie Chan films produced at Monogram from 1947 to 1949.

Coincidentally, both Oland and Toler worked with Anna May Wong at Paramount. Oland played Dr. Fu Manchu in three Paramount films including *Daughter of the Dragon* (1931), which stars Wong as the daughter of Fu Manchu. In *Shanghai Express* (1932), he was cast as rebel leader Henry Chang, a megalomaniac who rapes Wong's Hui Fei and is killed by his avenging victim. Toler played Wong's father, Chinese herbal doctor Chang Ling, in *King of Chinatown*.

Both Anna May Wong and Philip Ahn appeared in Charlie Chan films. Wong played a dancer in *The Chinese Parrot*, and Ahn appeared as Charlie Chan's son-in-law who fathers Chan's first grandchild in *Charlie Chan in Honolulu*. Film historian Charles P. Mitchell speaks highly of the Korean American actor's performance in that film: "Philip Ahn, a superb actor, is wonderful as Wing Fu, and it is a shame that his character never appears again in the series."[31] Ahn also assumed the role of murder suspect Captain Kong opposite Roland Winters' Chan in *The Chinese Ring* (1947). Ken Hanke comments on his radical transformation in this later film, stating, "it is a shock to see Philip Ahn, Charlie's erstwhile son-in-law…, now turned to a life of crime as the shady Captain Kong."[32] However, Ahn's alteration should not come as a shock for viewers and readers familiar with the actor's many ethnic transformations during the war years, a period in which his expressively nonexpressive persona was but a blank slate on which to project societal feelings of philanthropy (for the "good-natured" Chinese) and fears (of the "menacing" Japanese). The two films, one made before and one after the war, throw this schizophrenic dual persona in relief.

The popularity of the Charlie Chan films led to two offshoots in the B mystery genre: the Mr. Moto series at 20th Century-Fox and the Mr. Wong series at Monogram. Peter Lorre portrayed Japanese detective Kentaro Moto, a master of disguise and a jujitsu expert in eight films produced over a two-and-a-half-year period, from *Think Fast, Mr. Moto* (1937) to *Mr. Moto in Danger Island* (1939). Philip Ahn appeared in one Moto film, *Thank You, Mr. Moto* (1937), in which he played the role of a dutiful Chinese royal, Prince Chung, who owns precious ancient scrolls—which are keys to the lost treasures of Genghis Khan—and is pursued by smuggling outfits. *Thank You, Mr. Moto* gave Philip the opportunity to hone his acting skills by observing such accomplished thespians as Peter Lorre and Pauline Frederick (a stage actress who played Ahn's Chinese mother), as well as by working closely with director Norman Foster, an actor himself, who guided the self-trained Ahn toward an early form of the Method technique.

Moto films were ditched once Lorre moved to bigger roles and the threat of Japanese fascism in the international sphere undermined the legitimacy of a Japanese hero.[33] It is also notable that the Charlie Chan series terminated in 1949, the same year in which Mao Zedong's Communist Party took over China, effectively sealing off sinophilic representations in Hollywood. After the postwar U.S. occupation of Japan and the communist takeover of China, Hollywood segued from pro-Chinese to pro-Japanese sentiments, producing myriad films featuring geishas and Japanese war brides, such as *Japanese War Bride* (1952), *The Teahouse of the August Moon* (1956), *Sayonara*, and *The Barbarian and the Geisha* (1958).

Like 20th Century-Fox, another Charlie Chan studio, Monogram provided an alternative Oriental sleuth, James Lee Wong. Boris Karloff played Mr. Wong in the first five Wong films from *Mr. Wong, Detective* (1938) to *Doomed to Die* (1940). RKO publicity artist-turned-screen actor Keye Luke, who played Charlie Chan's "Number One Son" in ten films, was cast as Wong in the last entry in the series, *Phantom of Chinatown* (1940). In this film, Luke's character is romantically paired with Win Len (played by Japanese-Hawaiian American actress Lotus Long), a murdered archeologist's secretary who turns out to be a secret agent of the Chinese government.

It is ironic that Oriental detective films failed to achieve success and popularity when a real "Oriental" actor played Chan or Wong, as in *The House without a Key*, *The Chinese Parrot*, and *Phantom of Chinatown*. The genre remained the domain of white actors who impersonated slant-eyed, heavily accented masters of murder mysteries as well as purveyors of cryptic proverbs in what Eugene Wong calls a "racist cosmetology."[34] Despite the explicit racial insensitivity criticized by many Asian American scholars and media activists, however, one should not dismiss the contribution that this genre made to the career development of Asian American actors (including Keye Luke, Victor Sen Yung, Benson Fong, and, to a lesser degree, Philip Ahn).[35] These actors found steady employment and enjoyed on-the-job training thanks to the longevity of the Oriental detective series. The Charlie Chan series in particular established the unique style of the B detective genre through Orientalist icons and the generic mixing of crime, horror, comedy, family drama, and travelogue.

In contrast to the Chan, Moto, and Wong variations, it is quite extraordinary that the Asian American detective roles in *Daughter of Shanghai*—federal investigator Kim Lee and quasi-detective Lan Ying Quan—are not only played by real Asian American actors but are also devoid of degrading stereotypes. *Daughter of Shanghai* marked the "third beginning" of Anna May Wong's movie career, to borrow her own expression.[36] The first period of her career involved her struggle as a pioneering Asian American screen actress whose talent and beauty became largely subsumed within Hollywood's exotic racial and sexual imagery of a Madame Butterfly and a "dragon lady" in such films as *The Toll of the Sea* (1922) and *The Thief of Baghdad* (1924). Disheartened by Hollywood's treatment, in 1928 Wong left the United States for Europe to seek what would become the "second beginning" of her acting career. In Germany, France, and England, she ascended to international stardom, appearing in a variety of lead roles in stage and film productions, fluently speaking all the original language dialogue.[37] Back in Hollywood, the biggest disappointment for Wong came when MGM offered her the temptress role of second wife Lotus in the film adaptation of Pearl S. Buck's *The Good Earth* (1931), instead of the lead role of O-lan. After losing the role of a lifetime to Luise Rainer, Wong again deserted Hollywood to visit her ancestral homeland for the first time, to find out whether she was "playing a Chinese or merely giving an American interpretation of one."[38]

Upon her 1936 return from China, Wong signed a new contact with Paramount, which provided her sympathetic roles in a series of B detective and crime pictures between 1937 and 1939 (*Daughter of Shanghai*, *Dangerous to Know*, *King of Chinatown*, and *Island of Lost Men*) as it vied with 20th Century-Fox for the niche market of Oriental mysteries. As Robert McIlwaine rightly points out in *Modern Screen*, "Paramount is making the [Anna May Wong] pictures, not due to the current conflict in the Orient, but because of the tremendous success of those Charlie Chan features."[39] In these films, Wong played a series of positive roles exhibiting professionalism (*King of Chinatown*), investigative skills (*Daughter of Shanghai* and *Island of Lost Men*), and exceptional wisdom and devotion (*Dangerous to Know*).

The newspapers appropriately promoted her new Paramount roles as "Girl 'Chan'" or a "feminine counterpart of 'Charlie Chan,'"[40] emphasizing the novelty of an Oriental female detective. The idea of the series reportedly originated from the actress herself. According to McIlwaine, Wong first submitted the idea to Paramount in 1934. At that time no producers thought it worthwhile.[41] Three years later, the studio executives changed their minds and gave the green light to her proposition, probably because of the growing popularity of the Oriental detective cycle, fierce competition among the studios, and Wong's marketability as a B movie star that was enhanced by her much-publicized trip to China. This short-lived, Paramount lady detective persona was revived years later when Wong played the titular role of an art gallery owner/investigator in the now-extinct Dumont television series, *The Gallery of Madame Liu-Tsong*, which lasted thirteen episodes from August to November 1951.

Paramount's choice of Robert Florey to direct the first two Anna May Wong films was a logical one considering his reputation as a top-notch B filmmaker who could produce quality work under tight schedules and budgetary constraints. In addition, he had a keen interest in Asia, having made trips to the Far East twice, first in the spring of 1934 and then in the summer of 1937. On his first trip, Florey visited Japan, Hong Kong, Macao, and the Philippines and spent three weeks in Shanghai and other Chinese locations clandestinely shooting backgrounds for Warner Bros.' planned China-set films (only one of which, *Oil for the Lamps of China* [1935] was made — regretfully without using any of Florey's footage).[42] Accompanied by friend Nick Grinde, a director at Warner Bros., Florey revisited Asia three years later and toured film studios in Japan. After documenting and filming local talent, costumes, and backgrounds in hopes of future co-productions, Florey and Grinde headed for China only to be deterred by the outbreak of the Sino-Japanese War.[43] Paramount may have hoped to replicate the success of the Josef von Sternberg-Marlene Dietrich brand of exotica on a B scale by matching Florey and Wong, two ethnic/national others freshly returned from the Orient. Coincidentally or not, one of the French-born director's first jobs in Hollywood was as an assistant to Sternberg (who befriended and greatly influenced him) at MGM. Wong had her own connection to both Sternberg and Dietrich, with whom she collaborated in *Shanghai Express*.

How and why Philip Ahn became involved in the series remains less clear, yet one can infer that his friendship with Wong may have helped him secure the role of the first self-representing Asian American romantic hero in the history of American sound motion pictures. In his 1970 interview with Frank Chin, Ahn fondly reminiscences about his close relationship with Anna May throughout their high school days:

[A]t the time she bought a car, a beautiful old convertible Studebaker Oldster, but she couldn't drive. So she had me drive her to the studio and then take the car to school, and then pick her up in the evening and bring her back home. So while I was sitting around there waiting for Anna May Wong to finish work one day, Douglas Fairbanks spotted me and said he thought I would be good material for pictures and wanted to test me and use me in *The Thief of Baghdad*.[44]

Although Philip was forced to decline Fairbanks's invitation because of his mother's strong opposition, this early exposure to Hollywood through his classmate and neighbor undoubtedly influenced his future pursuit of a movie acting career.

Coincidence brought the two friends together at Paramount Studios in 1937. One year before, newcomer Philip had appeared in three Paramount films—*Anything Goes*, *The General Died at Dawn*, and *Klondike Annie*—and had established connections with director Lewis Milestone and star Mae West. In the aforementioned interview, the actor recollects his first encounter with the star:

I was walking across the [studio] lot and I saw a large limousine with a lot of people milling around it. I saw Mae West there, and she was beckoning. I supposed, "She can't be doing that to me," so I looked over this way, but there was nobody there.... But I figured it can't be me, so I started to walk away, and her bodyguard came up to me and said, "Miss West would like to speak to you." She asked me to come over and see her director. Later on I went and saw her director. She asked the casting director how much was the boy making on *Anything Goes*. I was making $100 a week in those days. So she said, "Pay the boy $250 a week."[45]

For a struggling college student just debuting as a minor actor, being beckoned by the studio's biggest star and the offer of $250 a week must have been beyond his wildest dreams.

Even so, Philip Ahn could not have imagined the lucky break awaiting him the next year: a lead role opposite Anna May Wong and a $900 salary for three weeks' work. Yet, despite his casting as the male protagonist, the actor's marginalized status was reflected on the *Daughter of Shanghai* payroll. Wong received top billing and earned $4,000, a salary more than four times higher than that of Ahn. Cecil Cunningham and Charles Bickford, who played the film's two chief villains, Ms. Hunt and Otto Hartman, also earned more than him: $1,000 and $1,500, respectively.[46] Although Wong's paycheck may sound inconsequential compared with the $150,000 per picture deal Claudette Colbert signed with Paramount in 1936,[47] *Daughter of Shanghai* was "her" movie, and Ahn was a supporting actor regardless of the significance of his role in the narrative.

One question still remains unanswered: why was the Korean American actor chosen to play the romantic lead in *Daughter of Shanghai* and *King of Chinatown*? His roles in both films are groundbreaking not only because he "gets the girl" but also because he is a man of power and status (an FBI agent in the former and a lawyer in the latter).[48] One might be tempted to find precedents for Philip Ahn's characters in the silent-era lead roles that Sessue Hayakawa played opposite his wife, actress Tsuru Aoki, in *Alien Souls* (1916), *The Honorable Friend* (1916), *The Soul of Kura-San* (1916), *Each to His Kind* (1917), *Bonds of Honor* (1919), *The Courageous Coward* (1919), *The Dragon Painter* (1919), *A Heart in Pawn* (1919), *Black Roses* (1921), *Five Days to Live* (1922), and *The Danger Line* (1924). One notable difference is that the Hayakawa-Aoki duo (both were natives of Japan) mostly played foreign nationals or immigrant workers, in contrast to the upwardly mobile Asian Americans depicted by American-born Ahn and Wong in the Paramount films.

Caught in between Sessue Hayakawa of the silent period and James Shigeta of the Cold War era, Ahn's romantic persona in the late 1930s stands out. Although both Hayakawa and Shigeta flirted with the seductive yet perilous promise and melodrama of miscegenation that was so appealing to white female audiences' repressed desires for exotic Asian lovers,[49] Ahn placated the mainstream spectatorial anxiety about white-yellow miscegenation by containing Anna May Wong's sexuality within same-race coupling. In other words, Ahn's upgrading to the male lead was auxiliary to Wong's portrayal of an active romantic heroine departing from traditionally coded images of "lotus blossoms" or Madame Butterflies who sacrificed their lives to free white protagonists from the burden of miscegenation. Although the Motion Picture Production Code of 1930 (the industry's self-censorship guidelines that would be strictly enforced by the Production Code Administration starting in 1934) specifically prohibited miscegenation between white characters and black characters, in practice the exclusion expanded to other racial minorities, such as Asians, Latinos, and Native Americans.[50] With few exceptions, Hollywood's interracial romances were destined to end in the tragic death of either or both members of the mixed couple, as in *The Bitter Tea of General Yen*, *Duel in the Sun* (1946), *Love Is a Many-Splendored Thing*, *The King and I*

(1956), *South Pacific* (1958), and *West Side Story* (1961). During this segregationist period, the only way that the Asian heroine could marry happily instead of committing suicide or being killed was to be paired off with a hero of her own race.

Keye Luke was an initial candidate for the coveted role of romantic lead in *Daughter of Shanghai*. William Hurlbut's early version of the screenplay, dated September 8, 1937, has a character description section that describes Kim Lee (then Duncan Lee)'s role as

> an American-born Chinese of the Immigration and Naturalization Bureau of the Dept. of Labor. Educated, poised, well-trained. Capable of playing the part of supercargo and interpreter aboard a tramp steamer. Must be a good actor who can portray courage, humor, sympathy and an attractive youth with whom Mei-Mei [later Lan Ying] can fall in love. Keye Luke would be ideal.

Interestingly, Ahn's name is attached to the description of a bit character named Ah Fong: "Quan Lin's secretary must be a good actor, suave, courteous and speaking good English. Dressed well. Philip Ahn type."[51] One can speculate that Paramount ultimately opted for Ahn, a fresh face, for the role of male protagonist because Luke's persona was too strongly associated with the rival studio's Charlie Chan series. Although it is not clear why the male protagonist's name was changed from Duncan Lee to Kim Lee in the final script, one cannot help but notice that the latter name implicitly foregrounds Ahn's ethnicity by using two of the most common Korean surnames. One should not rule out the possibility that the name was deliberately changed to acknowledge the casting of a Korean American actor in the role. According to the actor's brother Ralph, Philip privately regarded the Korean-sounding name as compensation for playing a different ethnicity.[52]

Once the new Oriental romantic couple was formed, Paramount's publicity machinery kicked into high gear to promote the duo. Thomas Harris elaborates the mechanisms for promoting stars as follows:

> [A] preliminary publicity buildup [starts] months or even years before the star is seen on the screen. Frequent devices used in such a buildup are a "discovery" usually concocted by studio publicists, a series of glamour pictures sent to all the print media, a rumored romance with another star already well known to the public, or a rumored starring

role in a major film. This publicity finds a primary outlet in syndicated Hollywood gossip columns and movie fan magazines.[53]

A similarly manipulative build-up was prepared for the creation of new ethnic star Philip Ahn. The most intriguing aspect of his star-making at Paramount is the studio's disguise of his ethnicity.

Paramount's pressbook for *Daughter of Shanghai* (distributed to the press as well as exhibitors) includes several references to his *Chinese* ethnicity:

> Two famous Chinese actors head the cast.... They are Philip Ahn and exotic Anna May Wong, the latter returning to the screen after a three year sojourn on the stage.... Two of Hollywood's outstanding Chinese actors [Ahn and Wong] are native born Californians!.... Chinese star makes debut in lead role—Ever hear of a Chinese who couldn't speak Chinese? Philip Ahn is one! Ahn [who plays] his first important role opposite exotic Anna May Wong...was born in Southern California, of Chinese parents.... Although he is Chinese, he does not speak the language.[54]

The *King of Chinatown* pressbook likewise states, "There are only five or six Chinese actors in Hollywood whose names anyone can remember, and ranking high on this list is Philip Ahn, who is teamed with another popular Chinese star, Anna May Wong, in Paramount's new crime thriller, *King of Chinatown*."[55] It is possible that Paramount publicists changed Ahn's ethnicity because a majority of American audiences at that time knew nothing about Korea and because such an esoteric identity would have had no publicity value. More importantly, however, the studio deliberately matched Wong's and Ahn's ethnicity to emphasize their homogeneity and compatibility as an ideal Oriental couple. The two California-born "Chinese" stars' coupling symbolically showcased not only the elimination of miscegenation threats to white America but also the formation of assimilated Asian Americans as a model minority imitating the white, middle-class, heterosexual union.

The rumor of his offscreen romance with Anna May Wong also played a pivotal role in Philip Ahn's publicity. Hollywood gossip columns and movie fan magazines widely spread the rumor that Wong and Ahn were romantically linked in real life. One newspaper article, dated October 20, 1937 and headlined "Anna May Wong and Old School Chum in Budding Romance," reported the following:

Anna May Wong and Philip Ahn, chums during Los Angeles school days and principals in an Oriental film, admitted today a romance that is "really not serious yet." "Of course, I'm very fond of Philip, we've been good friends for many years," Miss Wong said. "But marriage—" she wouldn't hazard a guess. Ahn, likewise, was indefinite. "But who can tell where love is concerned?" he added.[56]

Ahn was similarly ambiguous about the issue when he appeared as a guest on CBS radio's "Don Forbes' Hollywood Scrapbook" broadcast on November 11, 1938. He replied to the host's probing question: "All I can say is that she is one of the finest young ladies I know, and we have been friends since childhood. Further than that…I think you had better ask her. And that's the truth." [57] Not to admit or deny the alleged romance so as to keep the public's curiosity alive may have been a celebrity management strategy recommended by studio publicists. In various interviews, Wong subsequently denied the media's claim about her engagement to Ahn, comparing it to incest because she regarded him as a brother.

The true nature of their innermost feelings for each other remained a personal matter between the two Asian American performers. Nevertheless, it is significant that the studio and the press exploited the myth of an ideal Oriental romantic couple (onscreen and offscreen) for commercial and ideological purposes. As Anna May Wong's biographer Anthony B. Chan notes,

[T]he obvious reason for creating a supposedly intimate relationship between these two Asian Americans…was that audiences might have perceived [Anna May Wong's] on-screen relations with whites as a natural extension of yellow-white liaisons in actual life. To dispel any hint of miscegenation outside of rape and sexual captivity between the yellow Wong and white European American males, what better romance could have been created than this one between two old high school sweethearts…?[58]

As this socially constructed romance of the Asian American couple did not culminate in an offscreen marriage, and because they remained single, speculations about the pair's homosexuality followed. The campy scenes in *Shanghai Express* that suggest a lesbian romance between Marlene Dietrich's Lily and Anna May Wong's Hui Fei have often been cited as proof of the two actresses' offscreen gay relationship.[59] Although Philip Ahn's name has not been associated with such a high-profile white partner, critics continue to refer to his alleged homosexuality. For example, in her article about Anna

May Wong, Asian American scholar Cynthia W. Liu asks, "What was all the gossip about Wong's possible engagement to her high-school friend Philip Ahn, especially since Ahn himself was rumored to be gay?"[60] Another biographer of Wong, Graham Russell Gao Hodges, writes that the actress felt incestuous about the love scene with Philip and it is not clear whether "her aversion was because Ahn was gay or because Anna May preferred western men."[61]

However, the Korean-language print media presented a completely different interpretation of Ahn's lifelong bachelorhood. Newspapers and magazines invariably singled out his responsibility as *changnam* (eldest son) of Tosan An Ch'ang-ho as the primary reason why he missed out on nuptial happiness.[62] The reports eulogized his piety toward his widowed mother and younger siblings, as well as the legacy of his father. Philip Ahn was indeed faithful to his Confucian duties as the eldest son, who is expected to provide for and live with aging parents. Not only was he a good brother who supported his siblings in place of his father but he was also a *hyoja* (good son) who lived with and took care of his mother until her death in 1969.

The polarization of Ahn's sexuality in publicity and critical discourses attests to the complexities and contradictions surrounding Asian American masculinity and star image. Ahn often shuttled between two extreme stereotypes of Asian male sexuality (the beastly yellow rapist and the Oriental eunuch) throughout his screen career. His brief usurpation of normative heterosexual manhood in the late 1930s Paramount films assuaged white America's racial anxieties and provided a short-lived possibility of the "Oriental Clark Gable" persona. Eventually, as this idealized romantic union was discontinued onscreen and unconsummated offscreen, American commentators and critics conveniently attributed his bachelorhood to homosexuality without considering the particularity of ethnic tradition and familial situations emphasized by the Korean press. Their Korean counterparts, on the other hand, automatically ruled out the queer potentiality of Ahn's celibacy to keep their hetero-normative nationalistic imagination intact.

Ahn's transition from leading man to character actor during World War II offers insights regarding the sociocultural milieu that determined the making and unmaking of ethnic stars. Although the exploding wartime demand for Oriental villains boosted his career, making him one of the "Big Three" Asian actors of his generation (along with Richard Loo and Keye Luke), Ahn never had another opportunity to play an Asian American romantic hero in postwar Hollywood. Anna May Wong and Philip Ahn did reunite once more in a postwar film noir, *Impact* (1949), as part of the supporting cast. Ten years after their previous union in *King of Chinatown*, the duo was transformed into a middle-aged Chinese maid and her aging uncle, sadly demonstrating the impossibility of reviving their pasts.

THE GAZE OF RECOGNITION AS ALLEGORY OF ASIAN AMERICAN SPECTATORSHIP

Let us now return to specific textual examples in *Daughter of Shanghai*, particularly the dance scene that articulates a racial reconfiguration through a complicated gaze structure. *M.G. Herald*'s review on December 18, 1937 offers a satirical comment on the title of the picture.

> No war picture is this. No expedition is made to Shanghai. The only reason for the title apparently is that Anna May Wong, an American-born Chinese, is introduced to the ribald habitués of a tropical island honky-tonk as "the daughter of Shanghai-exotic dances."[63]

Paramount's interoffice memo from producer Harold Hurley to A.M. Botsford, dated July 14, 1937, shows the studio's desire for an exotic title to sell this Anna May Wong vehicle, which then had the nondescriptive title, *Across the River*:

> I have talked with the Chinese consul regarding the Anna May Wong Story, *Across the River*, and have received his approval on it. We wanted to use the title *Daughter of the Tong* on it, but the consul won't go for it. We will need an action Oriental type title for the picture.[64]

Obviously, even before the title was decided on and the characters and the script fully developed, the studio had a clear vision of two components of this picture: an "Anna May Wong Story" and "an action Oriental type."[65]

Wong's character in the film is not a daughter of Shanghai, but a daughter of San Francisco's Chinatown. As Wong is a third-generation Chinese American, her character Lan Ying is an American-born Chinese who speaks English perfectly. However, in the early part of the film, her American identity is repressed: she has a Chinese name, wears only Chinese traditional dress or cheongsam, and faithfully fulfills her filial obligations to her "honorable" father. Lan Ying first enters the film as a living mannequin wrapped in a Chinese royal robe, which is expressly displayed for Quan Lin's VIP customer, Mrs. Hunt, who initially mistakes her as an "antique." Lan Ying comes to life and identifies herself as "only a modern copy." Pleasantly surprised, Mrs. Hunt comments, "Simply exquisite. You will make a perfect princess."

FIGURE 3.2 *Lan Ying (Anna May Wong) first enters the film as an Oriental spectacle staged exclusively for a white female voyeur, Mrs. Hunt (Cecil Cunningham) in* Daughter of Shanghai (*Paramount, 1937*). Courtesy of the Academy of Motion Picture Arts and Sciences.

Lan Ying replies, "I'd rather be Lan Ying Quan. Thank you." Mrs. Hunt agrees to pay Lan Ying's quoted price, $2,000, for the Peking treasure.

This intriguing sequence highlights the cross-racial specular coordinates between a white female voyeur and an Orientalized feminine body. Mrs. Hunt's dominance as an Orientalist (who has a habit of importing not only *objets d'art* from the Far East but also *Orientals*) is mediated both through her pecuniary power and her readiness to unleash an "imperial gaze." The white woman symbolically solidifies her racial hegemony by labeling the other woman as an "antique" or "princess," thereby objectifying the latter as a mythic spectacle.

Mrs. Hunt is a defiant woman whose spectatorial pleasure regarding Oriental femininity contests the "collusion of the male and imperial gazes" prevalent in classical Hollywood films.[66] Only four minutes into the narrative, *Daughter of Shanghai* challenges mainstream cinema's normative construction of the white male subject as the ideal viewer-spectator by filling that position with a female character.[67] Throughout the narrative, the power positions associated with looking and being looked at are flexible and slippery. Along that line, Lan Ying and Mrs. Hunt's looking relations are reversed: in the end it is Lan Ying who looks *back* at Mrs. Hunt and discerns her guilt. Mrs. Hunt is brought to justice only when the shared investigative gaze of Lan Ying and Kim Lee lays bare her cover as a respected socialite. In the scopic scheme of things, female protagonist Lan Ying plays an ambiguous, dual role. Throughout the course of the film she alternates between the object of the imperial gaze (the passive Asian female spectacle) and the purveyor of the investigative gaze (the active detective woman). Although Lan Ying's subject positioning in *Daughter of Shanghai* is associated with a certain degree of paranoia as she witnesses her own father's murder and enacts perilous masquerades, the racialized female subject commands a greater freedom and mobility to escape the constrictive domestic space than stuck-at-home, would-be investigators in such woman's films as *Rebecca* (1940), *Gaslight* (1944), *Dragonwyck* (1946), *Undercurrent* (1946), and *Secret Beyond the Door* (1948). Lan Ying's flexible identity-in-process, her oscillation between the passive object and the active subject, becomes the signifying vehicle for a veritable cycle of deorientalization and reorientalization in racial terms.

The first moment of deorientalization occurs when she is emancipated from the traditional role of a Chinese daughter upon the murder of her Confucian father. Lan Ying swiftly changes into Western clothing, takes over her father's business and servants, and freely articulates her critique of the authorities: "I've seen how the authorities handle things! First there's great excitement—an arrest is expected in a few days—and in a few days, everything's forgotten–until someone else is murdered."[68] Rebelling against the government's authority bestowed on Kim Lee, thereby resisting both white and Asian patriarchy, Lan Ying travels to Central America to investigate Otto Hartman, who operates a smuggling house for aliens at Port O' Juan.[69] Wearing a simple dress and a beret, Lan Ying enters Hartman's nightclub, where a honky-tonk number featuring a blonde dancer in a scintillating black evening gown (with a group of other women) is being performed on stage. She takes a seat near the stage, turning her back to the spectacle behind her. Virginia Dabney, the actress who played the blonde dancer, and director Robert Florey had fallen in love a few months before the film's production and would marry two years later. Although there is no onscreen white protagonist whose gaze mediates this dance sequence, Florey's offscreen gaze (collapsible with that of the camera) directly controls the desired female spectacle.

Lan Ying's averted gaze in this scene functions on two levels. At first, it seems to suggest that the Asian woman cannot reciprocate or return the white woman's (specifically, Mrs. Hunt's) Orientalist, imperial gaze. This appears to reaffirm the racial status quo in which the white woman, albeit sexually stig-matized, has a privilege to gaze at the Oriental woman whereas the reverse is not allowed. However, upon closer scrutiny, it is apparent that Lan Ying's askance gaze flits about the room, scanning the predominantly male sea of onlookers (comprised of whites, blacks, and Latinos) who are rapt in voyeuris-tic pleasure. In other words, the Oriental female detective looks *away* from the white woman to look *for* the white male suspect, Hartman, the object of her investigation. Therefore, Lan Ying's gaze is doubly articulated; she resists participation in the male-centered scopic regime by averting her eyes from the female spectacle while simultaneously exerting the investigative gaze in search of her suspect.

Lan Ying eventually masquerades as a dancer named Leila Chen and is hired by Hartman. She is reorientalized as the "Daughter of Shanghai," adorned in an exotic costume and accessories. Juxtaposed with Lan Ying's dis-guise is that of Kim Lee, who infiltrates the smuggler's ship, *Jennie Hawks*, in the garb of a seaman. He is subsequently hired as an interpreter for the cap-tain, who is Hartman's partner, after pretending to speak what he claims to be "Russian": "Alpha, Beta, Gamma, Delta, Epsilon." When Kim Lee visits Hartman's saloon with the captain, Lan Ying's dance number hits the spot-light. In the midst of her incense-drenched exotica, Lee and Lan Ying share a series of surprised looks (in shot-reverse-shots) that I define as the "gaze of recognition." The reciprocating, bilateral gaze mediates an ethnically codi-fied ocular transaction that allows each to penetrate the "veil of the other," to see through the other's role-playing and masquerade. Although Kim Lee initially appears to be a surrogate for a white male protagonist (comparable to Cary Grant lasciviously leering at Marlene Dietrich's hot voodoo conga in *Blonde Venus* [1932]), the bearer of the gaze that objectifies the erotic spec-tacle, he himself also becomes an object of Lan Ying's epistemological, know-ing gaze that recognizes his own performance.

The two ethnic characters' shared "gaze of recognition" also mirrors the extradiegetic gaze of Asian or Asian American spectators who are capable of identifying the Korean American actor Philip Ahn's cross-ethnic masquerade because of their foreknowledge of ethnic differences between Chinese and Korean (facial features, surnames) and the ethnic stars' offscreen personali-ties. What is significant about the given "scene of recognition" in *Daughter of Shanghai* is an extratextual manifestation of a historically specific alliance between two Asian American stars from different backgrounds yet united in a common cause against Japanese aggressions toward their respective ancestral lands—an implicit discourse that can only be unraveled by spectators armed with differentiated knowledge(s) and cultural affiliations. Anna May Wong's patriotism for her familial home country and anti-Japanese feelings during the Sino-Japanese War were no less publicized than those of Philip Ahn. According to a 1937 Paramount publicity clip, the actress abandoned her new apartment on the grounds that its view of a Japanese garden upset her sense of patriotism. The following year, studio press kits reported that the actress auctioned more than 200 costumes, jewelry, and other memorabilia to raise relief funds for China.[70] The epistemological gaze exclusively shared by Lan Ying and Lee—the only Asian characters in the multiracial crowd of the scene—during the "Daughter of Shanghai" dance number therefore allegorizes the privileged spectatorial position that is unintentionally provided for bicultural audiences who possess greater sensitivity to and understanding of interethnic dynamics among Asian American players.

The film's final scene, in which Kim Lee proposes marriage to Lan Ying, presents yet another instance that facilitates ethnic recognition by placing linguistic difference in the foreground:

> LEE: How would you like to live in Washington?
> LAN YING: Perhaps a change of climate is just what I need.
> LEE: Then it's settled.
> LAN YING: Does this mean you're asking me to marry you?
> LEE: (In Cantonese, untranslated) What do you think?
> LAN YING: (In Cantonese, untranslated) I am very happy you love me.[71]

Lan Ying's anticipated marriage to Lee and impending move from San Francisco's Chinatown to Washington D.C. signify the final deorientalization of the ethnic female subject and her ultimate assimilation into mainstream America.

Unlike Lan Ying, Kim Lee enters the film in Western attire—black bow tie and evening jacket—and is never associated with traditional Chinese culture throughout the narrative. Even when he impersonates an interpreter to infiltrate the smuggling ring, the foreign languages he claims to be capable of speaking are Russian, Italian, Spanish, and Portuguese. As a representative of the federal government, Lee epitomizes an ideal model of an interpellated Asian American identity, which Lan Ying is to share through nuptial contract.

Nevertheless, the sudden insertion of unsubtitled Cantonese dialogue in the curtain-closing moments decisively derails the scene from the conventional romantic dénouement of classical Hollywood films accompanied by the English-language pact of coupling—sealed with sweet-nothings, a kiss, or an embrace. Mainstream audiences can only guess at what is being spoken by

FIGURE 3.3 *Gentlemanly G-Man: Federal agent Kim Lee (Philip Ahn), a new Asian American hero, embodies assimilation and upward mobility in* Daughter of Shanghai *(Paramount, 1937).* Courtesy of the Academy of Motion Picture Arts and Sciences.

the new romantic couple, now symbolically transported to an ineffable, yet ghettoized and segregated space. Underneath this inscrutable bonding peppered with "sonic Orientalism" lies yet another masquerade beyond the diegesis: that of actor Philip Ahn who "passed" as Chinese. Despite the overt ethnic bonding between the two Cantonese-speaking members of the couple, the knowing spectator can see through the ideological transparency of the dominant cinematic code that erects a homogenizing and interchangeable Oriental other through the politics of cross-ethnic casting and linguistic masquerades.

The scene of the final union makes the Asian American romance even more one of otherness by physically alienating and desexualizing the couple. Despite Lee's symbolic power as a representative of law enforcement, the Asian male hero lacks physical prowess, which is a typical attribute of the white male protagonist. Although Kim Lee uses his intelligence and wits to overcome crises, whenever engaged in a brawl with white males he is decisively disempowered and repeatedly knocked to the ground. His final victory

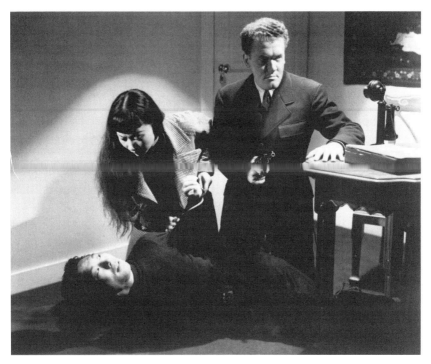

FIGURE 3.4 *The hypermasculinity of Irish chauffeur Kelly (Frank Sully) as a bulwark of protection for middle-class Asian American protagonists in distress in* Daughter of Shanghai *(Paramount, 1937).* Courtesy of the Academy of Motion Picture Arts and Sciences.

against the ring is achieved through his cross-racial male alliance with Kelly (Frank Sully), Mrs. Hunt's righteous Irish chauffeur, whose flailing fists protect Lee and Lan Ying from the villains. This parallels an early scene in which Quan Lin's razor-wielding, faithful black servant (Ernest Whitman) frightens away the smugglers harassing his Chinese master. In each case, the hypermasculinity of white ethnic (Irish) and black working-class men is mobilized to guard the safety and power of emasculated, middle-class Asian males. Thus, the portrayal of Lee and Lan Ying's reserved romantic union as lacking physical bonding serves to contain Lan Ying's subversive female subjectivity and sexuality through the patriarchal authority of Lee, who nevertheless represents an Asian American masculinity less potent than its Caucasian counterpart.

In a larger geopolitical context, Kim Lee's dependence on Kelly's physical strength in this penultimate, pugilistic scene seems to allegorize China's need for the aid of Western superpowers in its war against Japan. However, from the perspective of Asian American history, the Irish were the most hostile group to early Chinese immigrants during the second half of the nineteenth century.[72] Denis Kearney, founder of the Workingman's Party of California, and other Irish labor leaders were principal organizers of the anti-Chinese movement of the 1870s and influential lobbyists for the passing of the Chinese Exclusion Act of 1882. Therefore, the Chinese-Irish male bonding symbolized in Lee and Kelly's final handshake gestures toward interethnic reconciliation and an optimistic future for a multicultural America. Despite this liberal call for racial tolerance and inclusion, the film's dénouement carries a conservative message in terms of gender and class relations. All is well only when women are escorted to their "proper" places (home for Lan Ying and prison for Ms. Hunt), and working-class Chinese laborers remain excluded on- and offscreen.[73]

Although at first glance Paramount's *Daughter of Shanghai* and *King of Chinatown* appear to represent little more than a momentary lapse in conventional studio wisdom regarding the representation of Asian Americans, they reflect a unique set of attitudes among the historical, industrial, and cultural sectors, the interplay of which results in the portrayal of nonstereotypical ethnic role models to offset the "yellow peril" iconography flooding American screens. Of the two films, *Daughter of Shanghai* goes further in its deconstruction of orthodox textual and scopic strategies and in capsizing the racial status quo by employing active Asian American protagonists and their mutual "gaze of recognition," thereby allegorizing the differentiated spectatorship of bilingual and bicultural audiences. Although these films definitely indicate a forward-thinking vision of new identity formation in a minority group, they frequently revert to a less progressive discourse by recapitulating images of a sinister Chinatown, Orientalist female spectacles, and emasculated Asian American males—a discursive set of contradictions consonant with the prewar American public's schizophrenic oscillation between yellowphobia and yellowphilia.

That this dialogic interplay of meanings could operate so freely and so flexibly within the economically circumscribed world of the B film is indicative of the subversive potential of this genre during the vertically integrated, stringently censored classical studio era. Beneath the film industry's monolithic veneer of big-budget "house styles" and narrative conformity, there was a rich array of culturally and politically significant subject matter that remains, to this day, critically overlooked. Equally overlooked has been the significance of the first self-representing Asian American romantic couple in sound-era Hollywood cinema. The formation of the Anna May Wong-Philip

Ahn couple in the late 1930s deserves attention not only as a barometer of the shifting racial and international politics of the period but also as an ideal manifestation of Asian American stardom, which today's mainstream media still seems reluctant to duplicate.

4

STATE INTERVENTION IN THE IMAGINING OF ORIENTALS IN CHINA FILMS OF THE 1930s AND 1940s

A S OBSERVED IN THE PREVIOUS CHAPTER, among the various social, cultural, and historical determinants responsible for the rise of Hollywood's first sound-era Asian American romantic couple in Paramount's *Daughter of Shanghai* (1937) was the industry's conservative, self-regulatory code, which prohibited racial mixing between whites and nonwhites (a provision that would be relaxed during the 1950s, an era that witnessed the rise of the "Japanese War Bride" cycle). We now turn our attention from internal to external forces of censorship that screened, modified, and disciplined studio-era motion pictures in accordance with American foreign policy.

Despite the self-regulation principle of American motion picture censorship, which precluded the need for any federal-level censorship laws throughout its history, a cycle of "China films" (films set in China or Chinatown) popular during the 1930s and 1940s nevertheless fell under the careful scrutiny of the controlling nation-state for the sake of international relations. During the prewar era, Hollywood's China films were censored many times by the Production Code Administration (PCA)— the industry's centralized self-regulation agency responsible for enforcing the administration of the Production Code of 1930 under the auspices of the Motion Picture Producers and Distributors of America, Inc. (MPPDA)—as well as by Chinese and Japanese governments, partly because of political sensitivity regarding the Sino-Japanese conflict. No direct reference or allusion to Japanese military aggression against China could be made in pre-Pearl Harbor Hollywood films because of America's isolation policy toward East Asian conflicts and Hollywood's interest in gaining a foothold in both the Chinese and Japanese markets. Whenever conflicts between the Chinese government and Hollywood studios arose, the U.S. State Department (through the Nanking office of the American Legation) intervened as a diplomatic mediator and negotiated on behalf of American producers and distributors. After the Japanese attack at Pearl Harbor and the subsequent entrance of the United States into World War II, Hollywood became openly anti-Japanese and pro-Chinese. Along with the PCA, whose preemptive, pro-industry censorship mainly targeted the issues of sex and morality that might provoke local censors or religious boycotts, the Bureau of Motion Pictures of the Office of War Information (OWI)—the Roosevelt administration's propaganda agency—regulated the political content of wartime Hollywood films, directly influencing representations of Asian allies and enemies.

This chapter investigates how the interaction between the industry and the state affected the construction of racial, political, and ideological others; moreover, it considers how Philip Ahn's multiple onscreen personifications in a variety of China film texts both underscore and undermine the officially mandated, governmentally sanctioned narratives. The first part of the chapter focuses on diplomatic difficulties involving the Chinese government, the State Department, and the studios in regard to the production and distribution of 1930s Hollywood films set in China. I use, as a case study, the 1937 motion picture *The Good Earth*, which was produced under a formal contract between the Chinese authorities and MGM studios. MGM's successful negotiations with the Nanking censors through the American Legation sharply contrast the harsh repercussions suffered by Paramount, whose own China-themed films (including *Shanghai Express* [1932] and *The General Died at Dawn* [1936]) seriously agitated the Chinese government and its citizens. During the wartime era, the U.S. government's hypersensitivity toward cinematic images of allies and enemies was expressed in the OWI's close monitoring and revision of Hollywood productions. The latter part of this chapter examines specific textual examples from RKO's *China Sky* (1945), which features the first Korean role (played by Philip Ahn) in the history of Hollywood—an anti-American collaborator whose ethnicity was changed from Chinese in Pearl S. Buck's novel to conform to the wartime policy prohibiting negative representations of Chinese allies.

CONTRASTING CASES OF SINO-U.S. CENSORSHIP DEBATES: MGM'S *THE GOOD EARTH* AND PARAMOUNT'S *THE GENERAL DIED AT DAWN*

China was certainly neither the first nor the only country whose government imposed sustained pressures on the U.S. State Department and Hollywood studios in protest against unflattering stereotypes of their nation and people. Ruth Vasey's 1997 study, *The World according to Hollywood, 1918–1939*, reveals that Mexican, French, and Italian governments likewise attempted to influence Hollywood representations of their countries and nationals through official complaints, embargos on offensive films and/or their producers, and diplomatic negotiations. Vasey argues that the Mexican government's 1922 banning of the entire output of American producers who made films insulting to Mexico was responsible for convincing the movie industry of the need to regulate their products to satisfy international demands.[1] In October 1927, the MPPDA proclaimed the industry's new moral resolve, "The Don'ts and Be Carefuls," which would be replaced by the detailed Production Code three years later. The "Don'ts and Be Carefuls" includes a rule related to international relations, reflecting the caution caused by overseas protests and embargos: "[avoid] picturizing in an unfavorable light another country's religion, history, institutions, prominent people, and citizenry." Three years later, Article X of the 1930 Code put a slightly different spin on the above guideline: "The history, institutions, prominent people and citizenry of other nations shall be represented fairly."[2]

However, the existence of such a code and the pressure of foreign markets did not deter producers from recycling time-honored Chinese stereotypes, such as Fu Manchu, the bandit, the warlord, the houseboy, and the laundryman. Beginning in the early 1930s, the Chinese government became increasingly vocal in its criticism of Hollywood's treatment of China and took active political measures to safeguard its national prestige. One might hypothesize as to why such nationalistic reactions did not occur a decade earlier, as in the case of Mexico. Dorothy B. Jones—head of the OWI film reviewers and the author of the first book on the subject of Asians in American film, *The Portrayal of China and India on the American Screen, 1896–1955*—explains why China's protests occurred later:

[I]n the early days of American picture making, the Chinese as a people had not yet developed any appreciable degree of nationalism and were more concerned with family affairs than with matters having to do with the Chinese people as a *nation*.... By the early 1930s, however, when China began to take her place in the community of nations and to build up a functioning foreign service which could put her more closely in touch with other countries of the world, the Chinese government began to express itself with the manner in which China and Chinese customs and people were being portrayed in American motion pictures.[3]

Although the origins of Chinese nationalism can be traced back to Sun Yat-sen's declaration of "Three Principles of the People" (nationalism, democracy, and the people's livelihood) in 1905 and the May Fourth Movement of 1919 (the anti-imperial cultural movement of urban intellectuals), the so-called Nanking decade (1927–1937) witnessed China's forceful drive for modernization and nation-building in earnest.

In 1928, the Kuomintang (Nationalist Party: KMT) nominally unified China under the leadership of Chiang Kai-shek, with Nanking (Nanjing) as the capital. Aided by Western advisors, the Nationalists strove to modernize the country's military, finance, transportation, and communications infrastructure. Education was reformed, superstitions were tempered, and certain feudal customs, such as the practice of breast- and foot-binding, were abolished. The urban middle class quickly adopted Western lifestyles and ideas. Industries boomed under state initiatives. On the darker, flip side of the Nanking rule was the specter of military authoritarianism, corruption, and bribery, to which can be added the millions of drought-famine victims, the rebellions of warlords and local governments, the brutal suppression of the Chinese Communist Party (CCP), and Japanese encroachments into Chinese territories. Faced with domestic and international crises, the KMT government desperately sought to create positive national publicity and attain Western recognition, which was partly achieved through Chiang's influential allies, such as Henry R. Luce, publisher of *Time* and *Life* magazines.

The KMT saw film as an important means of state/party propaganda and tightened its control over the industry. In 1930, the ruling party initiated the Nationalist Film Movement to propagandize its cultural and ideological tenets and counter the CCP's Leftist Film Movement. In 1931, the National Board of Film Censors (NBFC) was founded under the auspices of the Ministries of Education and Interior to centralize film censorship. Three years later, the reorganized and renamed censorship board (Central Motion Picture Censorship Committee: CMPCC) was placed under direct KMT control.[4]

State-controlled Chinese censorship differed fundamentally from its American counterpart as implemented by the PCA. While the PCA, as a creation of the film industry, based its authority solely upon carefully laid-out, self-regulatory codes and had no power to penalize violating producers except for denying its certificates to their films, the NBFC/CMPCC could arbitrarily ban the exhibition of both domestic and foreign films.

According to Chinese film scholar Zhiwei Xiao, from June 1931 to June 1932 alone the Chinese censors banned a total of seventy-one domestic and foreign productions. Xiao elaborates, "While the majority of foreign films were banned for their offensiveness to Chinese sensitivities, most of the Chinese films were banned for moral reasons."[5] To promote the image of a unified, modern, and morally upright nation, the Nanking censors suppressed Cantonese dialects, superstitious genres (ghost and martial arts films), and overt manifestations of sexuality in domestic productions.[6] In 1934, the KMT decreed that the New Life Movement—Chiang Kai-shek's cultural doctrines consisting of propriety (*li*), righteousness (*yi*), honesty (*lian*), and a sense of shame (*chi*)—should be adopted as the principal theme of motion pictures to boost public morals at a time of national emergency.[7] As for Hollywood films, the authorities strongly objected to the Orientalist imagery of a capriciously conceived "China" filled with warlords, bandits, opium dens, civil wars, natural disasters, epidemics, and poverty; such imagery was inconsistent with the officially sanctioned, idealized vision of the New China.

In 1933, Sino-U.S. censorship disputes escalated when the NBFC (based on the reports of the Chinese Consulate at Los Angeles) threatened to refuse to endorse any subsequent films made by Paramount and Columbia unless these producers withdrew *Shanghai Express* and *The Bitter Tea of General Yen* (1932)—films that were considered objectionable to their nation and people—from *worldwide* circulation. The State Department made official its position in defense of the American motion picture industry:

> The American Government does not question the right of any government to prevent within that government's jurisdiction the exhibition of any motion picture which it may regard as contrary to its interests. Nor would this Government be disposed to object if permission to exhibit pictures of any particular company were made conditional on the suppression of a picture which, following a dispassionate and unbiased study thereof, is found to contain features which vilify or hold up to ridicule the people or government of a friendly power or which are likely to affect adversely international relations.... However...this Government could not admit the right of

any government to demand the suppression of an American picture outside the jurisdiction of the government making the demand, and any attempt to coerce American producers by unreasonable demands should be firmly opposed.[8]

The tension between the Chinese government and the State Department (the diplomatic window for the studios) became aggravated as the Chinese Consul General in Batavia (now Jakarta) advised his citizens not to see *The Bitter Tea of General Yen*, and the Chinese Consular officials in Havana influenced the Cuban authorities to expurgate the film (cutting offensive scenes and passages of dialogue). The Chinese government, the State Department, and Columbia Pictures executives gravitated toward a compromise only when the studio agreed to the Nanking authorities' demand to insert a prologue in the film's prints stating, "[This] picture represents a mere literary fancy devised by its author, and it does not in any way pretend to depict actual conditions in the real life of China."[9]

Not long after *The Bitter Tea of General Yen* and *Shanghai Express* were barred from China, MGM announced its plan to adapt Pearl S. Buck's epic saga *The Good Earth* (1931) for the big screen. The Chinese Consulate at Los Angeles was immediately alarmed because the Chinese intelligentsia and KMT officials universally considered the novel insulting to China. The studio entered into negotiations with Chinese delegates and applied to send their production team to China to shoot exterior background scenes and collect authentic props. Screenwriter Frances Marion and the Chinese Vice Consul of Los Angeles, Kiang Yi-seng, collaborated for five months to eliminate objectionable components, such as opium, "Lily Feet," banditry, squalor, and superstition, from the story synopsis.[10] After receiving permission from the Ministry of Foreign Affairs at Nanking through the Chinese Embassy of Washington D.C., a location team consisting of MGM director George W. Hill and twelve members of the production crew was dispatched to China in December 1933. The MGM staff soon discovered that the authorization they acquired via the Chinese representatives in the United States was useless and that they could not operate in China without permits issued by the Publicity Department of the Central Kuomintang Headquarters. Willys R. Peck, Counselor of Legation of the United States at Nanking, who had recently managed the diplomatic crises caused by *Shanghai Express* and *The Bitter Tea of General Yen*, intervened to mediate between various Chinese government officials and the MGM representatives. He regularly forwarded all relevant letters and detailed memoranda to the Secretary of the State in Washington, D.C. to report his progress and solicit instructions. The State

Department files in the National Archives and Records Administration at College Park, Maryland contain an exceptionally large volume of documents under the subject heading *The Good Earth*, attesting to the concerted diplomatic efforts waged during the film's production.

After the incidents of *Shanghai Express* and *The Bitter Tea of General Yen*, the Chinese censors began to take more demanding and stricter attitudes toward American producers and distributors. Months before MGM undertook the project *The Good Earth*, the Star Motion Picture Company had sent its representative to Shanghai in an attempt to make the same film. Negotiations broke off, however, and the NBFC announced its warning:

> All [American] film manufacturing companies should be notified that, whenever any picture based on the story *Good Earth* is to be prepared, the playbook shall be submitted in advance to the Commission for scrutiny and those pictures already made shall be immediately sent in and censored failing which a severe penalty would be imposed when such pictures are found anywhere in and out of China in future. The Commission hereby announces that it will refuse any application which the said manufacturing company may make hereafter for censorship of its products.[11]

As a result of this utmost vigilance against any film based on the "blacklisted" source material, Nanking's pressures on MGM regarding the production of *The Good Earth* were weighty from the outset. The Chinese government made various demands in exchange for permitting the MGM crew's photographic excursion in China. At first, it insisted that the studio should change the title to disassociate the film from the controversial novel. MGM rejected this proposition, yet reaffirmed its desire and willingness to accommodate any modifications of the original story recommended by the Chinese authorities.

On January 31, 1934, Dr. Hsu Mo, Political Vice Minister for Foreign Affairs, officially conveyed to the American Legation the following conditions prerequisite to MGM's filming in China:

> [1] Metro-Goldwyn-Mayer shall incorporate in the motion picture...any and all changes in the novel entitled *The Good Earth* which may be suggested by the interested Chinese authorities, whether such changes consist of omissions, additions or other alterations; and that the film should not be produced or shown if the changes desired by the interested Chinese authorities have not been made to their satisfaction;

[2] Metro-Goldwyn-Mayer shall have the collaboration of Chinese representatives appointed by the interested Chinese authorities at all stages in the production of the film, both in China and in the United States and shall follow any advice which may be given by these representatives;

[3] There shall be a prologue appearing at the beginning of the motion picture, which...shall state that the picture does not follow exactly the text of the novel called *The Good Earth*, and that such changes as have been made are the result of investigations of Chinese life made in China by qualified experts;

[4] In addition to the absolute requirements detailed above, the interested authorities expressed the hope that the entire cast of actors and actresses employed in the production of the motion picture shall be Chinese persons.[12]

Clearly, the Chinese government demanded that their representatives collaborate with the studio not only in China but also in the United States. This condition is in accord with a tentative proposal that the Nanking government was considering at that time: to send a representative of the NBFC to Hollywood to preview and "pre-censor" films ultimately intended for exhibition in China.

Needless to say, the American motion picture industry and its interests in China strongly opposed this novel idea of "source censorship" by a foreign government. In a confidential letter to Counselor Peck at Nanking, dated January 17, 1934, the American Consul General of Shanghai, Edwin S. Cunningham, reported the reaction of the Shanghai representatives of American film producers and distributors:

Attempting to look at the question from the American end, they cannot see why China should be allowed to censor American production which is uncensored by the American Government. They also see danger in establishing a precedent whereby Mexico, Bulgaria and other nations might claim the same right of a resident censor to protect their national dignity. They also think it possible that the censor would be interested in studying American studios and technique for the furtherance of the Chinese industry.... The Chinese censor would endeavor not only to cut out "derogatory" features, no matter how factual, but might also attempt to interject Kuomintang principles and propaganda.[13]

In other words, the American film industry disapproved of Chinese resident censorship in Hollywood for several reasons: (1) it conflicted with the principle of self-censorship; (2) it might generate, in a domino-like fashion, similar demands from other nations; (3) it might help advance a rival national industry; and (4) it could be misused to become propaganda for a foreign government.

Despite this protest against the imposition of official Chinese censorship in American film production, individual studios unsure or nervous about the content of their China-related projects had already been voluntarily consulting the Chinese Vice Consul Kiang Yi-seng of Los Angeles, who informally acted as an overseas radar for the Nanking censors. The Vice Consul diligently monitored Hollywood's output and advised the censorship board to take preemptive measures against "anti-Chinese" films even before prints were made available for review in China, as in the cases of *Shanghai Express* and *The Bitter Tea of General Yen*. In his communiqués with Counselor Peck at Nanking, Frederick L. Herron, Foreign Manager of the MPPDA, often complained about the Chinese Vice Consul's meddling disposition. On one occasion, Herron went as far as calling the young diplomat a "little whippersnapper...who has caused us so much trouble."[14]

Although the studios commonly consulted and collaborated with local consulate officials to forestall anticipated diplomatic difficulties, the Chinese government's plan to send official representatives to Hollywood solely for the purpose of supervising a particular film production was unprecedented. It is in this context that both the Chinese authorities and Counselor Peck of the American Legation repeat the word "innovation" when describing the project in correspondence found in State Department reports. One cannot help but marvel at the extent of the persistence and compliance on the part of MGM delegates when faced with unpredictable bureaucratic obstacles in China that hindered their mission for several months. Why did they not simply give up shooting in China and free themselves from an obligatory contract with the Nanking government?

The foremost reason was producer Irving Thalberg's drive for realism. Released after the death of the legendary MGM producer, *The Good Earth* was dedicated to Thalberg and dubbed as "his last great achievement." Thalberg apparently had the ambition to create the most authentic and elaborate depiction of China ever presented on the American screen. He sent his location team to northern China rather than Hong Kong to faithfully recreate the seasonal atmosphere of the original story, even though it would have been much easier to film in the British colony. The studio publicity literature describes the MGM expedition in China thusly:

The Chinese expedition was unique in its scope. While exteriors and expanses of countryside were being filmed by the photographic unit, accompanied by a special military escort provided by the government, Frank Messenger, business manger of the unit, and John Miller, the property man, essayed the task of purchasing the vast array of properties. Practically everything used in the picture was brought from China. More than 390 packing cases of goods were purchased and shipped back to the United States. In some cases the unit visited farms, inquiring of each farmer the price of everything. They paid in cash, backed up trucks and took away everything movable, utensils, tools, implements, doors and windows of houses and buildings, water wheels, baskets and clothes.[15]

Such elaborate operations were not possible without the permission and cooperation of the Chinese government, and so MGM virtually had no alternative but to accommodate their demands as fully as possible.

Moreover, the studio must have learned a lesson from the recent fiascoes of Columbia and Paramount's China films and would not have wanted to repeat their mistakes. By allowing Nanking's interference from the early stages of production, MGM may have hoped to circumvent an eventual, potentially fatal showdown with the Chinese censors in the distribution and exhibition stages, when any revisions would be more costly and difficult. Not coincidentally, MGM was notorious for "playing safe" with the PCA and foreign censors because it owned fewer theater chains (principally based in New York City) than rival major studios and thus felt greater pressure to churn out low-risk products appealing to independent and overseas distributors.[16]

In addition, the project seems to have been of political importance because government leaders on both sides of the Pacific apparently showed interest in it. Through their Chinese contacts, MGM directly lobbied General Chiang Kai-shek, who had "become greatly interested in the project...[and] sent a telegram, in the nature of an instruction, to the controlling Committee urging that a permit be issued to the Studio to take the desired pictures in China."[17] In a stalemated conference with the Chinese envoys, Counselor Peck inferred that the project had the attention of President Franklin D. Roosevelt himself when he said that "persons of great importance in the United States were interested in this project and if it failed, there would certainly be a strict inquiry in the United States into the reasons for such failure."[18]

Given these circumstances, it is not surprising that MGM, after lengthy discussions with Counselor Peck, committed to abide by the following principles in a written contract dated March 26, 1934:

[1] The Studio reaffirms its desire to make the projected motion picture a complete success from the viewpoint of Chinese as well as foreigners, that is to say, a picture which will place China in a favorable light before the world and which will meet with the hearty approval of the Chinese authorities and people.

[2] The Studio undertakes to cooperate to the fullest extent with a representative to be appointed by the Chinese authorities and the Studio further undertakes to consult with this representative at all times in the production of the film, both in China and the United States. The entire traveling expenses of the representative of the Chinese authorities will be paid by the Studio.

[3] The Studio agrees to accept any suggestions made by the representative of the Chinese authorities, during the making of the motion picture play *The Good Earth*, with a view to excluding features insulting or damaging to the Chinese people or incompatible with the object as stated in paragraph one and the Studio will also adopt any suggestions made by the Chinese representative for the improvement of the picture, if the suggestions seem to the Studio, as the sole producer of the play, calculated to increase the interest and effectiveness of the story.

[4] If the Chinese authorities desire a prologue (technically called "Foreword") to appear in the beginning of the motion picture *The Good Earth*, M.G.M. company will put in such a "Foreword" and consult with the Chinese authorities in regard to a wording which will not be detrimental to the picture.

[5] The Studio agrees...to submit the picture taken in China, or duplicates thereof to the Chinese authorities for approval before being exported to America.

[6] It is the intention and hope of the Studio to produce this picture with a complete Chinese cast.

[7] The Studio agrees not to make use of the film scenes made on this expedition in China for any other production except the film *The Good Earth*.[19]

As Dorothy B. Jones points out, it was "the first time in the history of Hollywood that such a formal agreement had been signed by a studio with a foreign government on the making of a film, and the policy inherent in this move was far in advance of its time."[20] Based on the agreement, the Chinese government consecutively sent two representatives, Major General Tu Ting-hsiu (Theodore Tu) and Huang Chao-chin, to Hollywood to supervise the MGM production. Although the all-Chinese cast request was eventually dropped because of its impracticality, General Tu, along with Paul Muni, the lead actor who would soon racially impersonate the Chinese farmer Wang Lung, was involved in the casting of Oriental players for sixty-eight nonprincipal speaking parts, among whom were Philip Ahn and his younger brother Philson. Much publicity circulated in the Chinese press about the fact that Chinese officials were present during the entire three-year production period of *The Good Earth* and that MGM was cooperating to the fullest extent with the wishes and advice of the Nanking representatives.[21] As MGM anticipated, *The Good Earth* passed the Chinese censors with flying colors in January 1937 and was released in China with only moderate deletions of a few scenes depicting poverty and violence.

That the first Chinese supervisor Tu Ting-hsiu, a faculty member of the Central Military Academy (the so-called West Point of China), was a friend of Chiang Kai-shek and that his appointment was personally approved by Chiang attest to the degree of attention the KMT ladled upon the MGM project. One of the family newspaper clippings of Philip Ahn's college years includes an intriguing article that reported on an encounter between General Tu and Ahn as a USC student.[22] During his college years in the mid-1930s, Ahn was active in extracurricular activities, displaying his leadership skills as president of the Cosmopolitan Club and chairman of the University Committee on International Relations. Among the many multicultural campus events he presided over was a welcome luncheon for General Tu, who gave a speech on the Sino-Japanese conflict to USC faculty and students. As a prestigious figure in the Korean American community, both as the son of Tosan An Ch'ang-ho and the well-known Hollywood actor, Philip Ahn would host and entertain many VIPs from the parental homeland, such as President Park Chung Hee, dancer Ch'oe Sŭng-hŭi (a.k.a. Sai Shoki), and actor Sin Yŏng-gyun, among many others. However, he was no less active in welcoming and assisting Chinese guests. For example, when actress Lei Ling Ai visited Los Angeles in 1941 to raise money for United China Relief funds as well as to promote her films, Ahn accompanied the Chinese Vice Consul Hsu Shao-chang to greet her at the airport. The *Los Angeles Times* report (dated August 10, 1941) on the airport reception dubbed the Korean American actor as one of the "members of the Chinese colony," demonstrating his prominent stature as an honorary Chinese.[23] During the Sino-Japanese War, Ahn's political activism synthesized the causes of Korean independence and Chinese resistance against Japanese aggression. He not only participated in interethnic rallies combining Korean American and Chinese American communities but also appeared in various pro-Chinese cultural programs, such as the "Rally for China" variety shows performed in Los Angeles in December 1938. Thus, Ahn's reception given to General Tu on the occasion of his patriotic speech at USC foreshadows his later role as a surrogate Chinese onscreen, as well as in community affairs.

Not long after that 1938 reception, Ahn and General Tu would professionally encounter one another again on the sets of *The General Died at Dawn* and *The Good Earth*—two films that were being made simultaneously. Paramount Studios had a temporary loan of General Tu from MGM to serve as technical adviser for *The General Died at Dawn* in a vain attempt to appease the Chinese censors. Remembered by director Lewis Milestone (who had cast him in his earlier film *Anything Goes*), Philip Ahn secured a substantial supporting role as the titular general's right-hand man Oxford in *The General Died at Dawn*. When he had a few days off from the Paramount production, the actor dropped by the MGM set to play a bit part in *The Good Earth*'s chaotic mob scene set during the 1911 Revolution. In the scene, Ahn's Republican military officer administers random executions of looters who have broken into the great house; these looters are a ragtag group of hungry thieves, including the female protagonist O-lan (Luise Rainer). The life of O-lan is saved in the nick of time as the troops receive an order to leave the premises just before her turn of being ransacked and executed comes up. Ahn's brother Philson (an on-and-off actor-for-hire) played the more substantial minor role of Wang Lung's neighbor in *The Good Earth*; his paycheck for the role helped this engineering student pay his tuition at the University of California, Berkeley.

Philip Ahn's role in both films is that of a well-disciplined, callous soldier who impassively performs his duties, whether indiscriminately executing looters (*The Good Earth*) or commanding a mass suicide in honor of his dying general (*The General Died at Dawn*). Although the former actions, albeit atrocious, may be justified in the name of law and order as well as national pride (as his character says, "We Republicans are not bandits. Order must be maintained throughout the city"), the latter fanatic behavior has little redemptive value. In fact, despite the fine dialogue written by high-profile screenwriter/playwright Clifford Odets, the powerful performances of glamorous stars Gary Cooper and Madeleine Carroll, and Oscar-winning cinematographer Victor Milner's expressionistic stylings and novel "dog-earing" of the screen (in which five separate images can be seen at once), *The General Died at Dawn* proved to be entirely offensive as far as the Chinese were concerned.[24] The titular character General Yang (Akim Tamiroff) is a monstrous, megalomaniacal warlord who destroys his own province and drives tens of thousands of Chinese into starvation when poor farmers fail to pay taxes, and he mercilessly orders the mass suicide of his guards when his own death is imminent. To top off this grotesque characterization, Akim Tamiroff's yellowface (equipped with a partially rubber mask molded from Philip Ahn's eyes)[25] and mangled accent are disturbingly phony. General Yang's loyal guards, led by a sinister-looking Philip Ahn, are reduced to zombie-like automatons lacking any outward display of humanity. The only good Chinese, Mr. Wu (Dudley Digges), a Shanghai hotel owner who works for the underground patriots, is perpetually dressed in traditional garments and lacks the prowess and bravery of the white protagonist— American newspaperman/adventurer O'Hara (Gary Cooper).

The General Died at Dawn bears a remarkable resemblance to Paramount's earlier China-set film, *Shanghai Express*, not only because of its exotic milieu and atmospheric use of "local color," its use of a train as the setting for major actions, and its shady blonde heroine and caricatured Chinese villains but also for the enraged reaction it evoked from the Chinese government. In November 1936, having been advised by Vice Consul Kiang of Los Angeles, the Nanking censors banned all Paramount products and demanded the withdrawal of *The General Died at Dawn* from worldwide circulation. The CMPCC also issued a formal letter of indictment to the studio's local representatives, claiming that Paramount had "the deliberate intention of insulting China." It blamed the American producer for making two consecutive films—*Klondike Annie* (1936) and *The General Died at Dawn*—that were derogatory to China despite repeated warnings against similar pictures in the past.[26] In its petition to the Committee, Paramount emphasized that the latter title was made under the technical supervision of General Tu, the Chinese government's official delegate to Hollywood, and the studio had accommodated all alterations recommended by him. Precisely because of his involvement with this scandalous film, General Tu was recalled before the completion of *The Good Earth* and replaced.

After a series of diplomatic bargains, the censorship controversy was finally settled in 1937 when Adolph Zukor, chairman of the board at Paramount Studios, gave the following assurance to the Chinese:

> [T]his picture was produced prior to my arrival at the studios of this corporation to assume active charge of its productions. It has always been the policy of this company to respect the sensibilities,

characteristics and customs of foreign countries. I wish to give you my definite assurance that this policy will be continued and that so long as I am in charge of this company, I will personally see to it that this policy is maintained and that nothing will be incorporated in any picture which we may produce in the future which will in any way affect adversely the sensibilities of the people of your country and of its government.[27]

Alarmed by diplomatic difficulties stirred up by *The General Died at Dawn*, Joseph I. Breen, then-chief of the PCA, even circulated a memo among studio heads that cited the film as a bad example not to be followed in future delineations of Chinese characters.[28] Nevertheless, the controversial film would reappear in American movie theaters in 1942, six years after its original release. The re-release can be attributed to the exploding demand for films about China, the most important Asian ally of wartime America.

By the time of its reissue, however, the task of supervising the industry's relations with foreign governments was handed over from the State Department to the OWI, which was created in June 1942. The Bureau of Motion Pictures (BMP) was set up under the OWI to oversee the making of government propaganda shorts and to coordinate relations between the film industry and federal agencies (including the military). The BMP was also in charge of clearing all contacts between Hollywood and foreign governments (friendly and neutral powers). Although Franklin D. Roosevelt had assured the industry that he wanted no censorship of motion pictures,[29] Hollywood producers feared Washington's intervention through the OWI in the production, distribution, and exhibition of their films. The censorship scare worsened in December 1942 when Lowell Mellett, former newspaperman and chief of the BMP, "advised" the studios to submit *all* synopses, treatments, final scripts, and finished films to his office for review. Pressured by sharp criticism from moguls and trade newspapers, the OWI stepped back, clarifying that submissions were on a voluntary basis.[30] The BMP repeatedly emphasized that its mission was not to censor but to increase the producers' factual understanding of the war and to help shape their efforts toward the winning of the war. However, as historian Clayton R. Koppes points out, the OWI had "more than patriotic [persuasion] at its command" because its Overseas Branch had definite sway over the Office of Censorship in the selection of films to be exported outside the United States, thereby controlling wartime overseas exhibition.[31]

The BMP boasted in their first year activities report (1942–1943) that they had successfully persuaded the studios into taking up a number of suggested picture ideas beneficial to the war information program (including RKO's *Hitler's Children* [1942], MGM's *Pilot #5* [1943], and Warners' *Mission to Moscow* [1943]) and dropping certain projects detrimental to the war effort, such as exploitative espionage pictures and films alluding to French and British imperialism (including Columbia's *Trans-Sahara*, Warners' *Free French Story*, and MGM's *Kim*). It also states, "Most of the studios now have established a procedure whereby every completed treatment and every completed script automatically clears through our office. All the studios at least submit those scripts which present problems from the standpoint of the war."[32] This report clearly suggests that the OWI exerted considerable sway in regulating the political content of wartime Hollywood films, complementing the PCA's internal censorship based on religious and moral principles. At times, the OWI's liberal New Dealers and the PCA's conservative Republicans (led by anticommunist, anti-Semitic Catholic Joseph I. Breen) gave the producers contradictory recommendations, leaving them confused and split in loyalty. The OWI propagandists pressured the studios to rectify ethnic stereotypes of the Allies (particularly the British and the Chinese) and to increase the visibility of Russia—an ideologically sensitive subject that had been avoided in Hollywood. As Koppes puts it, "The results too often were ludicrous: a classless Britain (or worse, a romanticized aristocracy) devoid of imperial ambitions; a progressive, unified China under Chiang Kai-shek instead of a desperately poor society plagued by corruption, brutality, and civil war; and a benign Soviet Union led by an avuncular, farsighted Stalin."[33]

Although *The Good Earth* had successfully passed both the PCA censors and those of Nanking in 1937, when the film was submitted for export in 1943, the OWI recommended that the Office of Censorship not permit its overseas distribution. The OWI review dated August 25, 1943 points out that the film contains numerous references offensive to Chinese sensibilities, such as to slavery and concubinage.[34]

The propaganda agency was particularly critical of *The General Died at Dawn* being reissued in August 1942 with a hastily added foreword: "Brave new China, led by Chiang Kai-shek, fought to rid itself of the last of the war lords. The Chinese people fought then as they do now, against evil dictators." In her OWI review dated October 5, 1942, Lillian Bergquist writes, "It is clear that this film does a grave injustice to the government of China—not by portraying her badly—but by not portraying her at all.... Many people who see it will be misled into believing that General Yang *was* the government of China—or at the very least, that the present government is excessively young and insecure."[35] The OWI was also responsible for handling the complaints filed by the Chinese Consuls and Counselors of Los Angeles, New York, and

Washington D.C. concerning the redistribution of the notorious film that had already gotten under their skin six years ago. Following the lead of Willys R. Peck of the American Legation, Lowell Mellett of the BMP directly mediated the disputes between the Chinese delegates and Paramount Studios. As a result of his conscientious diplomacy, Paramount succumbed and withdrew the picture by the end of 1942.

MGM's *The Good Earth* and Paramount's *The General Died at Dawn* provide intriguing case studies to chart out the multi-dimensional interests and positions of the studios, the State Department, the OWI, and the Chinese government in relation to film production, distribution, and exhibition. Hollywood's China films of the 1930s served as both textual and extradiegetic sites of diplomatic tensions and negotiations between the U.S. State Department and the Nanking government. Despite the industry's principle of self-censorship, the State Department's moderate, defensive intervention in the 1930s prefigures the OWI's active control of wartime Hollywood. The OWI regulation, although much less stringent, was the closest that American movie censorship came to the state control of its Chinese counterpart.

One of the recurring points of contention between the State Department and the Nationalist government was the fundamentally different principles of filmmaking and censorship in their respective nations. Chinese officials of the Nanking censorship board, well aware of the U.S. federal government's inability to exercise any legal restraint over the production of motion pictures, used that knowledge to justify the necessity for taking strong action against American films and their producers. American diplomats, in turn, considered the KMT to be unreasonable in pushing for their national propaganda (progressive and modernized images of China) in Hollywood entertainment. The situation drastically shifted after the creation of the OWI in 1942. The federal government managed to establish a system to press for wartime propaganda for America and its allies while not violating the First Amendment. The OWI did so by coercing "voluntary" collaboration through its control of export and overseas exhibition, a major source of studio revenues.

It is ironic that the Nanking government no longer needed its "resident censor" in wartime Hollywood—a system that it proposed back in 1934 and even tested during the production of *The Good Earth*. The OWI reviewers took over that role and often criticized Hollywood producers for the unfair treatment of China. For example, in her script review of Paramount's *China* (1943) dated November 16, 1942, Majorie Thorson objects that "it is the Americans, who, in the final analysis, are responsible for the Chinese victories in the story." She also disapproves of the fact that the leading Chinese character, Lin Cho (Philip Ahn), is described as "hard," "predatory," and "fanatic"—a chauvinistic, callous guerrilla chieftain who looks down upon women (particularly his bride) and betrays no emotion when his younger sibling is killed.[36] Accommodating the OWI's suggestion, Paramount inserted a foreword dedicating the film to the heroism and courage of Chinese allies. The studio also eliminated the negative traits of Chinese guerrillas who in the final print are portrayed as intelligent and self-sufficient fighters (Ahn's Lin Cho is turned into a sympathetic and brave single man). Perhaps as a gesture to humor both the OWI and the Chinese government and to make up for its past mistakes, Paramount pays direct tribute to Chiang Kai-shek in *China*, using as its ideological mouthpiece the female protagonist—an American teacher named Carolyn Grant (Loretta Young)—who eulogizes the Generalissimo as "the finest [man] that ever lived."

"I AM KOREAN": PHILIP AHN'S COMING OUT IN RKO'S *CHINA SKY*

It is true that Philip Ahn's wartime persona of Japanese villains left such a lingering impression as to cancel out many audiences' memories of his diverse roles. For example, Lewis S. Van Gelder, a Los Angeles resident, admits, "I had no idea what a Japanese World War II pilot was supposed to look like, never having met one.... My only frame of reference was the standard late-show movie image of ... Philip Ahn coughing up mouthfuls of chocolate syrup as slugs from Errol Flynn's wing guns stitched across their fighter cockpits."[37] Historian Bruce Cumings sums up the actor's versatile career in one sentence: "When the interrogator squinted his eyes at a downed American flyer and said, 'We have ways of making people talk, GI,' that was Philip Ahn talking."[38] What Van Gelder and Cumings remember are not specific scenes of particular films but meta-images of the diabolic Japanese culled from bits and pieces of various war films and synthesized onto one iconic face—one that stood for that of the enemy in the American moviegoers' collective unconscious for years.

Overshadowed by this notorious Japanese persona are Philip Ahn's many roles in the "China cycle" of films popular during the 1930s and the 1940s: *The General Died at Dawn*, *Stowaway* (1936), *China Passage* (1937), *The Good Earth*, *King of Chinatown* (1939), *Barricade* (1939), *North of Shanghai* (1939), *China Girl* (1942), *A Yank on the Burma Road* (1942), *China*, *The Keys to the Kingdom* (1944), and *China's Little Devils* (1945). One cannot help but notice that Ahn's career at Paramount began with the very two films—*Klondike Annie* and *The General Died at Dawn*—that so offended the Chinese authorities. This experience runs parallel to Anna May Wong's involvement with *Shanghai Express*, which remains the most commemorated achievement of her career to this day, despite her ancestral land's condemnation and banning of it. During her 1936 stay in China, Anna May was compelled to apologize for her "guilty" association with the offensive film, explaining that her ghettoized stature in the American film industry forced her to accept demeaning roles out of professional and financial necessity. In all fairness, one should give due credit to both Ahn and Wong who, despite their reluctant compromises in the face of institutionalized bigotry, pioneered Asian American stardom through sheer determination and professionalism.

Just as Wong expressed her dissatisfaction with Hollywood's racial politics by pursuing an alternative career in Europe and assimilating various aspects of Chinese culture during her 1936 trip, Ahn resisted the system in his own way. The actor's family archive retains the draft of a short article entitled "Oriental Actors in Hollywood," authored by Philip Ahn. Although it is not certain if this draft actually made its way to print, its contents clearly indicate that it had been written with the intent to highlight Asian American perspectives in trade papers or newspapers. In the undated article, Ahn criticizes Hollywood's practice of casting white actors in major Asian roles while confining real Asian actors to bit and minor parts. He particularly decries James Cagney's prejudiced statement, published earlier in *Variety*, which claims that Oriental actors had not been cast in important roles in *Blood on the Sun* (a United Artists release of 1945 in which the star-producer played the lead and Ahn appeared in a bit part) because Orientals "can't really act."[39]

In his 1970 interview with Frank Chin, Philip Ahn recollects another instance of racism prevalent during the studio system era:

> [W]hen I was working in *China*, I had a portable dressing room on the set. [The set crew] took it upon themselves to take my dressing room and move it...for some other actor. I reported to work and sat in my chair because I couldn't find [my dressing room]. The assistant director finally came to me. He asked, "Well, Mr. Ahn, will you get dressed? You're going to be in the next shot." I asked, "Where am I going to dress?" He says, "Oh, over there, back there," pointing to a couple of pieces of cloth put up. I said no. I just sat there and I wouldn't change. They finally got a tractor and pulled the dressing room, and I changed in my room. These are some of the things we experienced. We subtly fought for the advantage of our race.[40]

In addition to these outward expressions of resistance, Ahn internally reinterpreted Oriental stereotypes for his own political cause (namely, the Korean independence movement) and obliquely inscribed his diasporic identities in many of the cross-ethnic roles he played during World War II.

Philip Ahn's schizophrenic movement between Chinese and Japanese masquerades during the war years culminates with one of his most complex and challenging roles: Dr. Kim in *China Sky* (1945). Although Ahn failed to make good on his dream of bringing Pearl S. Buck's *The New Year* (1968) to the screen in his final years, he appeared in all of the three major adaptations of her novels by Hollywood studios: MGM's *The Good Earth* and *Dragon Seed* (1944), as well as RKO's *China Sky*. In the former two films, his roles were little more than bit parts; he appeared briefly in fleeting scenes as a soldier of the Republican troops (*The Good Earth*) and a leader of Chinese villagers (*Dragon Seed*).

Based on a story originally printed in *Collier's* magazine, *China Sky* represents an anomaly in Ahn's list of China films because he played a Korean character for the first time not only in his career but also in the history of Hollywood. Ahn's role is Dr. Kim, a Korean assistant who works in an American charity hospital called House of Mercy, located in the remote mountain village of Wan Li. A communications and supply center for Chinese guerrillas, the ancient village endures Japanese bombing nearly every day. Kim resents being subordinate to two American doctors, including Dr. Gray Thompson, a righteous idealist played by Randolph Scott. Toward the beginning of *China Sky*, Thompson returns from his fundraising trip in the States with his beautiful bride Louise (Ellen Drew) to the disappointment of his colleague Sara Durand (Ruth Warrick), who secretly loves him. Echoing this love triangle is a competition between Dr. Kim and guerrilla chief Chen-ta (Anthony Quinn) over nurse Siu-mei (Carol Thurston), Kim's fiancée. Trapped in a loveless engagement, Siu-mei falls in love with Chen-ta, who turns up at the hospital with a seriously wounded Japanese prisoner, Colonel Yasuda (Richard Loo). Conniving and treacherous, Yasuda sees through the personal flaws and weaknesses of Louise (a jealous, selfish, rich girl who hates Sara and the Chinese and is desperate to escape from Wan Li) and Dr. Kim, whom he boldly confronts during his treatment, having mysteriously insinuated that "we have much in common":

> YASUDA: You are not Chinese.
> KIM: I am Korean.
> YASUDA: You may deceive these stupid people here. Me, you cannot
> deceive.

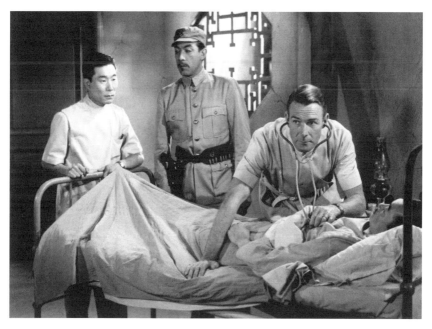

FIGURE 4.1 *Dr. Kim (Philip Ahn)'s jealousy and hatred for Chen-ta (Anthony Quinn) and Dr. Thompson (Randolph Scott) lead to his fatal downfall in* China Sky *(RKO, 1945).* Courtesy of the Academy of Motion Picture Arts and Sciences.

KIM: My mother is Korean.
YASUDA: And your father?
KIM: (angrily) My father is dead.
YASUDA: But he lived to give your life and he was Japanese.
KIM: I am known as Korean and that's how I wish it to be.

Kim initially rejects Yasuda's call for collaboration, but quickly changes his mind when the Japanese colonel incites his jealousy of Chen-ta and his hatred for Americans. The Korean-Japanese doctor administers medicine to the prisoner as a way to bring on a relapse and thereby prevent Yasuda from being handed over to Chen-ta. However, Yasuda then blackmails Kim by threatening to expose his half-Japanese heritage to his fiancée and enlists Kim to persuade Louise to send a coded message under her husband's name, that would supposedly bring an airplane in which to escape. Thanks to Dr. Thompson's intervention, Kim discovers that he has been double-crossed and that the message was not to send a plane but to instruct Japanese paratroopers to attack the guerrillas' ammunitions stockpile. When Kim yells, "This treachery I will not share," Yasuda shoots him and escapes. While Kim receives his

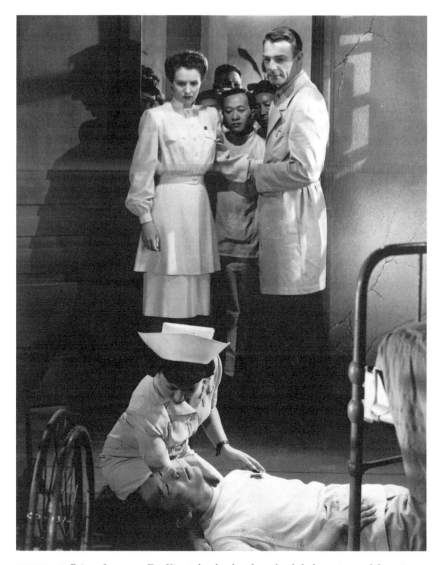

FIGURE 4.2 *Price of treason: Dr. Kim takes his last breath while his estranged fiancée-nurse Siu-mei (Carol Thurston) and American superiors (Ruth Warrick and Randolph Scott) watch in* China Sky *(RKO, 1945)*. Courtesy of the Academy of Motion Picture Arts and Sciences.

redemption, peacefully dying in the arms of Siu-mei, Dr. Thompson, joined by farmers and Chen-ta's guerrillas, defeats Yasuda and his paratroopers.

It is ironic that Hollywood's first Korean role Tosan's son played was a Japanese collaborator. However, Philip Ahn seems to have interpreted the role positively. In a December 1944 article in the *Los Angeles Daily News*, David Hanna reports on an interview he conducted with Ahn:

> His last stint in *China Sky*, he feels, is one of the most important he has played—psychologically, that is. It is the role of Dr. Kim Phillip, a man who is half Japanese and half Korean. This influence of both nationalities weighs heavily on his conscience, but ultimately his loyalty to Korea asserts itself.[41]

Ahn saw Dr. Kim's redemption as a manifestation of the character's "good" Korean side. To support this theory, Ahn strategically inserted a Korean word in a scene that displays the doctor's guilty conscience. Unlike Yasuda, who speaks heavily accented English, the American-trained Kim speaks the language fluently. Pearl S. Buck describes the earlier incarnation of this character (Chung Ming-liang, a Chinese doctor) in her novel as "a little more like an American...his English was perfect...His American clothes made him seem not quite Chinese."[42]

Nevertheless, Dr. Kim utters one superfluous, foreign word when he remorsefully soliloquizes, after betraying his colleagues, "May *hananim* forgive me for what I have done." In the final script, dated July 12, 1944, the English word *Buddha* was used rather than *hananim*.[43] The substitution of *hananim* for *Buddha* is significant for two reasons. As an encoded message to bilingual and bicultural audiences, the Korean word signifying "God" serves as an implicit, self-reflexive manifestation of the actor's true ethnicity, which had been habitually masked. At the same time, the change from *Buddha* to *God* reflects Ahn's religious identity as a devout Presbyterian.

In the script review of *China Sky*, the OWI expressed its concern over several religious references uttered by Asian characters of different ethnicities—Chinese, Japanese, and Korean—who appeal to Buddha for blessings and the vindication of their actions. By replacing *Buddha* with *hananim*, a foreign word incomprehensible to mainstream audiences, RKO producers could avoid evoking a particular religion in association with an immoral character. One cannot be certain if the idea of using a Korean word came from director Ray Enright, screenwriters Brenda Weisberg and Joseph Hoffman, or Philip Ahn. One can imagine, however, that the latter contributor had enough creative leeway to select which Korean word to speak and purposely chose the Korean equivalent of God instead of Buddha. It was likely a conscious decision on the part of the Christian actor to implicitly defy Hollywood's typecasting of Orientals as all-encompassing Buddhist others—a practice

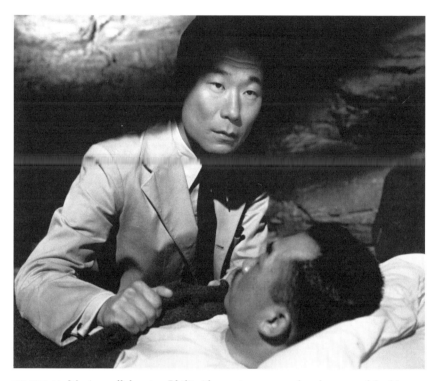

FIGURE 4.3 *Musing collaborator: Philip Ahn portrays a complex character of dual heritage whose treachery comes with remorse in* China Sky *(RKO, 1945).* Courtesy of the Academy of Motion Picture Arts and Sciences.

oblivious to and at odds with the heterogeneity and multiplicity of religions in Asia. With the utterance of the word *hananim*, Ahn may also have wanted to emphasize the Koreanness of his character's "good" Christian half, momentarily capsizing the "corruptible" Japanese side. Although cut in the final print, Dr. Kim's last words in the earlier scripts epitomize Philip Ahn's interpretation of this split character: "Say to my mother—at the end—I was Korean."[44]

China Sky was indeed a kind of cinematic "coming out" for Philip Ahn. He identified himself as Korean three times in the narrative, self-consciously asserting and commenting on his own ethnic identity, which had been previously mistaken as Chinese or Japanese by mainstream audiences. The self-reflexivity in the above-quoted confrontation between Yasuda and Kim is multilayered. Chinese American actor Richard Loo tells Philip Ahn, "You are not Chinese," reflecting the voice of Chinese audiences who had seen the Ahn habitually playing Chinese characters. The Korean American actor publicly reveals his true ethnicity heretofore displaced in his screen roles by saying, "I am Korean"—words that, before that time, had never been uttered in American cinema. And Ahn virtually plays himself when he says, "My mother is Korean...my father is dead." Not only does the scene implicate the cross-ethnic recognition of otherness and commonality between the two Asian American performers but it also symbolizes the precarious status of Koreans in America in the wake of the Pacific War.

Despite the widespread activism against Japanese colonial rule displayed by Korean immigrants, U.S. governmental policies conflated Japanese and Koreans during pre-independence years. Having been classified as subjects of Japan in the 1940 Alien Registration Act, Koreans became identified as "enemy aliens" in the wake of America's declaration of war against Japan. Insulted and enraged, Koreans protested, demanding their reclassification, which would eventually occur when a January 1942 ruling by the U.S. Department of Justice exonerated them from enemy alien status.[45] Before the reclassification, however, the Korean National Association recommended that compatriots wear badges, identifying themselves as Korean to protect their security. Despite the initial misclassification, Koreans began to earn respect and recognition for their exceptional contributions to the war effort. A large percentage of the small immigrant group of 10,000 committed their savings and labor, purchasing more than $239,000 worth of war bonds between 1942 and 1943, serving the government as translators and instructors in the Japanese language, and volunteering for the National Guard and Red Cross.[46] In this specific historical context, Ahn's emphatic declaration of his ethnicity allegorizes a collective statement on the part of Korean immigrants in America during the war.

It is noteworthy that *China Sky* was released in 1945, the year Korea officially resurfaced on the map of American foreign policy with the beginning of a three-year military rule south of the thirty-eighth parallel. Since 1905, when Theodore Roosevelt had sanctioned the Japanese control of Korea in exchange for America's monopoly in the Philippines (through the Taft-Katsura Memorandum), the U.S. government had disregarded the Korean problem until the Japanese attacked Pearl Harbor in 1941. During the war, America expressed its support for the Koreans who were suffering under Japanese colonization, a concern made official in the 1943 Cairo Declaration, in which the three Great Powers (the United States, Great Britain, and the Republic of China) together promised that "in due course Korea shall become free and independent."

The value of Korea from the standpoint of America's war information program was obvious. Roosevelt addressed the nation on February 23, 1942:

Conquered nations in Europe know what the yoke of the Nazis is like. And the people of Korea and of Manchuria know in their flesh the harsh despotism of Japan. All of the people in Asia know that if there is to be an honorable and decent future for any of them or for us, that future depends on victory by the United Nations over the forces of Axis enslavement.[47]

Nearly four decades after his fifth cousin Theodore abandoned Korea to secure unfettered imperial interests in the Philippines, FDR reversed course and ended a long era of apathy precisely because Korea was found useful for generating anti-Japanese propaganda.

Months after the radio broadcast of the above Presidential speech, the OWI came up with a list of proposed film topics, which included Korea and Russia. In a document entitled "Korea: why should a picture be made on this subject?" and dated October 10, 1942, the OWI propagandists assert the following:

We Americans are well acquainted with Japanese stab-in-the-back methods; we have numerous documented instances of mass Japanese brutality; but to date we are not familiar with the day-by-day operation of the Japanese New Order. Ruled by Japan for 32 years, Korea is Exhibit A of the Greater East Asia Co-Prosperity Sphere, and is at the same time a blueprint for Germany's New Order in Europe. What has happened in Korea is precisely what may be expected in all countries which fall under Axis domination.[48]

United Artists was the first studio to accept the OWI's new "Korean assignment." In November 1943, concurrent with the Cairo Declaration, the film company released *Jack London*, an adventure biopic concerning the titular American novelist-turned-war correspondent. The film contains an intriguing sequence in which London witnesses, during the Russo-Japanese War (1904–1905), Japan's brutal incursion into Korea and learns of its plan to conquer China and the West using Korea as a stepping stone. This biopic was the first American film to represent Korea, aside from silent travelogues made during the first decade of the twentieth century. Despite its turn-of-the-century setting, *Jack London* unmistakably allegorizes contemporaneous geopolitical events in the narrative's sympathetic treatment of Russian captives and cautionary foretelling of Japan's long-term conspiracy to overtake the world (a warning that no one heeds at the film's closure, leaving the protagonist and audiences bonded in their superior knowledge).

However, in *Jack London*, Korea is nothing but a nondescript, poverty-stricken landscape populated with stoic-looking crowds wearing Chinese garb who silently watch as Japanese troops pass by with Russian prisoners. To familiarize white audiences with this obscure region, the film introduces a scene in which Captain Tanaka (Leonard Strong), an Oxford-educated Japanese officer, gives a peculiar geography lesson to Jack London (Michael O'Shea). As the officer projects a beam of light (through an apparatus reminiscent of a film reel), visually suggesting the image of the Rising Sun over a geopolitical map, a grossly distorted area of land labeled "Korea" is spotlighted. The mouthpiece of Japanese propaganda explains,

> Here is a theater of our present operations.... Soon we will have all of Korea—a stepping stone to Manchuria and then Mongolia.... We've got to control China. But in order to control China, we will have to crush your country and England. That may take many years, of course, fifty or hundreds perhaps. But it has all been carefully planned, scientifically.... This, the taking of Korea, is only the first step, the first act of the drama.[49]

In *Jack London*, Korea is thus literally spotlighted as an ill-conceived geographical icon, a defenseless pawn in the territorial game played by superpowers. In comparison, *China Sky* personifies Korea, in the figure of Dr. Kim, as an enemy by proxy—a perception of Koreans that many Americans held during the Pacific War. The confusion about Korean loyalty is expressed by the protagonist Dr. Thompson, when he is informed that Kim is collaborating with Yasuda: "I can't understand this. Why should Dr. Kim like to help the Japs? Koreans have done everything possible to defeat the Japs." Although the Japanese character and viewers are privy to Dr. Kim's secret, the Chinese and American characters remain in the dark about the reasons behind the collaboration.

Let us put a rhetorical spin on Dr. Thompson's question: Why should a Korean character help the Japanese in the film? In Buck's original story and earlier scripts, Kim is Chung, a corrupt, anti-American Chinese doctor who collaborates with the enemy for money. In Buck's novel, Dr. Chung rationalizes his act of treason:

> If all white people were compelled to leave, he, a Chinese, would be [the hospital] head. He began to see the usefulness of the Japanese. Alone, China could scarcely hope to drive out the white man. But if Japan drove them out, in the name of the conqueror of China, the

difficult deed would be done. It would then only remain for the Chinese to drive out the Japanese, and there would be left China, their own country.[50]

The treatment of this act of collaboration posed a major obstacle to the RKO production. In an earlier outline of the screenplay, writer S. K. Lauren cautions,

> Dr. Chung's treachery should be rationalized to a philosophical and reasonable plane—it should sound like some of the pro-Fascist philosophy we heard in this country prior to December 7, 1941—like Anne Lindbergh's *The Wave of the Future*. At the same time—not to offend the Chinese, we should make it clear that Chung is an isolated but characteristic phenomenon of every country fighting for its freedom—like a Quisling in Norway or a Laval in France.[51]

The screenplay subsequently underwent several major revisions. At one point, the studio completely abandoned Buck's original storyline and invented an alternative plot. Authored by Emmet Lavery, this version focuses on an interracial love triangle, under fire in China. The triangle consists of a wounded French flier, a mature Chinese female doctor, and a young female American Red Cross worker. RKO was planning to cast Paul Henreid as the Frenchman, Luise Rainer as the Chinese doctor, and Maureen O'Hara (later Claudette Colbert) as the American girl. Both the PCA and the OWI opposed the scenario for radically different reasons. In a memo dated November 9, 1943, Joseph I. Breen of the PCA observes the following:

> The basic story, frankly, is a plea for complete racial equality.... This is suggested by much of the action of the play and numerous lines of dialogue which seem to argue that all men are and should be completely equal in all things irrespective of origin, of race, color or religious or previous condition of servitude. There is the complete acceptability of the likelihood of marriage between the Chinese woman doctor and the white French aviator.... Shall the industry, as an industry, and by means of the approval of the Production Code Administration...take upon itself the responsibility of seeming to endorse a thesis of this kind with its many ramifications and its highly provocative and controversial aspects?...The thesis will be approved by many millions of people and, by the same token, very thoroughly disapproved by many millions more. The point to be considered, however,

is that here again, under the guise of entertainment, it would appear that we are engaging in propaganda for one side of a highly contro-versial question.[52]

The OWI liberals, on the contrary, applauded the script's progressive plea for racial tolerance and yet objected to the elements underlining American racism (the Chinese doctor's refusal to marry the French aviator and immi-grate to America on account of racial prejudices, the American girl's horror upon being told that she received Negro blood in a transfusion), insisting that such references could be picked up and used by Japanese propagandists.

Faced with a no-win situation, RKO dropped the idea of the interracial love triangle and went back to the original outline. The thorny issue of col-laboration was finally resolved with the introduction of a new identity. In a *New York Times* article, dated September 24, 1944, producer Maurice Geraghty is quoted as saying, "The principal opposition against the previous scripts was that they called for the showing of Chinese groups working in col-laboration with the Japanese enemy. All is sweetness and light on the score, now...because the collaborationists are represented as half-breed Japanese-Koreans."[53] In other words, Korean ethnicity was exploited as a way to avoid presenting a negative image of the Chinese, one of America's most prized allies during World War II. Under the double pressure of the OWI and the PCA, RKO studio heads and creative personnel opted to place the blame on Koreans—Japanese colonial subjects—rather than to risk dishonoring an Allied nation. Apparently content with the alteration, the OWI approved the revised script, stating, "*China Sky* could emerge as a superb tribute to United Nations unity, and as evidence of American understanding of the new China."[54]

Nevertheless, in April 1945, the OWI Overseas Branch declined to rec-ommend *China Sky* for Asian and European markets. The nations that were determined as unsuitable for the film's exhibition included the Philippines, China, Thailand, Japan, Korea, French Indo-China, Burma, Indonesia, Bulgaria, Czechoslovakia, Denmark, Holland, Belgium, France, Greece, Hungary, Italy, Yugoslavia, Norway, Poland, and Romania.[55] Although the ostensible reason was that the Office had to be selective because only a lim-ited number of films could be exported for early showing in liberated coun-tries, the OWI discreetly barred overseas exhibition of many propaganda films deemed detrimental to postwar foreign relations. This diplomatic policy (which most likely continued under the auspices of the PCA after the disso-lution of the OWI in August 1945) explains why Philip Ahn's propaganda films of the 1940s could not reach Korean audiences after World War II.

Although the wartime banning of American films was lifted in liberated Korea, the studios must have been discouraged by the prospect of shipping out anachronistic anti-Japanese propaganda to the region once Japan was occupied and converted into an ally. In an interview published in a November 6, 1966 issue of *The Houston Post*, Ahn says that when he visited Japan, he was told that "if my old [anti-Japanese] movies were shown I would be a national hero [in Korea]."[56] This prediction might have been realized had geopolitical circumstances not barred the distribution of World War II propaganda films in Korea.

Along with *China Sky*, *First Yank into Tokyo*, an anti-Japanese espionage drama, is another 1945 RKO film that provides pioneering representations of Koreans, the likes of which could not be found in pre-Korean War productions. In this film, Korean underground agent Haan-soo (Keye Luke) is partnered with American pilot Steve Ross (Tom Neal) who, after undergoing a surgically assisted racial transformation, infiltrates a prisoner-of-war camp on the outskirts of Tokyo. Together with Steve, Haan-soo heroically sacrifices his life to help an American atomic bomb scientist possessing crucial weapon formulas escape Japan, thus contributing to the U.S. victory in the war (the film closes with newsreel footage of atomic explosions in Hiroshima and Nagasaki).[57] Counterpoising the negative image of a Korean as a Japanese collaborator in *China Sky*, *First Yank into Tokyo* depicts brave members of the Korean underground working on the side of the Allies in China and Japan.

According to the aforementioned OWI report on Korea, a Korean Volunteer Corps of 30,000 was fighting alongside the Chinese, and another 40,000 Koreans were enlisted in the Russian army as of 1942. Four days after the attack at Pearl Harbor, the Korean Provisional Government (KPG), then in Chungking, formally declared war against Japan and issued the following proclamation to all Koreans at home and abroad:

> You must blow up Japanese ammunition plants! You must destroy railroads the Japanese use! You must shoot and kill every armed Japanese by day and by night! You must commit every act of sabotage which will hinder the Japanese war effort! Let us all give our all in this fight against our common enemy, Japan! To fight for America is to fight for Korea![58]

The plot of *First Yank into Tokyo* is not too farfetched because the Office of Strategic Services, a precursor of the CIA, collaborated on secret espionage and sabotage plans with the KPG's Independence Army (Kwangbokgun) in preparation for land battles in Korea and Japan—plans that were aborted with the dropping of A-bombs in Hiroshima and Nagasaki. As one of the Korean guerrillas tells the American hero in the RKO film, "In twenty-five years of fighting the Japanese, we Koreans learned many [things]"[59]—indispensable knowledge that was appropriated for the American war effort on- and offscreen.

The opposing images of Koreans in *China Sky* and *First Yank into Tokyo* attest to the instability of the U.S. commitment to Korea. The OWI encouraged the studios to explore the subject of Korea for the purpose of anti-Japanese propaganda. The U.S. government welcomed the resources, knowledge, and dedication of Koreans in America to advance its war effort. Yet, *First Yank into Tokyo* is the only Hollywood film paying tribute to Korean sacrifice and heroism in the war against Japan. In fact, the significance of Korea was incidental to both Washington and Hollywood. Moreover, precisely because of their official classification as being Japanese, these people without a nation could be easily mistaken as enemies by the general public. When relations with China were in question, Hollywood, with the OWI's endorsement, did not hesitate to scapegoat the Japanese colonial subject so as not to display anti-Chinese representations. As a result, the first Korean images on American screens in the two aforementioned films were curiously bifurcated into opposite archetypes—the friendly ally and the dubious collaborator (enemy by proxy)—as if prefiguring the simplistic opposition between South Korean allies and North Korean enemies in Korean War films made during the Cold War period.

Rather than simply serving as evidence of the U.S. government's "flip flopping" on the issue of Korea, however, these diametrically opposing Korean images in *China Sky* and *First Yank into Tokyo* further attest to the anxieties attending mainstream conceptualizations of racialized Asian others (whether friends or foes; victims or aggressors). This collective unease is symptomatically projected onto the hybrid body of Dr. Kim, who is marked with palimpsestic traces of three East Asian ethnicities (originally Chinese; known as Korean; and covertly half-Japanese). Despite the character/actor's repeated self-proclamation in the narrative, the contemporaneous racial logic of American cinema and society disallows the construction of a distinct Korean subjectivity.[60] Not surprisingly, both of Hollywood's first Korean characters—Dr. Kim and Haan-soo—die at or near the point of narrative closure, as if the threat that their liminal identities have posed to the familiar, comfortable dichotomy between good and bad Orientals and between the Chinese and the Japanese has been eliminated. In the context of the Production Code, Dr. Kim's death in *China Sky* also serves the purpose of sealing off the possibility of his marriage to the Chinese fiancée played by Caucasian actress Carol Thurston. This union would have been transgressive

FIGURE 4.4 *Star publicity card featuring Philip Ahn in* China Sky *(RKO, 1945) and the Korean flag.* Courtesy of the Ahn Family.

as it could be translated as miscegenation on an extra-diegetic level. The film ultimately validates yellowface romance between Thurston's Siu-mei and Anthony Quinn's Chen-ta at the expense of killing the authentic Asian other.

The Japanese collaborator Dr. Kim nevertheless represents the first and most substantial of a handful of Korean roles Philip Ahn played throughout his prolific career. Without exposing the political motivation behind the casting of Ahn as Korean rather than Chinese, RKO capitalized on the publicity angle of "correct casting" in a brief pressbook article entitled, "Korean as Korean," where Ahn's family background and his siblings' contribution to the war effort (Philson as lab chief at Hughes Aircraft, Susan as a naval gunnery officer, Soorah as a defense worker, and Ralph as a draftee) were introduced.[61] RKO also produced a publicity postcard featuring the image of the "RKOrean" actor. On January 7, 1945, *Miami Herald* reprinted the postcard in the "Seein' Stars" section along with images of Fred Astaire, Lucille Bremer, Gene Tierney, and Hattie McDaniel. The postcard feaures an illustrated close-up image of Ahn's apathetic, mask-like face and the collar of his *China Sky* doctor's uniform. The lower left-hand corner shows his name, and on the lower right is printed an address: RKOrea Studios, Hollywood, California. The upper right-hand corner shows a U.S. postage stamp with the image of a Korean flag. The card is postmarked, "Washington D.C., November 2, 1944." The newspaper caption reads: "Philip Ahn, Only Korean

Actor in Hollywood Received this 'First-Day Cover' (franked with the 5-cent U.S. stamp showing the flag of Korea)."[62]

In November 1944, when Susan Ahn received the postcard from her brother, she was so flabbergasted as to wonder if it was real. The first female gunnery officer in the U.S. Navy was, to say the least, impressed by the fact that the Post Office recognized Korea's existence and reproduced the accurate image of a Korean flag.[63] Susan perhaps overvalued the U.S. Postal Service's initiative in the production of this postcard, which would likely have been designed for the purpose of star publicity by RKO. Although the Los Angeles mayor had previously honored the Korean flag by raising it at City Hall to celebrate Korean National Flag Day on August 29, 1943,[64] it is indeed impressive that RKO used the insignia in their publicity months before the Korean Liberation in August 1945. The card symbolically locates Ahn's image as mediator between America (D.C. postmark) and Korea (flag), as well as between his ancestral homeland and his place of employment, Hollywood (RKOrea). It is ironic, however, that such a mediation is embedded in the sinister-looking image of Dr. Kim, who is half-Japanese and half-Korean, as if predicting the American military government's collusion with former Japanese collaborators, conservative landowners, and extreme rightists to expel the communist influence from the occupation zone south of the thirty-eighth parallel.[65] Regardless of the negative traits of Hollywood's first Korean character in *China Sky*, and the problem of misusing Korean ethnicity to appease the U.S. and Chinese governments, Philip Ahn's emphatic declaration "I am Korean" is historically significant, particularly because it expresses a pre-division, pre-Cold War Korean identity that all but disappeared in 1950s Korean War films.

5

HOLLYWOOD GOES TO KOREA

War, Melodrama, and the Biopic
Politics of Battle Hymn

A S EXAMINED IN THE PREVIOUS CHAPTER, during the period bracketed by the Japanese invasion of Manchuria in 1931 and the end of World War II in 1945, federal agencies, such as the State Department and the Office of War Information (OWI), carefully monitored the depiction of Asians in American motion pictures, fearing that negative portrayals would create adverse repercussions on international relations. This regulation of representational discourses attests to the degree that the cinematic portrayal of Chinese, Japanese, and even Korean characters was contingent upon political factors whose unearthing brings to light the abiding nation-state interests in two particular East Asian regions. Segueing from the emphasis on China and Japan in the 1930s and the 1940s to the emergence of a third geopolitical entity in the 1950s, one that took center stage during the American Cold War period of sociopolitical upheavals, we now turn our attention to Philip Ahn's ancestral homeland: Korea.

This chapter first provides an overview of the Korean War genre and then focuses on one case study: Douglas Sirk's *Battle Hymn* (1957). This film offers the most substantial representation of Korea and Koreans in classical Hollywood cinema and remains the best-known American film on the Korean War in South Korea. I also examine how the duality of Cold War-era America's perceptions about Korea was inscribed in Ahn's

Korean War roles, shuttling between sympathetic allies and villainous enemies, and how the diasporic actor's familial association with the northern region of Korea complicates this dichotomy.

Divergent perspectives on and details about America's role in Korea and the origins of the Korean War deserve book-length discussions of their own. Such a discussion, in all of its historical complexity, is beyond the scope of this book.[1] However, for the purposes of the following film analysis, it behooves us to briefly consider the background behind this often misunderstood war. The seeds for the civil war had been sown with the following geopolitical events: the 1945 division of Korea along the thirty-eighth parallel by the United States and the Soviet Union; the subsequent failure of the Joint Soviet-American Commission to reach an agreement on the question of reunification, and the 1948 establishment of two separate, ideologically opposing regimes: the Republic of Korea (ROK) in the south and the Democratic People's Republic of Korea (DPRK) in the north. What followed was an inevitable fratricidal clash, a war for reunification waged by leaders of the two Koreas: Syngman Rhee and Kim Il Sung. The North Korean invasion across the thirty-eighth parallel on June 25, 1950 was, instead, interpreted by Washington as an act of international aggression as part of a Soviet scheme to expand the communist control of the region, thereby threatening American interests in Japan, Taiwan, and the Philippines.

However, contrary to the official discourse then circulating in Cold War-era America, Joseph Stalin's role in the Korean War was actually that of "facilitator rather than initiator."[2] Various declassified documents from the Russian archives that have been made available for research since the early 1990s[3] prove that North Korean leader Kim Il Sung was the initiator and that he persuaded a reluctant Stalin to assist his military campaign to unify the Korean peninsula under northern control.[4] After several initial rejections of support, Stalin finally acquiesced to Kim's repeated appeals in January 1950, on the following assurances: that America would not intervene, that the Soviet Union would not get directly involved in the fighting, and that Kim would obtain Mao Zedong's consent prior to the invasion to ensure the presence of Chinese reinforcements when needed.[5] Just as Stalin would never have approved of Kim's attack had he known that the United States would defend South Korea, the Truman administration would not have committed American troops had it viewed the conflict as anything other than a communist conspiracy masterminded by the Soviet Union.

As Kathryn Weathersby puts it, for Washington policymakers, "the issue was not so much that South Korea should be kept out of Moscow's control, but rather that Soviet aggression against an independent state lying outside its sphere of influence...was a challenge to American resolve...especially when that state was closely linked to the United States."[6] In the context of the Cold War, what started as a civil war between the two Koreas eventually escalated into an international war involving combatants from twenty different nations. The Korean War was the first military action fought under the flag of the United Nations. Although South Korea and the United States provided 90 percent of the UN troops, sixteen other countries committed a variety of forces.[7] On the communist side, the People's Republic of China sent hundreds of thousands of troops across the Yalu River to aid North Korea, and the Soviet Union provided weapons, supplies, advisors, air cover, and diplomatic strategy during the armistice negotiations.[8] As William Stueck argues, "In its timing, its course, and its outcome, the Korean War served in many ways as a substitute for World War III...[one that displaced] the ultimate horror of a direct clash of superpowers"[9] but not without grim consequences of its own. By the time the truce was signed in July 1953 to end a prolonged stalemate, two million Koreans had perished, another ten million had been separated from their families, property losses in North and South Koreas had approached $4 billion, 37,000 American soldiers had lost their lives, and $54 billion had been exhausted for war expenses. Above all, as Bruce Cumings rightly points out, "The true tragedy was not the war itself...[but that] the war solved nothing."[10] More than fifty years after the end of the war, the Korean peninsula still remains partitioned, and the pain and suffering of divided families on both sides of the Demilitarized Zone (DMZ) continue.

THE KOREAN WAR IN AMERICAN POPULAR CULTURE: FROM *THE STEEL HELMET* TO *M*A*S*H*

For both Washington and Hollywood, the Korean War was quite different from World War II. Harry S. Truman infamously called the Korean War a "police action" to justify the mobilization of troops without a declaration of war passed by Congress. As a limited war for containment, it failed to gain the same popular support as the "Good War." The public had difficulty understanding the causes and objectives of American involvement in an obscure Asian country that few had ever even heard of. Neither did the government establish a centralized propaganda agency such as the Creel Committee (World War I) and the OWI (World War II) to enhance its war information program and coordinate media relations.

For Hollywood producers, the Korean War may have initially seemed a catalyst to revive its boom years during World War II—an opportunity to cash in on the war economy and win back audiences from television (a emergent rival medium) with newsreels on current events and widescreen, Technicolor war films. In the early months of the war, the studios "waged [their] own 'Korean' War" (to borrow a catchy *Variety* headline) to register potential movie titles with the Motion Picture Association of America (MPAA)'s Title Registry Bureau, such as "Communism in Korea," "The Battle of the Koreans," and "War of the Koreans" (20th Century-Fox); "Korea" and "Crisis in Korea" (David Selznick); and "Dateline in Korea" (Samuel Goldwyn).[11] In August 1950, the film industry pledged its full cooperation with the government's war effort, and major studios began providing technical and training assistance to the Army Signal Corps in the production of official military footage of the Korean War. In the same month, a group of prestigious producers, moguls, and stars (including Cecil B. DeMille, Y. Frank Freeman, Samuel Goldwyn, Louis B. Mayer, Joseph M. Schenck, Albert Warner, Harry M. Warner, Jack L. Warner, John Wayne, and Darryl F. Zanuck) collectively published a political statement entitled "Let Us Make No Mistake about It" in trade papers. The manifesto echoes the Cold War domino theory intrinsic to the Truman Doctrine: "The action in Korea shows us what would happen to us in the Pacific if Russia were to send her own forces against us. We could not hold Korea, we could not hold Japan, we could not hold the Philippines, we probably could not hold Alaska and perhaps not Hawaii."[12]

Despite this publicly expressed commitment and enthusiasm, Hollywood shrank from producing Korean War films. As Paul M. Edwards points out, "While more than 500 of the approximately 1,700 movies made between 1940 and 1945 were about World War II, the Korean War generated less than 100 films and no more than three dozen during the war."[13]

After all, Korea did not turn out to be as lucrative an opportunity as it first appeared. Partly it was because the Korean War did not offer the same national goals as World War II did, nor did it culminate with a glorious victory to which cinematic tributes could be paid. MGM's *Men of the Fighting Lady* (1954)—a Korean War film based on James A. Michener's May 10, 1952 *Saturday Evening Post* report, "The Forgotten Heroes of Korea"—contains self-reflexive comments about the industry's attitudes toward the war. The opening sequence features Michener (Louis Calhern) as he embarks on the Navy carrier *Fighting Lady* for the purpose of writing Korean War stories. Flight surgeon Commander Dowling (Walter Pidgeon), after praising the novelist's Pulitzer Prize-winning short story collection about the World War II experience, *Tales of the South Pacific* (1947), asks him the following question: "Why couldn't you stop while you were ahead? Even Shakespeare couldn't make this dirty little war romantic." This cynical remark reflects Hollywood's admission of its own inability to generate popular entertainment from the unpopular war.

However, audience apathy and the lack of convincing patriotic agendas were not the only reasons why Hollywood avoided the subject of the Korean War. The Korean War occurred at a time when the Red Scare and McCarthy-era witch-hunts had taken full effect in every walk of American society. In 1947, the House Un-American Activities Committee (HUAC) opened a series of hearings on alleged communist infiltration in the film industry and cited for contempt of Congress for "refusing to testify" (a group of left-wing screenwriters and directors today famously known as the "Hollywood Ten") who refused to testify. After the HUAC indictment of Alvah Bessie, Herbert J. Biberman, Lester Cole, Edward Dmytryk, Ring Lardner, Jr., John Howard Lawson, Albert Maltz, Samuel Ornitz, Adrian Scott, and Dalton Trumbo (all of whom would be sent to federal prison for six to twelve months in April 1950 after a series of failed appeals), the members of the MPAA and the Association of Motion Picture Producers issued the "Waldorf Statement" in November 1947, which expressed their commitment to dismiss the Ten, not to reemploy them, and to purge any subversive or disloyal elements from the industry. This statement signaled the beginning of Hollywood's dark period of blacklisting, which continued until the 1960s. By the end of 1951, 324 directors, writers, and actors (including Joseph Losey, Jules Dassin, Carl Foreman, Lillian Hellmann, Paul Muni, and John Garfield, to name a few) had been fired and blacklisted.[14] The culture of fear and mistrust stymied the industry's creative momentum and affected the content of American films. As David A. Cook puts it, "Safety, caution, and respectability were the watch-words of the studio chiefs, and controversial or even serious subject matter was avoided at all costs."[15]

Amidst this widespread Cold War paranoia, the Korean War was a risky subject for Hollywood from both commercial and political standpoints. The industry learned a lesson from the fiasco of pro-Russian films produced at the OWI's behest during World War II that were subsequently condemned by the HUAC as communist propaganda. Two former allies during World War II—the Russians and the Chinese—were abruptly turned into enemies during the Cold War era. This mutability of allies and enemies in a short period of time and the unpredictability of future foreign policies discouraged studios from depicting the contemporaneous conflict in Korea. A *Newsweek* report (dated August 28, 1950) elaborates the industry's position:

> What Hollywood fears in trying to cash in on the current international crisis is that by the time writers, directors, cutters, and distributors

have done their jobs, world conditions may have drastically changed. It currently prefers to play safe with reissues and sure-fire escapist fare—musicals, cowboy films, mysteries.

This apprehension is directly expressed in the Production Code Administration (PCA)'s October 17, 1950 memo on the subject of *The Steel Helmet* (1951), which was being independently produced by Robert L. Lippert:

In view of the critical war situation in the Far East and the unusual circumstance that this story is about a war which is presently being fought, it was the feeling of this office that Mr. Lippert should protect himself and the industry and should handle his portrayal of the North Koreans with extreme care and delicacy lest the picture be a stumbling block to our State Department in reaching a peaceful settlement with the North Koreans.[16]

As one of the two first Korean War feature films exhibited in American theaters (along with *Korea Patrol* [1951]), *The Steel Helmet* generated fierce controversy, demonstrating not only the difficulties of representing the first Hot War of the Cold War era but also the precarious relationship between the industry and the Department of Defense (DoD). In 1949, the DoD established the Motion Picture Production section (with Donald Baruch as chief) within its Public Affairs Office to facilitate cooperation between Hollywood and the armed services—a role undertaken by the OWI during World War II. Iconoclastic writer-director and World War II veteran Samuel Fuller submitted his script of *The Steel Helmet* to Baruch's office in October 1950, with a request for cooperation in the production of his film. The DoD disqualified the project for official cooperation on the grounds that it contained no public informational value and had a number of objectionable sequences. Fuller came back with a rough cut the following month and, this time, solicited government-owned combat footage for inclusion in his film. After a review of the incomplete print (which reflected some of the suggestions made by Pentagon publicists), the DoD approved Fuller's access to and use of the Army-owned stock footage in the Signal Corps Photo Center, Long Island, while declining the filmmaker's offer of courtesy credit.

Both the PCA and the DoD found themselves in hot water when a few conservative critics vehemently attacked *The Steel Helmet,* calling it communist propaganda upon its release in January 1951. At the center of controversy was one particular scene in which the infuriated (anti)hero—tough guy Sergeant Zack (Gene Evans)—machine-guns an unarmed North Korean prisoner of war (POW) in retaliation for the death of a South Korean orphan boy shot by a Red sniper. The film's foremost critic was Victor Riesel, a newspaper columnist, who deplored, "How can anyone talk of 'censorship' when a new movie called *The Steel Helmet* is just about to make the rounds portraying the bestiality of an American GI?"[17] Quoting a report published in the leftist newspaper *Daily Worker*, which identified *The Steel Helmet* as "further proof of the savagery of the U.S. war against the Korean people," Riesel criticizes Fuller's film for "[doing] great harm in this tense day of psychological, as well as shooting war."[18]

Cornered by the unforeseen controversy, the PCA put the blame on the DoD, insisting that

> because it has always been our understanding that the Army will not lend, or give, footage for inclusion in any motion picture which they have not approved, we were inclined to...presume that the Army's willingness to give [Fuller] stock footage carried with it, if not the approval, at least the suggestion that the Army had no *objection* to the film.[19]

Lieutenant-Colonel Claire E. Towne in the Pictorial Branch of the DoD Office of Public Information, disputed this claim:

> The picture was produced without cooperation of the Department of Defense or any of the Services, and without approval either actual or implied, on either the script or the finished picture, or on the premiere and/or subsequent showings.... We did, however...allow the producer to use a few hundred feet of stock material that has previously been cleared for newsreel, television, and other pictorial use. It was specifically understood that this act did not constitute approval of the picture.[20]

Despite or perhaps because of the heated controversy, *The Steel Helmet* was a smash hit and turned Fuller into one of the most sought-after directors in Hollywood overnight. Scripted in a week and shot on the fly in Griffith Park, California, in ten days on a budget of $104,000 and with a mere twenty-five extras, this pulpy, low-budget picture garnered $1 million in the first twenty-two weeks of state-side release alone.[21] Widely considered as the best Korean War film by critics and scholars, *The Steel Helmet* now occupies a seat in the pantheon of greatest American war films of all time. Fuller's film pioneered the tone of the Korean War genre: a downbeat, black-and-white psychological drama focusing on the conflicts and personality clashes within an isolated platoon unit. This formula was to be emulated by *Fixed Bayonets* (1951), *Men in War* (1957), *Pork Chop Hill* (1959), *All the Young Men* (1960), and *War Hunt* (1962).

In fact, Samuel Fuller can be claimed as a Korean War auteur, not only because he made two Korean War films, *The Steel Helmet* and its big-studio follow-up, 20th Century-Fox's *Fixed Bayonets*, but also because his entire corpus of films is filled with characters and incidents involved in Korea-related issues in one way or another. For example, *Hell and High Water* (1954) revolves around the fictionalized Chinese plot to drop an atomic bomb on Korea from a plane disguised as American. In *China Gate* (1957), a group of ex-Korean War veteran American Foreign Legionnaires arrive in Vietnam, "the hottest front in the world," to continue their battle with communists after Korea became "cold." In *The Crimson Kimono* (1959), the Nisei detective Joe Kojaku (James Shigeta) pits himself against his old Korean War buddy as they fight over the same (Caucasian) girl. The pedophile Grant (Michael Dante) in *The Naked Kiss* (1965) hides his pathological self behind the veil of an illustrious reputation, posing as a Korean War hero-turned-philanthropist. In *Shock Corridor* (1963), asylum inmate Stuart (James Best), who imagines himself as Colonel Jeb Stuart from the Civil War, is a "brainwashed" and subsequently disgraced Korean War defector.

Interestingly, *Shock Corridor* opens with the reflection of Philip Ahn's face on the glass frame of his character's diploma. As Chinese psychiatrist Dr. Fong, he assists protagonist Johnny Barratt (Peter Breck), a reporter obsessed with winning a Pulitzer Prize, in his plan to infiltrate a mental ward to investigate a murder case by pretending to be schizophrenic. During his brief screen time, Ahn utters a revealing line—"Lower your mask only for an instant and they'll know you're a phony"—which underscores the film's central theme (reality vs. performance), as well as the way in which his own career consisted of cross-ethnic masquerades.

Throughout Fuller's *oeuvre*, Korea functions as a kind of repressed "Lacanian real,"[22] returning relentlessly and circuitously in the form of traumatic symptoms dogging the American male psyche during the Cold War era. In his narratives, the Korean War and its strain on the male psyche are constantly displaced onto something *other* or at least onto something politically adjacent: World War II, the French-Vietnam War, Cold War paranoia, interracial conflicts and bonding, and madness and pathology.

Often dubbed as the "forgotten war" in the popular vernacular of keywords and catchphrases, the Korean War was not simply forgotten but intentionally repressed in American popular culture because it was "the counterpoint to the patriotic memories of World War II."[23] One of the most ignominious and repressed memories of the Korean War is the defection of twenty-one American GIs in the 1953 Operation Big Switch (POW exchange)[24] and the alleged collaboration of American POWs with the enemy. According to government statistics, of all 7,140 American POWs, 2,701 died in captivity.[25] Having survived torture, death marches, starvation, lack of medical care, and indoctrination by their North Korean and Chinese captors, the 4,000-odd surviving POWs were repatriated to the cold, unreceptive arms of the U.S. government and citizenry. Starting with their sea voyage back home, the returnees were subjected to strenuous, repeated debriefing interrogations during which they were pressured to inform on fellow prisoners. Although only 14 of 565 men charged with misconduct faced an actual court martial (ten of them were convicted), many repatriated POWs continued to be harassed by FBI agents and military interrogators for years after they resumed civilian life.[26]

In lieu of glorious victory parades and celebrations to distract the public's attention, the media sensationalized the Korean War POW stories with such headlines as "Cowardice in Korea" (*Time*, November 2, 1953), "Brain-Washed Korean POWs" (*Scholastic*, May 12, 1954), "Brainwashing: Time for a Policy" (*Atlantic*, April 1955), and "Why POWs Collaborate" (*Science*, May 11, 1957).[27] In his much-quoted book, *In Every War But One* (1959), journalist Eugene Kinkead argued that U.S. servicemen had never been so dishonorable in any war as in Korea where "one out of every three American prisoners was guilty of some sort of collaboration with the enemy...[and] one man in every seven...was guilty of serious collaboration."[28] Although more objective studies subsequently revealed that the behavior of the Korean War POWs was no worse than those in captivity during previous wars, this unfortunate group was an all-too easy scapegoat of the Red Scare and McCarthyism of 1950s America. The popular media (particularly film and television) perpetuated the distorted images of treacherous Korean War captives as weak, pampered victims of "momism" and brainwashing.[29]

Unlike World War II films that depict POW escapes and heroism, the Korean War counterparts focus on the themes of brainwashing and collaboration, as in *Prisoner of War* (1954), *The Bamboo Prison* (1954), *The Rack* (1956), *Time Limit* (1957), and *Sergeant Ryker* (1968). Out of this forgotten subgroup emerged one indisputable masterpiece of American cinema: *The Manchurian Candidate* (1962). Based on Richard Condon's 1959 bestseller, this compelling Cold War satire features a fantastic and disturbing plot revolving around a Korean War veteran named Raymond Shaw (Lawrence Harvey) who, having been brainwashed into becoming a communist killing machine, assassinates a presidential candidate.[30] Despite the film's explicit mockery of Joe McCarthy and extreme rightists, its notorious 360-degree rotating brainwashing sequence set in the Manchurian amphitheater, where drugged and hypnotized American captives are conditioned to kill their combat buddies in cold blood, did little to exonerate Korean War POWs from McCarthy-era stigmatization.

The Korean War remains one of the most unpopular wars in American history. Although public dissent could not be expressed freely as it would be during the Vietnam War precisely because of the repressive social milieu fostered by McCarthyism, as public opinion polls conducted in August 1953 show, a majority of Americans (62 percent) felt that it was not worthwhile fighting in Korea.[31] Undoubtedly, the stalemate in Korea was one of the major factors that precipitously lowered Truman's approval rating from 87 percent in July 1945 to 23 percent in November 1951, forcing him to give up his hopes for reelection in 1952. When the three-year conflict ended in bitter disappointment and frustration, there was little left to remember or celebrate. Except for Douglas MacArthur's final victory prior to his controversial dismissal—Operation Chromite (the Inchŏn Landing of September 15, 1950)— virtually no major battle in the war, before or after, brought glory to UN/U.S. forces. This lack of memorable victories resulted in the decontextualization of Korean War combat films (no specification of geographical and temporal backgrounds and the frequent recycling of World War II newsreel footage).

The war's political unpopularity and absence of military glory probably encouraged Hollywood producers to approach the topic in a circuitous way. In fact, one prevalent characteristic shared by many Korean War films is genre-mixing. In particular, the emphasis on melodramatic themes of family, marriage, and romance provided an effective means to avoid representing the realities and controversies of the war itself. For example, Samuel Goldwyn's production *I Want You* (1951) is entirely set on the homefront of small-town America, although much of the narrative tension derives from the offscreen war. As the boss of a construction company, Martin Greer (Dana Andrews) is asked by his employee George Kress (Walter Baldwin) to write a letter requesting that the draft board defer his teenaged son's posting to Korea. Martin refuses because his conscience does not allow him to lie that the young man is "indispensable" for his business. He faces an even more vexatious moral conundrum when his own mother (Mildred Dunnock) applies the same plea on behalf of his younger brother Jack (Farley Granger); his rejection of that request ushers in family conflicts. In the end, Martin gives up his own "indispensable" classification and reenlists along with his World War II buddy. Throughout the film, the presence of the war is felt only indirectly through radio broadcasts and letters from the draft board. Ending with the image of a reconciled family gathered at Jack's wedding before his departure for Korea, *I Want You* waives the opportunity for audiences to witness the inevitably tearful familial separation and bloody combat experience.

On the contrary, MGM's *The Rack*—ostensibly a POW film—begins in the immediate aftermath of the Korean War with the repatriation of Captain Edward Hall, Jr. (Paul Newman), who faces collaboration charges. Although considerable screen time is devoted to court-martial procedures, the film's emotional core in the rocky relationship between Hall and his disciplinarian father, an army officer of the old school (Walter Pidgeon) who cruelly yells at his son upon being informed of the latter's collaboration, "Why didn't you die like your brother did?" Defense attorney (Edmond O'Brien) rationalizes Hall's collaboration by pointing out not only the enemy's inhumane treatment of POWs and cunning system of mental torture but also the inadequacies of his upbringing (Hall lost his mother at the age of twelve and grew alienated from his habitually absent, militaristic father). During the trial, Hall is asked to read his autobiography written in the camp in which he confesses that "my father never kissed me, he didn't hold us or do what we saw other fathers doing with their kids. I never felt warm.... I wish my father had given me a chance to show how much I loved him." Unable to control his emotions, the vulnerable officer breaks down and sobs while being watched by courtroom spectators, including his repentant father, who belatedly takes his son in a conciliatory embrace in the following scene. Given this heavy dose of melodramatic affect, the film can be easily categorized as a "male weepie" in addition to a POW film and a courtroom drama. Following the cathartic release of emotional tensions in the father-son relationship, Hall is found guilty of treason and delivers a moralizing speech in which he accepts the verdict as a just one. Ultimately, the film reaffirms the judicial authority of the state, exonerating paternal/social responsibilities and indicting the personality flaws of individual POWs.

In his article, "The Korean War Film as Family Melodrama," Rick Worland argues that the frequent integration of combat action and family melodrama in Korean War films "creates an off-balance combination of resolve and regret that complicates readings of these films as jingoistic reinforcements of official policy."[32] The very limitations and ambiguities of the war turn into assets in certain Korean War family melodramas, such as *I Want You* and *The Bridges at Toko-Ri* (1954), which explore the moral dilemmas and emotional turmoil of skeptical yet dutiful soldiers who must leave their beloved ones without knowing why they should fight. However, Worland's exclusive focus on all-American family dynamics in his discussion of the melodramatic trend does little justice to another important offshoot of Korean War melodrama: Oriental romance.

Several Korean War films center around the theme of East meets-West romance between an idealized Asian woman and an American serviceman, including George Breakston and C. Ray Stahl's *Geisha Girl* (1952), King Vidor's *Japanese War Bride* (1952), and Joshua Logan's *Sayonara* (1957). In these films, the Korean War functions as a mere excuse for cross-Pacific encounters between a GI Joe and a Lotus Blossom. The dialogue between American fiancée Eileen Webster (Patricia Owen) and her soon-to-be unfaithful boyfriend Lloyd Gruver (Marlon Brando) in *Sayonara* emphasizes this point. During her reunion with Gruver in Kobe, Japan where the combat-weary officer is sent for extended rest and recuperation (R & R),[33] the anxious girl-next-door confronts him by asking, "Why aren't we married now?" The indecisive fiancé mumbles, "Oh, I suppose the Korean War might have a little something to do with it." Eileen's pointed response to what she considers to be a pathetic excuse seems to be directed not only to Gruver but also to the producers of *Sayonara* and other Oriental romance films: "Wasn't Korea, maybe, *convenient?*" Gruver's psychological crisis in Korea in the ten-minute opening sequence, when the ace pilot is distressed to realize that "there was a guy with a face in one of those planes" he shot down, quickly and conveniently fades away once the narrative moves to occupied Japan. There, Gruver falls in love with a stunningly beautiful Japanese dancer, Hana-ogi (Miiko Taka), whom he marries against all odds.

In the Oriental romance type of Korean War melodrama, the white male desire for the exotic, submissive Oriental woman is often displaced onto the neighboring geographical space—defeated, occupied, and tamed Japan. In addition to offering retreat and recreation, and rest and recuperation from the physical injuries and psychological strain endured in Korea, Japan is codified as an excessively feminine arena for enacting romances with Madame Butterflies. As Gina Marchetti points out, "Instead of questioning the morality of the Korean War or exposing the conflict between conscience and duty within the military, the narrative shifts from war to romance, obscuring the issue of war in the process but still making the romantic relationships understandable only through a reference to war and racial otherness."[34]

Considering the paramount concern with race in this particular sub-genre, it is not surprising that Philip Ahn's presence is prominent in two Oriental romance films, *Japanese War Bride* and *Love Is a Many-Splendored Thing* (1955). Both films mobilize the Korean War as a convenient excuse for the encounter between or separation of the American male protagonist and the demure Oriental beauty. In these films, Ahn plays the disempowered

Asian patriarch who reluctantly surrenders his Japanese granddaughter or Eurasian niece to American suitors. In both films, his consent is a nominal prerequisite to the heroine's interracial marriage as well as her physical and mental migration from the East to the West.

Japanese War Bride opens with the title "Korea" against a shot of a dark, deserted battlefield on which dead bodies are piled up. As the camera pans across the grim scene of massacre, a flashlight (projected from the offscreen patrol) hits the face of a surviving GI, who faints after seeing shadowy figures before him. This forty-five-second, noir-like opening sequence gives way to a well-lit Japanese hospital scene where the wounded soldier, Lieutenant Jim Sterling (Don Taylor), awakens from the nightmare in Korea to see the smiling face of a pretty local Red Cross nurse, Tae Shimizu (Shirley Yamaguchi). After two weeks under her care, Sterling recovers enough to confess his feelings for her and propose a date. In the next scene, the American GI visits the house of Tae's grandfather, Eitaro Shimizu (Philip Ahn), a lame, wealthy, aged patriarch, with whom Tae and her widowed mother live. Following the Japanese custom, Sterling officially asks Shimizu for permission to marry Tae. While the two men converse in the center of the room, Tae in a traditional kimono quietly prepares tea in a peripheral space. Shimizu takes the suitor to an adjoining dining room where two monkeys are brought in. He insists on sacrificing the animals with a samurai sword in honor of the American guest. When Sterling leaves the room in disgust, Tae follows and informs him that the grandfather was only pretending to kill the monkeys to frighten him away.

Back in the house, the old patriarch apologizes to the guest, explaining his intention: "I have seen a good bit of the world and know how different our ways are from yours. My granddaughter is a product of our ways and customs. I wished to present you a symbol of the vast difference that lies between you both." Shimizu reluctantly grants his consent to the marriage only after adding his cautionary reservation: "I do not wish to stand in the way of happiness...but I cannot say that I believe you're doing the right thing." His concerns are proven valid later when Tae suffers severely from prejudice and bigotry in her in-laws' rural Californian home. Nevertheless, the film underscores the superiority of egalitarian American family values by showing the Shimizu residence as a repressive environment where women are subjugated to and silenced by the patriarchal order. Throughout the entire scene described above, Tae's mother is relegated to the background as a subservient, silent spectator who dares not say a word in the matter of her own daughter's marriage. As soon as the grandfather exits and the couple is left alone, Sterling symbolically emancipates Tae from the suffocating Japanese tradition by telling her never to bow to him again and kissing her hand gently.

Ahn assumed an almost identical role, albeit of a different ethnicity, three years later in 20th Century-Fox's *Love Is a Many-Splendored Thing*. This time, he is the middle-aged uncle (on the father's side) of Jennifer Jones's Han Suyin, a Eurasian doctor who practices in Hong Kong. The widowed heroine's devotion to medicine and her desire to return to mainland China to help her people are gradually replaced by an overpowering, romantic love for Mark Elliot (William Holden), an unhappily married American correspondent. Distressed by the scandal and stigma haunting their relationship, Suyin temporarily leaves Hong Kong/Mark for Chungking where she is summoned for family business. Mark pursues her and formally proposes marriage at the house of Suyin's Third Uncle (Philip Ahn), the head of the family. The Chinese uncle cynically responds in this way to Suyin's plan to emigrate to America for a new life: "Ah, yes. We can begin in flight, pull out roots and wither and die." When the determined niece declares that she would rather face the future without hope than the present without Mark (thus choosing her Caucasian lover/America over familial ties/China), he concedes and advises her to leave nothing behind in her homeland. Ahn's Third Uncle admits his inability to oppose this marriage by saying, "We cannot stem the tide of change."

In *Love Is a Many-Splendored Thing*, Ahn plays a decisively emasculated patriarch whose feudal, aristocratic world is slowly crumbling in the midst of political and generational revolution signified by the impending arrival of the communists and the abandonment of the extended family by his two nieces, Suyin and Suchen (Suyin's younger sister who has opted to live with a foreigner in search of protection from the communist threat). Although she helps the uncle save face by soliciting his permission for her marriage, Suyin leaves him in the dark about Mark's marital status. In fact, Suyin asks for his permission only to honor traditional protocol because, as she tells Mark, "it would hurt [the Third Uncle] not to make this gesture." As with Shimizu in *Japanese War Bride*, Third Uncle's reservations turn out to be prophetic. Mark fails to get a divorce and is transferred to Korea as the war breaks out. Dismissed from the hospital by the bigoted management, Suyin is reduced to a Madame Butterfly who steadfastly waits for the return of her white lover. Although Mark initially underestimated "the little war" (which he like many Americans thought would not last more than two or three weeks), he is killed during an air raid on a Korean battlefield, tragically ending the "many-splendored" romance.

In both *Japanese War Bride* and *Love Is a Many-Splendored Thing*, the Korean War plays a pivotal role in either the initiation or termination of interracial romance. Ahn's Shimizu and Third Uncle are overwrought symbols of the Old World (the "backward," decaying, premodern East) from which the gallant, democratic American hero must save a nonwhite woman with the promise of romantic love and egalitarian marriage.

In addition to his usual cross-ethnic impersonations in the aforementioned films, Philip Ahn played Korean in several films and television programs set during the Korean War. The first Korean War film he appeared in was *Battle Zone* (1952)—an update of Raoul Walsh's silent World War I drama, *What Price Glory?* (1926)—that centers on the rivalry of two Marine combat photographers over an Italian Red Cross nurse. Ahn's bit part is the Korean assistant/interpreter who helps U.S. combat cameramen infiltrate a North Korean town to take photographs of enemy facilities. Although the charcoal "Korean-facing" of U.S. soldiers on their espionage mission and the disguise of one of the South Korean runners who turns out to be a North Korean spy remotely evoke the actor's own career of professional masquerades, his role in the film is so negligible that his character is not even given a name.

In *Battle Circus* (1953), a nonsatiric precursor to Robert Altman's *M*A*S*H* (1970) produced by MGM, Ahn plays another nameless Korean character, a wounded North Korean POW transported to the 8666th Mobile Army Surgical Hospital (MASH) unit. This time, his brief appearance is injected with dramatic significance, as it affects both the narrative and the relationship of the two protagonists—Lieutenant Ruth McGara (June Allyson) and Major Jed Webbe (Humphrey Bogart). Frightened and confused, Ahn's prisoner runs away from an x-ray machine and threatens the MASH staff in the operating room with a hand grenade. Ruth bravely approaches him, trying to calm him with reassuring words: "Don't be frightened. Nobody's gonna hurt you. You'll be all right." Suspense builds up as shots of Ruth apprehensively advancing are intercut with reverse shots of the scared prisoner gesturing to detonate the grenade. What makes this scene all the more interesting is that two long shots are inserted to show Webbe and another male doctor continuing their operation in the foreground while the North Korean man and the American woman—two panic-stricken "others"— are confronting each other in the background. Ahn's bestial otherness is accentuated through the exposure of his bare torso and his repeated barking of untranslated Korean dialogue, *"na chukiji mothae!"* ("You can't kill me!"). The intense specular confrontation between Philip Ahn and June Allyson in the scene evokes that classic moment when the woman looks at the monster, a trademark of horror film and the subject of Linda Williams's canonical 1984 essay "When the Woman Looks." According to Williams, "The horror film offers a particularly interesting example of this punishment in the woman's terrified look at the horrible body of the monster...a surprising (and at times subversive) affinity between monster and woman, the sense in which her look at the monster recognizes their similar status within patriarchal structures of seeing."[35] The scene in *Battle Circus* described above clearly visualizes this mutual recognition of racial and gendered otherness in a space dominated by militaristic and medically trained white masculinity. Bogart's Webbe, a hard-drinking cynic afraid of marital commitment, develops a serious relationship with Allyson's "goody-goody" Ruth only after she proves her bravery to him by taking the grenade away from Ahn's "monster."

Given the fact that the two aforementioned films were released within a year of one another, the diametrical bifurcation of Ahn's Korean roles (the friendly South Korean ally vs. the menacing North Korean enemy) becomes especially pertinent. The issue is complicated precisely because Ahn is a descendant of the pre-division Korea diaspora. As mentioned in earlier chapters, both of his parents came from a province north of the thirty-eighth parallel; his delivery in Korean was strongly imbued with northern accents. The political and educational activities of his father Tosan An Ch'ang-ho gained ardent support from pre-division northern residents and migrants at home and abroad. He founded two schools (Chŏmjin Elementary School, the first Korean co-ed school, in 1899 and Taesŏng School in 1908) in P'yŏngyang, a city held dear by the patriot. After the division and the establishment of the hostile regimes, Tosan was claimed as a hero by both South and North Koreas. Under the southern Park Chung Hee regime, his status was officially canonized with the 1963 award of the Korean National Medal of Honor and the 1973 dedication of Tosan Memorial Park in Seoul.

North Korea's Kim Il Sung did his own share of honoring the martyred patriot by appointing Tosan's sister, An Sin-ho, to the cabinet post of Vice Chairperson, Central Committee for Women. Her tombstone lies in the Memorial Park for Patriots in P'yŏngyang. Although Tosan and his family in California were vocal proponents of American democratic ideals as well as its political and economic systems, he became the subject of investigations by the U.S. federal government on the false charge of being a communist during his last visit to America in 1925—an investigation triggered by an informant letter to the Immigration Service allegedly sent by Syngman Rhee and his cohorts to diminish Tosan's influence in the Korean American community. When Tosan was arrested by the Japanese in Shanghai in 1932, the colonial police also used the pretext of his alleged "communist" affiliation to obtain the support of local authorities to transport the exiled anticolonial leader to Korea under Japanese rule.[36]

This knowledge of Ahn's family history complicates our reading of his communist roles in Cold War-era films and television programs. One of the most provocative examples is his casting as a Chinese brainwasher in the "Good Thief" episode (original airdate: November 25, 1955) of the ABC series *Crossroads*. Ahn's character, Comrade Sun, indoctrinates half-starved and shivering American POWs with communist propaganda:

> What are you doing here in Korea? Are the Korean people your enemy? And the Chinese? Did your country have possessions in Korea that it must protect? You have been betrayed. All of you. You are puppets in the hands of imperialistic warmongers who seek to keep China from finding a place in the sun.

In *The Shanghai Story* (1954), Ahn plays Major Ling Wu, a villainous Red officer who brutally tortures American and European civilian internees (and nearly rapes an Italian woman) in Shanghai immediately after Mao's takeover of China. The paired villainy of Philip Ahn and Richard Loo in the film unmistakably recycles the familiar tropes of World War II anti-Japanese propaganda by simply recasting the same actors in different uniforms. Thus, Ahn's star text is a sign consisting of palimpsestic traces *sous rature* (under erasure), to borrow Jacques Derrida's deconstructionist terminology, whose fluid meanings are constantly deferred/different.[37]

This point is particularly salient in his performance in the "Mister Pak Takes Over" episode (broadcast on June 13, 1955) of ABC's *TV Reader's Digest*. This Korean War story, based on real-life events, opens with a documentary image of Koreans being checked for security by the U.S. troops, against the voiceover of Captain Vincent Herbert (Kenneth Tobey) as he introduces the titular character, Pak Chang (Philip Ahn), a new Korean interpreter in his battalion headquarters: "For years, he worked for officers of the Japanese Imperial Army. G-2 suspects a good deal of anti-American propaganda may have rubbed off on him. He lived in North Korea for quite a spell and G-2 thinks he got loaded with communist propaganda." The voiceover goes on to sketch in details about Pak's defection to South Korea during the war and his eventual enlisting in the ROK labor battalion. When Pak arrives at the camp, he identifies himself as a "good interpreter" who is fluent in Korean, Japanese, and many Chinese dialects. Distrustful of his loyalty, the commander demotes Pak to menial labor (cleaning and serving coffee), a position in which he poses no intelligence risk. However, the middle-aged Korean proves to be a useful interpreter as well as a skillful interrogator when two Chinese POWs are brought into headquarters. Thanks to Pak's linguistic facility and intimidation tactics, the Americans are able to make the recalcitrant POWs talk. The interpreter clears his reputation once and for all and earns the esteem of his American supervisors when he contributes to a victory in major combat by intercepting the enemy's radio transmissions and snaring them with the faux military orders he delivers in northern Manchurian dialects. In the final scene, Captain Herbert corrects his initial mistrust and pays tribute to the Korean by promoting him to "Mister" Pak and serving him a cup of joe in person.

Pak's transformation from a Japanese collaborator and a North Korean resident to an ROK attaché and an impostor enemy transmitter is indicative of the many traces of different ethnicities and ideological persuasions in Ahn's screen persona. The mainstream media have, unwittingly turned the actor into a decentered, poststructuralist subject capable of resisting oppositional binaries (collaborator/patriot, communist/capitalist, and North/South) and destabilizing the corresponding relationship between signifier and signified. This argument is particularly applicable to the aforementioned television episode in which Ahn not only plays an interstitial subject (traversing ethnic, geographical, and political boundaries) but also incorporates Korean dialogue in place of Chinese dialects.

In the twilight of his life, Philip Ahn had one final opportunity to contribute to the Korean War representation by appearing as Korean characters in three episodes of the popular CBS television series *M*A*S*H* (1972–1983): "Hawkeye" (January 13, 1976), "Exorcism" (December 14, 1976), and "Change Day" (November 8, 1977). In the Emmy-nominated episode "Hawkeye," the titular MASH surgeon (Alan Alda) crashes his jeep in front of a Korean farmhouse as he swerves to avoid hitting some children in the road. Suffering a head concussion, Hawkeye makes futile yet inspired efforts to communicate with the Korean family (headed by Philip Ahn) that gives him temporary shelter. The only word the Korean characters understand is "Oŭjŏngbu," the name of the town where the 4077th unit is located. One of the little girls is sent to deliver Hawkeye's note to Oŭjŏngbu. While waiting for the arrival of help, Hawkeye tries to stay awake, spilling out stream of consciousness nonsequiturs in his nonstop babble, which leaps from one subject to another—from the history of his ancestors in Maine to medical school teachers to Boston's musical theater repertoire to the bone structure of the opposable thumb—all to the bewilderment of the Korean family. Framing his soliloquy as a conversation with his unresponsive, stoic audience, Hawkeye injects numerous references to American popular culture (including Doris

Day, Paul Muni, "Yankee Doodle Dandy," and *South Pacific*), performing songs and impersonating actors that are part of a cultural idiom not shared or recognized by rural Koreans.

Although this jarring juxtaposition of baffled, nonexpressive Koreans and the motor-mouthed American clown is playfully staged to incite the laughter of mainstream audiences, Korean-speaking viewers might find humor elsewhere. When his dinner is ready, Ahn's farmer invites Alda's Hawkeye in Korean: "Please shut your big mouth and eat with us." The use of the slang expression "ipdak h'ula" (literally much big mouth or shut up) triggers a fit of giggles from his wife (Shizuko Hoshi) in their secret teasing of Hawkeye's verbosity. When the American army doctor has difficulty handling spicy Korean dishes, Ahn's character once again gently ridicules this inadequacy: "American GIs are weak at spicy food." In the epilogue, a restored Hawkeye returns to the family's farmhouse to pay back their hospitality with presents from the camp: cooking oil, tobacco, comic books, and candy. Despite the American doctor's gratitude and compassion for the poor family, his prejudiced perception of Korea is displayed when the farmer's wife offers him some of the food she is cooking. Hawkeye takes a bite, compliments her cooking, and then suddenly becomes suspicious: "Where did you get meat? Wait a minute! Where is the dog?" He is relieved to hear the dog bark outside and resumes eating.

Throughout this episode, Alda's character is necessarily narcissistic, putting on a one-man variety show for his own sake (to keep himself awake and alive) and, by extension, for the mainstream television audience, rather than for the Korean family. The situation is both absurd and humorous because he jabbers and croons nonstop as if there were no cultural and linguistic barriers between himself and his hosts, who patiently carry out their daily chores amidst the noise and constant interruptions. When Hawkeye returns after recovering from his head injury, his narcissism is replaced by a kind of gentle xenophobia expressed in his final statement, which evokes the ethnic stereotype of dog-eating barbarians. This last superfluous joke thus undermines the positive image of an ordinary Korean family that has shown nothing but kindness and goodwill to a strange American guest.

Another *M*A*S*H* episode, "Exorcism," introduces the equally stereotyped Korean custom of shamanism. Philip Ahn appears as a superstitious old man who gets hit by an American army vehicle when he steps in front of it in an attempt to scare away evil spirits. Major Frank Burns (Larry Linville), a jingoistic, xenophobic, inept doctor, objects to admitting the Korean patient into the O.R., calling him a "whiplash hustler" (the name given to locals who fake injuries in the hopes of receiving compensation from the U.S. military). After the old man's granddaughter, Kyŏng-ja (Virginia Ann Lee), testifies to her grandfather's innocent intentions, Hawkeye insists on operating on him. However, the patient refuses to undergo the operation until a *mudang* (shaman priestess) is brought in to exorcise spirits from the premises. Bending army regulations, Hawkeye calls in an exorcist to humor his patient. After the performance of an exotic "pagan ritual," not only does the superstitious patient agree to surgery but also previously inoperative equipment around the camp (the P.A. system, a medical gauge, an overhead light, and a lighter) mysteriously begin to work again. As in the aforementioned episode, which juxtaposes Ahn's simple rural existence with that of Alda's sophisticated urban consciousness, the "Exorcism" episode interweaves Korean backwardness and superstition with American modernity and medical proficiency. Although the latter episode in part validates indigenous mysticism and calls for racial/cultural tolerance (as denoted by Colonel Potter [Harry Morgan]'s order to reinstate the Korean spirit post in front of the MASH unit), it perpetuates the fictitious image of absurdly superstitious Koreans who are injured and then saved by sympathetic Americans.

As an iconoclastic antiwar satire and countercultural comedy, *M*A*S*H* (both the film and the television series) simply uses the Korean War as a convenient backdrop to ridicule the military establishment and religious orthodoxy, as well as to express the American public's disillusionment with the government in the wake of the Vietnam War. In terms of ethnic representations, little progress has been made from the 1950s Hollywood Korean War films to the 1970s TV show. Although the perennial popularity of this television classic attests to a growing willingness on the part of American audiences to embrace otherness within generic limitations, *M*A*S*H* habitually misrepresents the Korean language and culture in a mishmash of multi-ethnic extras and props, not to mention the stereotyping of Korean people in archetypal roles (farmers, peddlers, hustlers, thieves, orphans, houseboys, prostitutes, and "mooses" or female slaves). The only two significant recurrent Korean characters in the entire series are both played by non-Korean actors (Patrick Adiarte as Ho Jon in the first season and Rosalind Chao as Soon Lee in the eleventh season).

In "Hawkeye" and other episodes, untranslated Korean dialogue (often delivered poorly by non-Korean actors) serves as a comic sonic backdrop. This intermittent transmission of linguistic difference, however, offers distinct reading positions for bilingual, bicultural spectators who harvest meanings from what is intended as incongruous jargon. Although these floating signifiers (cut free from predetermined and delimiting signifieds) ostensibly construct a monolithic sense of otherness and inscrutability for mainstream audiences, Korean speakers' ears may be keen to the different enunciative patterns of Korean and non-Korean actors. The episodes featuring indigenous characters represented by diasporic Korean actors such as Philip Ahn or Soon-Tek Oh[38] thus provided extratextual pleasure for audiences armed with ethnic reading competency. One Korean American commentator, Philip W. Chung, for example, recollects the following:

> One of the worst experiences for [our family] was watching M*A*S*H. These supposedly Korean characters would appear and the non-Korean actors portraying them would mangle the Korean language beyond comprehension. This pissed off my parents and me. But whenever Soon Tek was on M*A*S*H speaking his flawless, dignified Korean—it was exhilarating to see. We felt proud to be Korean.[39]

The termination of the indefatigable television series on February 28, 1983 (when the episode "Goodbye, Farewell and Amen" was aired) signaled the virtual demise of the Korean War genre in American popular culture. True, television shows of the 1990s continued to feature Korean War veteran characters, such as Maurice J. Minnifield (Barry Corbin) in *Northern Exposure* (1990–1995), Martin Crane (John Mahoney) in *Frasier* (1993–2004), and Harold Weir (Joe Flaherty) in *Freaks and Geeks* (1999–2000). Such films as *For the Boys* (1991), a fictional biopic of USO entertainer Dixie Leonard (Bette Midler), and *Truman* (1995), a historical biopic of Harry S. Truman, also contain brief Korean War segments. However, no Hollywood film or television series exclusively focusing on the Korean War has been produced since the early 1980s, when the last major Korean War feature *Inchon* (1981) was released and the last episode of M*A*S*H was aired.

Despite this historical and cultural amnesia, the repressed eventually returned in the twentieth 007 installment, *Die Another Day* (2003), which can be seen as a new, updated Korean War film situated in the context of the Bush administration's war on terrorism. The film's megalomaniacal North Korean enemy Colonel Moon (Will Yun Lee/Toby Stephens) and his secret solarized laser weapon, "Icarus," not so subtly allegorize real-life dictator Kim Jong Il and his nuclear program. Red Scare iconography and tropes of 1950s and 1960s Korean War POW films are vividly recast during the credit sequence in which James Bond (Pierce Brosnan) is shown being mercilessly tortured by a North Korean brainwashing team. The outbreak of a second Korean War is halted in the nick of time through the imaginary "preemptive strike" of the British-American coalition represented by Bond and Jinx (Halle Berry).

The most recent example of this uncanny reincarnation of the Korean War genre is Jonathan Demme's 2004 remake of John Frankenheimer's classic, *The Manchurian Candidate*. Adapted into a 1991 Desert Storm setting, Demme's film nevertheless evinces the collective nightmare of brainwashing, a particularly Korean War, not Gulf War, phenomenon.

"Ours Is the Thanks That You Are With Us": East Greets West in Douglas Sirk's Battle Hymn

Of the handful of Korean War films featuring Philip Ahn, Douglas Sirk's *Battle Hymn* deserves special attention. Despite the lofty status of its director in American film history and genre study, *Battle Hymn* has received remarkably little critical attention—a fact that reinforces the marginalized status of Korean War films in general. Sirk's biographer Jon Halliday dismisses the film during his interview with the auteur, expressing his complete bewilderment over the filmmaker's involvement in it.[40] In her book-length study of Sirk's melodramas, Barbara Klinger mentions the title once in a list of Sirk's films that feature Rock Hudson.[41] As one of the eight Sirk/Hudson Universal collaborations (along with *Has Anyone Seen My Gal?* [1952], *Taza, Son of Cochise* [1954], *Magnificent Obsession* [1954], *Captain Lightfoot* [1955], *All That Heaven Allows* [1955], *Written on the Wind* [1957], and *Tarnished Angels* [1958]), *Battle Hymn* is a peculiar yet compelling blend of war film, religious drama, biopic, and melodrama. It is based on the same-title 1956 memoir by Colonel Dean E. Hess of the U. S. Air Force, an ordained minister-turned-combat pilot who flew hundreds of missions during World War II and the Korean War. As the hero's two nicknames—"Killer Hess" and the "flying parson"—suggest, Hess's contradictory vocational allegiances offer rich thematic material for filmmakers itching to unfold a dramatic story against a wartime backdrop.

However, *Battle Hymn* is not simply a film that mines the relationship between war and religion. It is also a story about Korea and Korean children. As Sirk labels it in his interview with Halliday, *Battle Hymn* is a "Korean picture,"[42] arguably the only one of its kind produced by a major Hollywood studio. After achieving moderate box-office success upon its original release,[43] the film was quickly forgotten by the American public and critics alike, falling outside the canon of both auteur and genre studies.[44] *Battle Hymn*'s unprecedented gravitation toward Korean themes, however, was better appreciated in South Korea where it remains the best-known Hollywood Korean War film, with the possible exception of the 1955 melodrama, *Love Is a Many-Splendored Thing*.[45]

As a fledgling cinephile growing up in South Korea during Chun Doo Hwan (Chŏn Tu-hwan)'s authoritarian regime (1980–1987), I watched *Battle Hymn* every June 25 (or *yuk-i-o*, the Korean War Commemoration Day). In support of Chun's notorious "Three S Policy" (a cultural edict encouraging sex, sports, and screen so as to divert the public's attention from political oppression), two rival South Korean network channels, KBS and MBC, filled their weekend and holiday schedules with escapist Hollywood fantasies. As a unique phenomenon of postcolonial cultural displacement and historical ventriloquism, television programmers of the 1990s opted to air *Battle Hymn*, rather than domestic films about the war (such as *The Marines Who Never Return* [*Toraoji annŭn haebyŏng*; 1963], *Red Muffler* [*Ppalgan mahura*; 1964], *South and North* [*Nam gwa puk*; 1965], and *Kilsottŭm* [1985]),[46] on the day commemorating the most significant event of modern Korean history. My father, who attended Seoul National University in the immediate aftermath of the war, is a member of the generation who saw the film in theaters upon its original 1957 release in South Korea. According to him, college students of the late 1950s divided Hollywood films into two categories—"requirements" and "electives"—naturally assigning *Battle Hymn* to the former. It would not be an exaggeration to say that *Battle Hymn* is as much an integral part of the memories of June 25 for South Korean audiences (of my parents' generation as well as my own) as *It's a Wonderful Life* (1946) is to their American counterparts celebrating Christmas.

The fewer than 100 American films comprising the Korean War filmography rarely foreground any ethnographic details of Korea's native populace. As Paul M. Edwards points out, in most cases such films as *Fixed Bayonets*, *Men in War*, and *War Hunt* merely use the war as an excuse to "cast men in conflict with themselves, with each other, or with the elements."[47] Whether that conflict is between pleasure-seeking army doctors and marriage-minded nurses (as in *Battle Circus*), loner enlisted men and disciplined squad leaders (*The Steel Helmet* and *Pork Chop Hill*), or black and white soldiers (*All the Young Men*), their stories focus on the exploits of the U. S. Army, Air Force, Marines, and (less frequently) Navy—men and women thrown into obscure, unidentifiable foreign settings. In most cases, Koreans are either completely absent or marginalized as nameless, faceless communist soldiers or defenseless South Korean refugees and homeless kids. These cardboard Korean cut-outs are reduced to "all-look-alike" allies or enemies whose presence is of little dramatic importance—a point made aphoristic in Samuel Fuller's *The Steel Helmet*, when the cynical Sergeant Zack spouts, "He's a South Korean when he's running with you, and he's a North Korean when he's running after you!"

Battle Hymn is an exception to the rule, however, for its subject—Dean Hess—developed unusually close ties with Koreans (including President Syngman Rhee as well as Korean generals and pilots) and became deeply involved in providing shelter and care for numerous children who had lost hope of returning home and finding their families. Hess's enhaloed status as a Korean War hero can be attributed not only to brilliant combat stats in his 250 Korean missions (for which he earned the Silver Star, the Legion of Merit, and the Korean Order of Military Merit) but also to his philanthropic dedication to orphans. That dedication culminated in December 1950 with a large-scale airlift (nicknamed Operation Kiddy Car) that transported 1,000 children from a crumbling Seoul to safety some sixty miles off the southern coast of the peninsula on Cheju Island, where he helped establish the Orphan's Home of Korea (Han'gukboyukwŏn). Hess shuttled between his duties as a commander of the training program for the embryonic ROK Air Force and as a provider and fundraiser for the orphanage. Even after he left Korea in May 1951, Hess continued to help the children and donated $60,000 from the proceeds of his published memoir and its filmed adaptation for the construction of new orphanage facilities in Seoul. In the early 1960s, Hess adopted a six-year-old girl from the Orphan's Home of Korea. He is still remembered by many Koreans as the "Father of War Orphans."

Hess's extraordinary devotion to Korean orphans and pilots, as well as his outspoken love for their land, were clearly responsible for the otherwise anomalous ethnic representation in his biopic. Unlike many enlisted men (cinematic or otherwise) who were either confused about what they were fighting for in Korea or were only motivated by a sense of duty, Hess confessed in his memoir that he had "undergone a complete metamorphosis—become part Korean" because of his "strong bond of brotherhood with [his] Korean flyers" and his compassion and paternal feelings for Korean children.[48] *Battle Hymn* differentiated itself from other Korean War films featuring Asian waifs, such as *The Steel Helmet, Mission over Korea* (1953) and *The Young and the Brave* (1963), by allowing twenty-five orphans from the Cheju orphanage to represent themselves. As the studio publicity puts it,

> [They] were not recruited from Central Casting in Hollywood. They were sent directly from Korea as "Ambassadors of Good Will" by President Syngman Rhee. They had no chance to be spoiled; they were just themselves.[49]

The film's authenticity was strengthened once the self-representing children injected indigenous dialogue, dance, and songs into the otherwise

FIGURE 5.1 *Rock Hudson plays Colonel Dean E. Hess, the "Father of Korean War orphans" in Douglas Sirk's biopic* Battle Hymn *(Universal, 1957).* Courtesy of the Academy of Motion Picture Arts and Sciences.

artificial Korean mise-en-scène fabricated in studio sets or staged in the Arizona desert. Producers at Universal made additional efforts to maximize the biopic's verisimilitude by employing Hess as technical advisor and acquiring the support of the DoD, as well as the U. S. Air Force and Army. This full military cooperation resulted in spectacular air combat and bombing sequences whose realism was further enhanced by the fact that Hess himself operated his plane (an F-51 bearing the number 18),[50] doubling for his double Rock Hudson in the flying scenes.

FACTS, FICTIVES, FABULATIONS: *BATTLE HYMN* AS HISTORICAL BIOPIC

In his important book-length study of classical Hollywood biopics, George F. Custen argues that "an odd mixture of careful research, of compromised whimsy, and of outright fabrication characterized the sets, the costumes, the characters, manners and mores, and narratives of most biopics."[51] *Battle Hymn* is no exception. Despite its veneer of verisimilitude, the film proves to be yet another instance in which history undergoes reconstructive surgery to serve the dramatic purposes of a commercial Hollywood product.

In the film's introductory sequence General Earle E. Partridge of the U.S. Air Force appears against a sound stage setting where an F-51 Mustang is parked in an obviously ersatz "natural" landscape. With an air of amateurish awkwardness, he introduces the film, directly addressing the camera:

> During the war in Korea, I was in command of the Fifth Air Force, operating under the United Nations' command. This plane was just one of the many involved in our operations. Its pilot I shall never forget. I am pleased to have been asked to introduce this motion picture, which is based on the actual experiences of this pilot, Colonel Dean Hess of the United States Air Force. The remarkable story of Colonel Hess, his poignant and often secret struggle with a problem peculiarly his own, his courage, resourcefulness, and sacrifice have long been a source of inspiration to me and to fighting men who have known him. But the story of Colonel Hess is more than a dramatic demonstration of one man's capacity for good; it is an affirmation of the essential goodness of the human spirit. For this reason I am happy it is told. It begins in the summer of 1950, five years after the end of World War II, and one month after the invasion of South Korea. It is a quiet sunny Sunday morning in the pleasant little town of West Hampton, Ohio....

Custen singles out the "introductory assertion of the truth" by title cards or voiceover narration as a distinctive generic convention of the biopic. *Battle Hymn* pushes this convention forward by prefacing the narrative with a staged documentary sequence in which the biographee's wartime commander, General Partridge, is cast as the purveyor of truth, someone of high credentials who can verify the authenticity of the story.

However, when closely examined, this opening sequence reveals the film's dubious relationship to the truth and to history. According to the Air Force General's ostensibly reliable testimony, the story begins in West Hampton, Ohio, one month after the June 25, 1950 outbreak of the Korean War. A dissolve from the studio set to an outdoor shot of a pastoral mansion against General Patridge's last lines smoothly stitches the talking-head introduction to the following scene of Dean Hess (Rock Hudson) delivering a sermon to his congregation—a service with which he later feels dissatisfied. After confiding his doubts and skepticism to his wife Mary (Martha Hyer), Hess reminisces about a nightmarish scene from World War II in which he accidentally bombed a German orphanage during a combat mission, killing thirty-seven children. After the flashback ends, Hess writes a letter to the Air Force, volunteering for service in the Korean War not as a chaplain, but as a combatant.

The two crucial bits of information supplied to us by the presumably trust-worthy narrator General Partridge—July 1950 and West Hampton, Ohio—are both narrative inventions. World War II veteran Hess was called back to duty in the Air Force as early as July 1948 and was transferred to Japan in April 1950, two months before the North Korean invasion across the thirty-eighth parallel. As the commanding officer of the Fifth Air Force under which Hess served in Korea, General Partridge is in a position to know better than anyone that Hess was *not* in Ohio during the "summer of 1950...one month after the invasion of South Korea." He is "lying" about this temporal setting for dra-matic purposes.

A second deception involves the ideal, small-town location called West Hampton, Ohio. Although it is possible that town names have changed, no such place is to be found on Ohio state maps. Hess was indeed an Ohio native, but his hometown was Marietta. Hess began preaching at the age of sixteen in churches in Marietta and in neighboring rural villages such as Paw Paw. After graduating from Marietta College with a degree in theology and a certificate from the civilian pilot program in June 1941, Hess was ordained in the Christ Church and was invited to several churches in Cleveland as a cir-cuit preacher while working as a factory foreman on weekdays to pay back his education debts. On December 7, 1941, when he was informed of the Japanese attack on Pearl Harbor, Hess made a crucial decision, one that altered the course of his life. After finishing his usual Sunday sermon, he announced to a troubled congregation that it would be his last since he would be joining the fight to defend his country. Although he occasionally assumed the role of surrogate chaplain to his fear-addled men and said prayers for fallen pilots during World War II and the Korean War, he never again returned to the pulpit after the Pearl Harbor attack. In fact, Hess was com-pleting his doctoral degree in history and psychology at Ohio State University in Columbus when he was ordered back into Air Force uniform in 1948. The vision of Hess ministering to his own church in a fictional small town, West Hampton, embodies a dream that was never realized, a course that was not taken due to the intervention of calamitous world events.

The film condenses and overlaps World War II and the Korean War by altering the timeline of Hess's decision to substitute his ministerial career with that of a combat flyer from December 1941 to July 1950. As Paul M. Edwards observes, one of the foremost characteristics of Korean War films is their focus on a "two-war man...a pilot or older officer...who served in World War II [and] often carried guilt about his experiences there [which] he works out...on the battlefields of Korea."[52] The transference of guilt between the two wars and the ultimate moral victory of the American hero constitute *Battle Hymn*'s thematic backbone. Director Douglas Sirk conceived the film as a "rondo" which begins with the "destruction of a children's orphanage and killing [of] children" in one war and ends with "saving children's lives and building an orphanage" in another war.[53] To maintain this structure, Sirk inserted a flashback near the film's beginning showing Hess (who is addressed by his co-pilot as "Killer") confronting the horrific consequence of an accident during a bombing mission over Kaisersburg, which cost the lives of thirty-seven German orphans. The Nazis' radio propaganda, reporting the death of the children, ominously indicts the American pilot. "His hands will be stained forever with innocent blood of those harmless infants."

Although this incident is based on Hess's actual experience during World War II, its emotional and psychological effect on his life is perhaps exaggerated in the film to squeeze out a typically Sirkian moment of melodramatic affect. In his book, Hess explains his own feelings about the bombing incident:

> [A] writer in the Air Force Times conjectured that guilt stemming from this incident may have been partially responsible for the aid I rendered Korean orphans in the airlift that became known as Operation Kiddy Car. I do not know. Certainly we all are sympathetic to the needs of children, and when I was told that that building in Kaiserslautern was a day school and orphanage, that particular mission over Germany left a mark in my mind like a brand. But at the time of the bombing it seemed like just another mission, accomplished with a degree of success because at least one bomb had found its intended target in the railroad yard.[54]

Unlike his cinematic counterpart, the flesh-and-blood Hess did not visit the orphanage site destroyed by his raid to verify the validity of the propaganda broadcast, nor did he volunteer for Korea out of guilty feelings about this incident. Like West Hampton, Kaisersburg is an equally fictional hamlet based on the real German town that Hess bombed—Kaiserslautern. Hamburg-born émigré director Sirk even conferred an imaginary Germanic identity on Hess by identifying Kaisersburg as the hometown of the hero's dead grandmother, embellishing the significance of the German trauma.

Despite Sirk's personal investment in the German sequence, Hess—as his memoir attests—was comparatively more disturbed by another accident that occurred in Korea. While providing close air support for U.S. Army troops in the early months of the war, he unintentionally strafed South Korean refugees (due to misinformation received from a liaison pilot), as he describes:

> I had fired one short burst of my guns before I caught a quick close-up glimpse of my target: a column of refugees, now scrambling into the ditch. My finger leaped from the trigger as though shocked, and I turned quickly and looked again as I pulled away. A girl of ten or twelve lay on the road, obviously dead and mangled.[55]

Hess revisits this horrific sight in the latter part of his book, stating that the girl he "machine gunned from the air will remain in [his] mind forever."[56] This incident helped forge a cross-racial, brotherly bond between Hess and one of his co-pilots, Ernest Craigwell, a black lieutenant who similarly dispatched a group of Korean civilians (including women and children), mistaking them as enemy troops.[57] Hess was able to console the lieutenant who was paralyzed by shock and agony by confiding his own guilty experience.[58]

In the cinematic re-creation, Craigwell becomes Lieutenant Maples, played by James Edwards, an African American actor who occupies an iconographic place in Korean War films.[59] Craigwell's screen surrogate Maples is forced to shoulder the sole burden of slaughtering refugees as Hess's Korean trauma is omitted in the process of cinematic adaptation. While the biopic emphasizes the reciprocal nature of the combat traumas of two different wars and different races (Hess in World War II and Maples in the Korean War), it excises the white male protagonist's child-killing in the latter war. Through this omission, Hess's psychological turmoil is resolved, and his moral redemption in Korea is rendered untainted—a personal victory that cancels the memory of the inglorious armistice agreement of July 1953, which ended the Korean War in a stalemate. As in other films, such as Paramount's *Submarine Command* (1951), in which a guilt-ridden World War II naval officer played by William Holden—after deserting his wounded captain on the deck during a crash dive—redeems himself in Korea, *Battle Hymn* utilizes the Korean War as a curative second chance in which the traumatized hero can write over his mistake and regain self-esteem.

When Douglas Sirk was asked about his view of the Korean War, he answered as follows:

> The Korean War was there. There was no reason as an afterthought to preach that the Korean War was bad, or good. It was almost history. The war as a fact was unalterable. There is nothing about taking sides,

and *Battle Hymn* certainly doesn't concern itself with the fact of war but with a character in war.[60]

Battle Hymn has continuously been ignored as a minor work of little distinction by neo-Marxist critics who favor Sirk's family melodramas, such as *All That Heaven Allows*, *Written on the Wind*, and *Imitation of Life* (1959)—films that shrewdly criticize the Eisenhower era's conformist culture and materialistic values behind the façade of overly sentimental and hyperbolic soap opera narratives. Reflecting this critical position, one online reviewer of *Battle Hymn* directly confronts Sirk's claim to political neutrality by labeling it as "a propaganda film that shows the army as decent saviors of the world, protectors of the innocent; it displays the urgent need for heavy armaments and the engagement in warfare with totalitarian threats to that innocence."[61] Incidentally, another reviewer on the same Web page provides a completely different evaluation, confessing how *Battle Hymn* made so significant an impact on him as to lead him back to religious conviction.[62] The latter position echoes the eulogizing tenor expressed in a letter of recommendation by the Motion Picture Association of America's Director of Community Relations, Arthur H. DeBra, in February 1957, who described Sirk's work as a "fine motion picture [that can] give deep emotional satisfaction...a life-long experience in one single evening."[63]

These divergent audience responses provoke the following question: Is *Battle Hymn* an example of political propaganda justifying American militarism and its failed "police action" (which cost the lives of 37,000 U.S. soldiers and $54 billion), or is it an innocent spiritual tale paying tribute to the faith and goodness of benevolent souls? These two countervailing reading positions reflect America's lack of consensus concerning the Korean War itself. For instance, General Omar N. Bradley, Chairman of the Joint Chiefs of Staff, memorably described the situation in Korea as "the wrong war, in the wrong place, at the wrong time, with the wrong enemy."[64] General James A. Van Fleet, on the other hand, thought that "Korea has been a blessing. There had to be a Korea either here or some place in the world."[65] Historian Bruce Cumings, the most cited and contested scholar of the Korean War, would likely not agree with Sirk's bald assertion that "the Korean War was there" and "the war as a fact was unalterable." In *The Origins of the Korean War*, Cumings argues,

> For the Truman liberal, Korea was a success, "the limited war." For the MacArthur conservative, Korea was a failure: the first defeat in American history.... The American split verdict on the Korean War is

an agreement to disagree, a stitched-together mending of a torn national psyche. Above all it is a compact to forget—a selective forgetting that preserves psychic order. You remember one verdict, and forget or condemn the other.[66]

The above-quoted passage evokes modernist historiographers' contention that there is no such a thing as an "objective history" or History with a capital H per se. According to Hayden White, "[H]istory is no less a form of fiction than the novel is a form of historical representation."[67] History writing is inherently fictional because it adopts the same linguistic conventions and narrative *tropes*—metaphor, metonym, synecdoche, and irony—that are used in novels and dramas.[68] As Robert C. Allen and Douglas Gomery perceptively point out, "*Facts of the past* do exist independently of the mind of the historian, but *historical facts* are only those data selected from the past that a historian finds relevant to his or her argument."[69]

Likewise, the "true" Korean War story in *Battle Hymn* is a composite of mediated, selective, and even altered historical facts concocted and assembled from biased perspectives so as to serve the economic needs of studio heads and producers; the authority of cultural watchdogs, such as the PCA and civil interest groups; the publicity machinery of military sponsors, such as the DoD, the U.S. Army, and Air Force; the ego-stroking of technical adviser Dean Hess; and the artistic ambitions of Douglas Sirk and the film's screenwriters.[70] *Battle Hymn*'s "selective forgetting" of Hess's Korean War trauma (the killing of a ten-year-old girl and other refugees) is a narrative imperative that accommodates the collective needs of the abovementioned groups and guarantees a satisfactory dénouement in accordance with the dominant ideology.

The cinematically embroiled acts of forgetting and fabulation reflect the historical amnesia of the U.S. government and military as proven in the Associated Press (AP)'s Pulitzer Award-winning 1999 exposure of the Nogun-ri massacre. According to the collaborative testimonies of Korean survivors and veterans of the 7th Cavalry Regiment, over the course of three days (July 26–28, 1950), U.S. soldiers and pilots killed hundreds of South Korean civilians huddled underneath the railroad bridge near Nogun-ri, 100 miles southeast of Seoul.[71] The mass killings occurred due to the retreating American troops' panic about North Korean guerrillas who often disguised themselves as civilians and infiltrated refugee groups—a recurring image in Korean War films from *One Minute to Zero* (1952) to *Battle Hymn*.[72] The surviving victims' demand for a full investigation and compensation went unanswered for years by both the South Korean and U.S. governments.[73] The AP revelations pressured the two governments to embark on a joint investigation of the case, which resulted in President Bill Clinton's January 2001 statement expressing deep regret for "an unidentified number of innocent Korean refugees"[74] having been killed in Nogun-ri and conveying the U.S. commitment to build a memorial for all innocent Korean civilians sacrificed during the war, as well as to provide a $750,000 commemorative scholarship fund as "a living tribute to their memory."[75] Korean victims and politicians protested the U.S. government's hasty closing of the incident without offering a formal apology and compensation to the Nogun-ri survivors, as well as its denial of the existence of any military orders to fire on refugee columns, despite the testimony of ex-GIs and declassified records proving otherwise.[76]

President Clinton's will to memorialize *all* South Korean deaths in his "statement of regret" is reminiscent of Colonel Hess's wish to erect a monument dedicated to 200 orphans who died within the first three months after they were brought to the Cheju orphanage because of a lack of food and medicine. Hess writes, "Someday perhaps we'll build a monument there; and if I have my way, the stone will be simply inscribed: 1950 Orphan's Home of Korea. Dedicated to the Memory of Those Whom We Could Not Save."[77] At the end of the film, a captioned dedication ("dedicated to those we could not save") appears above Hess's signature, granting his wish cinematically and reemphasizing the biopic's authenticity. Both Clinton's and Hess's commemorations of innocent Korean victims suggest a particular picture of Americans during the Korean War: the self-affirming saviors and benefactors for South Korea who mourn those who could not be saved. Ironically, a translation of Hess's memoir was published in South Korea in 2000 in the midst of the Nogun-ri controversy; Korean media reports focused on selected passages from the book in which Hess testifies to his killing of South Korean civilians as evidence against the U.S. military.[78] Koreans insist on remembering what Americans either intentionally or unwittingly forget and what Hollywood films never depict. In fact, in several South Korean films set during the war, American GIs are portrayed negatively as rapists, womanizers, or even killers, problematizing the myth of the benevolent American protector as promoted in such Hollywood Korean War films as *Battle Hymn*.[79]

Making Women Oriental: Why Mrs. Hwang Became Miss Yang

Battle Hymn's oscillation between fact and fiction, between remembering and forgetting, becomes more pronounced in its representation of Korean characters. The most significant Korean role in the film is En Soon Yang (Yang ŭn-sun, played by Anna Kashfi), a beautiful young Korean schoolteacher who helps Hess relocate and take care of hundreds of orphans who have flocked around his camp seeking food and shelter. Hess first encounters Miss Yang in the mayor's office, where he and his sidekick Sergeant Hermann (Dan Duryea) request heavy equipment needed for the airfield construction. Although they manage to find the right office thanks to Hess's witty decision to inquire about the "Boss Man" to a Korean who does not know the English word "mayor," Hess and Hermann are unable to make their needs understood to a group of civilians waiting for the absent mayor. From the baffled group Miss Yang emerges and approaches them, offering help in impossible English. Surprised and relieved, Hess tells her what he is looking for. Miss Yang's translation of Korean and command of English enable him to locate the needed equipment. Answering Hess's thank-you, Miss Yang politely bows and says, "Ours is the thanks that you are with us." Hess again encounters the Korean woman when he gives a ride to an old man, oddly named Lu Wan (Philip Ahn), and a couple of kids to a Buddhist temple. When Hess and his company arrive at the temple, Miss Yang and several foundlings under her supervision are about to leave the place for a refuge in the south. Hess persuades the reluctant Miss Yang and Lu Wan to stay and help him take care of hundreds of homeless children that he has rounded up in the camp. Aided by Sergeant Hermann and Lieutenant Maples, Hess remodels the damaged temple as a provisional nursery and supplies the orphans with food and medicine rerouted from military sources.

Miss Yang's secret feelings for the white colonel are revealed in her sad reactions when, one day, Hess casually tells her that his wife is expecting a baby at home. While Miss Yang is temporarily excused from the embarrassing moment, Lu Wan informs Hess that she has lost everything because of the war—her home, friends, and romance. When the Korean woman is left alone with the colonel again, she hands a pine twig to him, saying that the tree symbolizes eternity for Koreans. Against a romantic yet doleful soundtrack, she speaks of a legend about the twin pine trees of her hometown, Cheju Island. Miss Yang seems to refer to her own relationship with Hess when she tells him that the trees are said to have been brought together out of the graves of two lovers who could not have each other in this life.[80] As foreshadowed, the woman later dies in Hess's arms after she risks her own safety to protect an orphan girl during an air raid. A monument dedicated to her memory by Hess stands at the Cheju orphanage, to which the proud hero returns with his wife and Sergeant Hermann in the film's last scene. Against the children's choir singing the "Battle Hymn of the Republic," the camera tilts up to show the twin pine trees shooting up toward the sky, as if commemorating the undying spirit of the sacrificial Korean woman.

As the above synopsis illustrates, Miss Yang plays a pivotal role in coloring Hess's militaristic and humanitarian adventures in Korea with a tint of romance and melodrama, blending Sirk's trademark genre with war iconography. The actress who played Miss Yang, Anna Kashfi, received second billing to Rock Hudson—the most substantial Korean female role that Hollywood ever churned out. As examplifed by such Oriental romance films as *Japanese War Bride*, *Sayonara*, *Love Is a Many-Splendored Thing*, and *The World of Suzie Wong* (1960), Hollywood's favorite *femmes orientales* have always been either Japanese or Chinese. In comparison to occupied Japan and colonial Hong Kong, bastions of touristic and sexual pleasure, Hollywood's Korea is represented as a jagged and masculinized mythic space populated by macho-posturing American GIs, beastly communist enemies, and destitute South Korean orphans and refugees. This despecularized space—a blighted Oriental frontier wide open for American adventures and explorations—is surely no place for Geishas or China Dolls.[81] The only women that American servicemen encounter in Hollywood's Korea are peasant mothers, prepubescent girls, or communist saboteurs, excluding the possibilities of Korean women as potential love objects.[82] *Battle Hymn*, however, provides a rare exception in which a Korean woman is cast as a perfect vision of Oriental beauty, a feast for the Western male gaze.

Miss Yang's character can easily be described as an offshoot of Madame Butterfly, an Oriental feminine archetype that has been recycled countless times from the silent motion picture *The Toll of the Sea* (1922) to the long-running Broadway musical hit *Miss Saigon*. Following the tradition of white male adventurers in the East, Hess forms a surrogate family with a local woman and nonwhite children. Hess and Miss Yang's metaphorical coupling is accentuated when their favorite orphan, Chu, calls them, respectively, *abŏji* (father) and *ŭmma* (mom). Although Miss Yang only translates the word "father" to Hess, it is obvious that she enacts the maternal role to the male protagonist's (surrogate) children. Similar to the original Butterfly Cho Cho-san, the Oriental woman despairingly realizes that the man she loves has a Caucasian wife. Her inevitable fate is to sacrifice her life. The Korean woman's death not only frees Hess from the temptation of adulterous miscegenation but also allows his wife Mary to take over her role of mother in the last scene when the white couple is affectionately welcomed by Chu and other orphans. The film inscribes Miss Yang as a doubly exotic subject by defining her as a product of an interethnic marriage between a Korean man and an Indian woman—a half-breed child who was born in India but grew up on Cheju Island, Korea's miniature version of Hawaii with a climate and culture considerably different from that of the mainland. Her half-Indian ethnicity seems to have been devised to justify the cross-ethnic casting of Anna Kashfi, who played a Hindu girl in Paramount's *The Mountain* (1956) and was promoted by Universal Studios as a Calcutta-born actress who had made two films in India.[83] The actress regretfully bears no resemblance to a Korean, and her occasional utterances in the Korean tongue are no less awkward than those by Rock Hudson.

Readers of Hess's memoir might notice that the name En Soon Yang bears an unmistakable resemblance to the flesh-and-blood woman On Soon Hwang (Hwang On sun), a well respected social worker (now known as the "Korean Mother Theresa") who became directress of the Cheju orphanage and chaperoned the twenty-five Korean orphans to Hollywood during the film's production. Hess describes her in this way:

> Clearly an able and sympathetic person was needed to take charge. Madame Rhee [Syngman Rhee's wife], whose intense interest in the orphanage grew daily, suggested an old friend of hers, Mrs. On Soon Hwang, who had been studying social-welfare procedures in England. She proved to be a wonderful choice. From a wealthy, educated family, she had returned to Korea to find her home leveled and her son gone—apparently killed by the Reds. She gave our orphans the mothering and the warm love which they had been so sadly lacking. She was a woman in her early fifties, whose lovely face reflected her strong, patient character and great warmth.[84]

Unlike her considerably younger cinematic counterpart who dies before Hess completes the Operation Kiddy Car mission, On Soon Hwang—who is twenty years Hess's senior—was brought into the project after the children were airlifted and relocated in an abandoned school building in Cheju, which was turned into the Orphan's Home of Korea. Mrs. Hwang appears briefly in the film's last scene as one of the orphanage supervisors or teachers silently bowing to Hess and his wife. The indomitable woman continued her work for almost fifty years, mothering more than 7,000 orphans. In real life, Hess not only kept corresponding with Mrs. Hwang and made donations to the orphanage after the war but also was reunited with her (as well as some ex-war orphans) in 1975 and 1999, when he revisited South Korea as the guest of the Korean National Tourism Corporation and the ROK Air Force.

Despite its affirmative surface as a tale of cross-cultural understanding and love,[85] *Battle Hymn* strategically erases the contribution of a female social worker by filling her role with an exotic Madame Butterfly. The transformation of Mrs. Hwang to Miss Yang is indicative of Hollywood's representational

FIGURE 5.2 *As an offshoot of* Madame Butterfly, *Miss Yang sacrifices her life for the sake of the white male protagonist's surrogate children in* Battle Hymn *(Universal, 1957).*
Courtesy of the Academy of Motion Picture Arts and Sciences.

tendency to sexualize the East as a "virgin" woman. As Ella Shohat observes, in Western cinema the Orient is decisively gendered as feminine and is often allegorized as a "'virgin' coyly awaiting the touch of the colonizer."[86] Apparently, a middle-aged, married, Western-educated woman who professionally assists the white protagonist as a colleague does not coincide with this virginal image of the Orient. The film walks a tightrope by transforming Mrs. Hwang into a glamorous younger woman who could romantically match Hess, suggesting an allure of miscegenation and adultery—an unholy combination that would be strongly opposed by the PCA and religious censors. After a dose of melodramatic tension, such an intriguing possibility dissipates with Miss Yang's premature death during a communist air raid toward the film's end. The anxiety could have been avoided altogether by representing Mrs. Hwang as she was. This, of course, was not an option because there was no place for a despecularized and desexualized woman in classical Hollywood narrative, which often mobilizes (Asian) female bodies for voyeuristic or fetishistic purposes. Moreover, *Battle Hymn* aligns itself with the political agenda of U.S. military expansionism in Asia by rendering racial and sexual others as submissive and grateful colonial subjects in need of white rescuers.

"WHO ARE YOU?": THE ENIGMA OF THE OLD MAN

If Korean femininity is reduced to the conventional Butterfly figure, what can be said about Korean masculinity? Along with Miss Yang, Lu Wan is an important Korean character who not only assists Hess with the orphans but also inspires him with spiritual wisdom. Lu Wan is a man in his seventies who introduces himself as a maker of ivory statues loved in Pusan. Although the old Korean man is a converted Christian, he seeks temporary shelter in a Buddhist temple on his way to the southern port. Hess appeals to Lu Wan's Christian belief to persuade him to delay his return to Pusan for the sake of the orphans. Lu Wan emanates an aura of keen insight from their first meeting by conjecturing Hess to be "a man of God," to which Hess replies, "Just another pilot." Lu Wan's sagacious encouragement of faith deeply impresses Hess when one day, after combat, he confides to the old man:

> HESS: There is nothing as terrible as war. I killed today.
> LU WAN: Yes, war is evil. I see what is in your heart. Colonel, may a poor carver of ivory babble for a moment? Understand that it is only babble that may have no more worth than a handful of sand. In times like these, can a man of good conscience ask others "protect me, kill for me, but do not ask me to stain my hands"? What must one do if a choice of two evils is all there is to offer? To accept the lesser sometimes can be our only choice. In order to save, at times we must destroy. And in destruction, create a new life.
> HESS: Is that the answer?
> LU WAN: The true answer is not in my babble. It is in the Book: "Oh Lord, Thou has seen my wrong. Judge Thou my cause."
> HESS: *Who are you?*
> LU WAN: Just a weary old man most anxious to get to his store in Pusan.

In this emotionally powerful scene, the film self-consciously introduces an intriguing question: who is this mysterious old sage? Although Lu Wan is self-effacing in his modest words, his spiritual power to move an ordained former minister to near-tears attests to the fact that he represents something larger than his self-appellation of "a poor carver of ivory" and "a weary old

FIGURE 5.3 *Philip Ahn as enigmatic ivory carver Lu Wan. Although Ahn was only fifty-one years old at the time of the film's production, he played a man in his seventies, representing a figure of Old Korea in* Battle Hymn *(Universal, 1957).* Courtesy of the Ahn Family.

man." In the following section, I propose three hypotheses that help unravel the enigma of the old man.

First Hypothesis: Dr. Kay Won

The first possibility is that Lu Wan is a substitute for Major Kay Won (Kae Wŏn-ch'ŏl), a young Korean doctor of Hess's unit who was instrumental in caring for the medical needs of the orphans. Along with Hess and Mrs. Hwang, Dr. Kay was one of the key founding members of the Cheju orphanage. In his memoir, Hess singles out Dr. Kay as the Korean to whom he was most attached:

> Of all the Koreans, it was most difficult to part with Dr. Kay Won. Having worked with both the orphans and our field personnel, he was closely linked with my two divergent interests. He gave me a promise, unnecessarily, that he would continue to look after the children's medical needs—a promise he is still faithfully fulfilling today. [87]

As with Mrs. Hwang, another important Korean figure's contribution to the orphanage was omitted from the narrative to give sole credit to Hess. Although Lu Wan assumes his share of responsibility in caring for the children, he does not possess the vital skills necessary to save the children as did Dr. Kay, who "worked day and night, trying with scanty facilities and medicines to treat wounds and diseases of many kinds."[88] Also, Lu Wan's dedication to the orphans is depicted as weaker than that of Hess, because the old man responds hesitantly to Hess's initial request and then leaves the children prematurely for his business in Pusan (he returns only after he finds out that his store in the southeastern coastal city has been burned). The old man's on-and-off volunteer babysitting is a pale substitute for the doctor's prolonged professional care.

By replacing Mrs. Hwang and Dr. Kay with Miss Yang and Lu Wan, the film conforms to Hollywood's convention of sexualizing Asian women and emasculating Asian men. The role of Dr. Kay in his mid-twenties (six years Hess's junior) is thus transferred to an old man in the twilight of his life. Despite his spiritual maturity, Lu Wan lacks the technical proficiency and physical potency needed to match Hess. Through this radical aging of Dr. Kay's role, the film decisively enfeebles Korean masculinity, thus empowering American masculinity in comparison. This spectral absence of a Korean medic contrasts with the emphatic presence of young doctor Chung (Benson Fong) in MGM's World War II film, *Thirty Seconds over Tokyo* (1944)—a Chinese professional who plays a crucial role by saving the lives of American pilots who have crashed on Chinese shores after bombing the Japanese capital in the famous Doolittle Raid of April 1942.

Second Hypothesis: President Syngman Rhee

There was indeed a real Korean "old man" who was mentioned repeatedly in Hess's memoir: Syngman Rhee. During the Korean War, Hess befriended President Rhee and his Austrian wife Francesca (whom he once called "my Korean sweetheart" to the shock of an American Embassy secretary),

and they became close allies. The ROK President awarded Hess with two dec-
orations—the Korean Order of Military Merit and the Korean Public Welfare
Medal—in recognition of his heroic status both as combat pilot and as god-
father of Korean orphans. Hess's memoir is punctuated with enthusiastic
eulogies for Rhee, such as the following:

> Here surely was the greatest man I would ever know. Seventy-five
> years before he had been born into a medieval world, in a nation four
> thousand years old. Most of his life he had struggled to break Japan's
> death grip on the land of Korea. He had suffered six years in prison,
> seven months of which were spent in solitary confinement and tor-
> ture. Here, in prison, his conversion to Christianity had become his
> strength.... When we parted...I was sure that I had met a man upon
> whom history will confer many honors.[89]

Hess's above description of Rhee not only shows that the first ROK president's age at that time roughly coincided with that of the Lu Wan character
but also indicates that the two "old men" (real and cinematic) share the
same religious beliefs.

Furthermore, actor Philip Ahn's presence implicitly links his screen char-
acter to Syngman Rhee, who had a close yet rivalrous relationship with An
Ch'ang-ho. As the foremost figures in the independence movement along
with Kim Ku, Rhee and An worked side by side in the Korean Provisional
Government in Shanghai, which was established in 1919 following the
March First Movement, consisting of nationwide mass demonstrations against
Japan's colonial rule in Korea. They were also pioneering but rival leaders of
early Korean American communities, respectively based in Hawaii and
California. During Rhee's presidency, Philip Ahn engaged in a regular correspondence with him, discussing the Korean film industry and the possibility
of Ahn's participation in it. In a letter to Ahn, dated December 10, 1948, Rhee
wrote, "I regret that your father is not here to see the results of his lifelong
labors to bring about the freedom and independence to our people. He was a
fine man and dedicated his life to the cause of Korean freedom."[90] Implicitly
linked to both Syngman Rhee and An Ch'ang-ho, the figure of Lu Wan perhaps embodies the spirit of the Korean independence movement, of which
many Christians (including both Rhee and An) and American missionaries
were in support.

In Hollywood's "China films" made during World War II and the Sino-
Japanese War,[91] the Chinese Nationalist (KMT) leader Chiang Kai-shek,
another converted Christian, was openly praised by American characters.

For example, in *China* (1943), an American female teacher living in China (Loretta Young) passionately expresses her admiration for Chiang, saying he is one of the finest men who ever lived. This eulogy for the Chinese leader clearly parallels Hess's veneration for President Rhee, which—though reiterated throughout the pages of his book—is never mentioned in Sirk's film. Unlike China films packed with Chinese generals, freedom fighters, and doctors, *Battle Hymn* lacks Korean male figures with authority and power. For example, the mayor of Seoul is conveniently absent when Hess visits his office looking for assistance. Interestingly, a framed photo of Syngman Rhee is displayed on the background wall—a fleeting, unidentified image that likely goes unnoticed by most audiences. The name of General Kim, chief of the ROK Air Force, is mentioned in an earlier scene by a Korean pilot, but the man himself never appears in the film. General Kim Chung Yul (Kim Cho˘ng-yo˘l) was in fact Hess's close friend who shared with him military information during the war. The film's credits list the name of Chinese American actor Richard Loo for the Korean general's role, a ghostly character who might have existed in the earlier stage of production but is absent in the final print.

The only general whom Hess meets in Seoul is Timberidge (Bartlett Robinson), commander of the U.S. Air Force Headquarters, who preaches the imperative of discipline to ROK pilots for whom he shows little respect. The American general tells Hess,

> These Koreans will listen to a man with the same kind of nerve they have. That's why I called on Killer Hess.... They are new to boot, Dean. Besides, they are a hot bunch. They are overanxious. They already cracked up a couple of planes we gave them. And they won't get more. We have none to spare outside of combat.

The absence of powerful Korean men, such as President Rhee, General Kim, and the mayor of Seoul, contributes to the cinematic construction of South Korea as an occupied land dominated by American military authority represented by General Timberidge and Colonel Hess. Although Hollywood readily represented China's autonomous fight for freedom in films made during World War II (when the nation was a privileged U.S. ally along with Great Britain and Russia), no such recognition was made in Korean War films. On the contrary, in those films South Korea was often personified by old men, women, and children lacking self-sufficiency and the ability to defend themselves or their country.

Third Hypothesis: Hess's Alter Ego

Another interpretation is to see Lu Wan as Hess's alter ego, as his religious side repressed in the military act of slaughtering. In his memoir, Hess confides to the reader the intense inner conflicts he experienced as a minister-turned combatant. After his first killing during a World War II mission, he muses to himself:

> Now I was committed. My hands were stained, albeit for a cause. But where was the disgust and remorse I was sure that I, like all men after initial combat, must suffer? Shouldn't I, who had dedicated years of my young life to the ministry, suffer an especially sharp pain? Didn't those enemies have a love for life? Didn't they also have families and loved ones? True, I had resolved long ago that I had chosen the lesser of two evils: to fight, rather than to allow fascism to overrun the world. But now, though I was sure that men had died from my own efforts, it seemed impersonal, detached.[92]

He asks many such questions throughout the two wars, both justifying his cause and reconciling his two conflicting identities as a man of God and a man of war. Lu Wan's emotive words of comfort to Hess after his mission are assembled from bits and pieces of Hess's own sayings scattered throughout his book:

- "I had resolved long ago that I had chosen a lesser of two evils" (p. 4).
- "I had declared, 'how in all good conscience can I ask others to protect [our cause]—and me—while I keep clean of the gory mess of war?'" (p. 5).
- "[W]e in essence were shoving off other young men forward and saying, 'You get the blood on your hands. You accept the guilt; we'll stand by while you do it and pray for you'" (p. 34).
- "If it is true that in order to save we must at times destroy, I had done my part" (p. 63).
- "'Oh, Lord, Thou has seen my wrong, judge Thou my cause,' cried Jeremiah. Could I not ask the same?" (p. 244).

Considering the remarkable similarity between Lu Wan's and Hess's words, it is obvious that the old man is the voice of Hess's religious self, condoning or reconciling the sin of his other self, Hess the combatant. In their first encounter, it is Lu Wan who calls Hess "a man of God," which the latter denies by saying "just another pilot." In his memoir, however, it is Hess who defines himself as Lu Wan does: "I continued to think of myself, even here, participating in all this slaughter, as a man of God."[93] Thus the film uses Lu Wan as Hess's cross-racial double, a ventriloquist lending voice to his inner thoughts. This argument is corroborated by studio publicity: "[T]he screenplay device of having an aged Korean, converted to Christianity, serving as Colonel Hess's 'conscience' and giving voice to his beliefs and philosophies rather than have Hess express them directly, perfectly preserves the grand illusion of the picture without sacrificing anything in the way of integrity or entertainment."[94] This theory is further corroborated by the fact that Hess himself was called "Old Man" and "papa-san" (not so much for his age but for his rank) by his American airmen, ROK trainees, and seven Korean kitchen girls.[95] In other words, Lu Wan is a bodiless spirit, a disembodied voice standing for Hess's religious conscience. He is more a "screenplay device" than a person, one that facilitates Hess's redemptive journey in Korea. It is partly thanks to Lu Wan's symbolic function that Hess is able to "find himself." As he writes to Mary in the film, "Through the agony of war I have finally done what I never before was able to do. In reaching beyond myself, I found myself." The moment when Hess asks Lu Wan who he is then can be interpreted as Hess's search for his own identity.

The doubling of the two actors—Rock Hudson and Philip Ahn—provides an opportunity to tease out queer readings of their respective masculinities. *Battle Hymn* was produced at a time when Rock Hudson's own sexual identity was in crisis. His marriage to Phyllis Gates—allegedly arranged by the studio—was near dissolution, culminating in divorce in 1958, one year after the film's release. The marital and psychological crisis of the closeted, gay man is subtly allegorized in Hudson's screen performance as Hess, who forges more profound and meaningful relationships with men than with women. Hudson's Hess runs away from his complacent small-town life and pregnant wife to return to the militaristic world of intense homosocial bonding. Although heterosexual seductions continuously stalk Hess in the form of Miss Yang, an attractive woman apparently in love with him, he seems completely unresponsive and oblivious. Rather, Hudson/Hess enjoys engaging in spiritually fulfilling conversations with James Edwards/Lieutenant Maples and Ahn/Lu Wan, whose religious devotion and biblical wisdom reinstate his own faltering beliefs. He also consoles his two-war buddy and wingman, Don DeFore/Captain Skidmore, at his deathbed—a lengthy, tearful farewell that can be identified as the film's one true "love scene." The contrasting yet mirroring masculinity of Hudson and Ahn is particularly intriguing precisely because both actors' offscreen identities are affiliated with the discourse of homosexuality.[96] While the white male star Hudson had to assume the mask of ultra-heterosexuality and normativized manliness to conceal his gay self, the Asian supporting actor Ahn was often cast in sidekick roles that called for an effeminate bodily comportment assimilative of amorphous queer sexuality. Thus, what Ahn's Lu Wan ventriloquizes for Hudson's Hess is not simply the latter's religious conscience but also a potential for expressing queer masculinity, repressed in the homophobic culture of the Eisenhower era.

The symbolic casting of a disempowered old man in place of the young, modern doctor Kay and of the freedom fighter-turned-President Syngman Rhee, as well as the mirror-like positioning of him as Hess's religious (and queer) alter ego, can be attributed to the disappearance of Korean masculinity in cinematic spaces dominated by American GI heroes who assume the roles of saviors for South Korean women and children. The old man's name Lu Wan is not a Korean name (it sounds more Chinese than Korean). His identity is spectral, rather than real. His time lies in the premodern past as evidenced by his traditional garments of Chosŏn Dynasty vintage. Thus, he is a figure of Old Korea, a waning existence quickly being replaced by a younger generation (represented by the orphans) who befriend GIs, eat American candy bars, and sing English-language songs. Although the film honors his spiritual function as an Oriental guru, it denies him any technical or political agency (associated with Dr. Kay and President Rhee) and ultimately defines his existence as anachronistic by displacing him amidst the Americanized children dressed in Western clothing in the last scene.

FROM CHU TO SAM:
THE AMERICANIZATION OF KOREAN ORPHANS

If Miss Yang is prematurely eliminated and Lu Wan is symbolically buried, who is left to represent Korea when Hess returns to visit his little beneficiaries in the film's last scene? Undoubtedly, it is Hess's favorite orphan Chu, played by Jung Kyoo Pyo (Chŏng Ku-p'yo), the only Korean child to receive credit in the film. In a burst of joy, Chu jumps into the arms of his returned white father and addresses him in pidgin English, "Me, Chu." The child also quickly befriends Hess's wife, who introduces herself as "Me, Mary." This happy reunion implies the possibility of a new multicultural family. Actor Jung Kyoo Pyo was in reality adopted by an American couple. In February of 1957, *Life* magazine reported the following:

When Universal Pictures set out to make *Battle Hymn*, a haunting story of a gentle warrior, it imported 25 Korean orphans to Hollywood as extras—and thus America acquired Sam. Sometimes called the Tiger, but by rights called Jung Kyoo Pyo, Sam was 5 years old, uninhibited, chubby and charming. He was also a clown who could steal scenes from veteran actors and usually leave them happy.... A childless American couple, Harold and Terry Friar, saw Sam in Los Angeles and loved him. He had already made some adjustments to America. He loved comic books and ice cream. So the Friars adopted him and soon Sam had them eating a seaweed supper, an old Korean delicacy. They have grown quite fond of it since.[97]

As the report indicates, Jung Kyoo Pyo was Americanized as Sam Friar, a fast-assimilating young boy who found a new home in California. His memory of the Cheju orphanage would quickly fade, and he would forget his past as Jung Kyoo Pyo, an orphan who endured poverty and hunger in war-torn Korea. Kyoo Pyo/Sam is just one of 5,348 Korean war orphans who were "rescued" and adopted by altruistic Americans between 1951 and 1965.[98] As Darrell Y. Hamamoto argues, since the Korean War, the mainstream U.S. media has increasingly mobilized the image of the Asian war orphan as a propagandistic device "graphically dramatizing the evils of communism to good-hearted Americans." According to Hamamoto, "The figure of the Asian orphan evokes liberal humanist compassion, depoliticizes the meaning of war, and, most important, confers a sense of moral superiority to the American saviors."[99]

Chu functions not only as a symbol of his foreign savior's moral pride but also as an allegory of his nation's infantile status in the eyes of American politicians and civilians. In his writings, Hess himself uses the child metaphor to describe his feelings for the ROK Air Force: "My affection for the infant ROK Air Force was exactly that of a parent—fierce, possessive, single-minded."[100] This rhetoric can be expanded to allegorize the unequal relationship between the United States and the Republic of Korea. As Bruce Cumings puts it, the ROK was "more an American creation than any other postwar regime in Asia...[and the United States] is the country that has defined South Korea's existence since 1945."[101] Until the surge of anti-American sentiments sparked by the 1980s nationalist *minjung* (literally translated as "people") movement, the United States had long been perceived as the "liberator," "blood ally," and "benefactor" by South Koreans.

Gratitude and betrayal seem to be the two most frequently mentioned emotions exchanged between Americans and South Koreans in the past six decades. The Korean resentment over the U.S.-initiated national division in 1945—the greatest American betrayal since the 1905 Taft-Katsura agreement, which conceded Korea to Japanese powers in exchange for the U.S. monopoly in the Philippines—quickly morphed into heartfelt gratitude for

U.S. intervention in the Korean War and its postwar aid for South Korean rehabilitation. Syngman Rhee's letter to Harry S. Truman, dated July 19, 1950, effectively summarizes the official discourse of Korean appreciation for its benefactor:

> I cannot find words to express, for myself and for all the people and government of Korea, our profound gratitude for your prompt and continued actions in bringing aid to Korea in these desperate days.... No Korean can ever forget the courage and sacrifice of [American soldiers] who in the great traditions of the United States of America have come to the defense of the weak against the cruel aggressor and have fought and given their life blood that liberty and freedom should not perish from the earth.[102]

The South Korean self-appellation as "the weak" and the U.S. self-identification as "the protector" together contribute to the erection of a parent-infant metaphor that still dictates the two nations' asymmetrical relations.

In the wake of nationwide anti-American protests (the largest of its kind since the 1980s) following the killing of two fourteen-year-old Korean school girls by a U.S. military armored vehicle in June 2002 and the subsequent acquittal of the two American soldiers responsible for the accident, many Americans have experienced a strong sense of betrayal. In CBS's *60 Minutes* February 9, 2003 coverage of rising anti-Americanism in South Korea (entitled "Yankee Go Home"), reporter Bill Simon recapitulates the old metaphor. Having defined South Korea of the 1950s as "a baby that needed a father" in his interview segment with a Korean politician, the reporter's voiceover goes on to say that "being a gentle father" is no longer easy when "South Koreans are attacking American bases here, assaulting American soldiers, and burning the American flag in public squares." After the airing of this report, U.S.-based Korean Councils were bombarded with protest calls and emails from enraged viewers who expressed anti-Korean sentiments and resentment over the U.S. participation in the Korean War. Similar emotional responses can be found in open letters from Americans posted in the English-language Web pages of major Korean daily newspapers.[103] It seems that the American public's desires and expectations of South Korean gratitude for the U.S. sacrifice during the Korean War are so abiding that any instances proving otherwise ignite sharp feelings of betrayal even today, a half-century after the cease-fire.

The tensions stemming from the love/hate familial romance between the two nations are ironed out and concealed through the idealized representation of grateful children in *Battle Hymn*. Like Miss Yang and Lu Wan, both diligently bowing and conveying their thanks to Hess, the orphans do their best to repay the benevolence of their surrogate father, Hess, who is reported to have been called by Koreans "Mister United States."[104] Two orphan girls stage a traditional dance accompanied by the children's choir of "Arirang" (Korea's most popular folk song), an endearing performance that Hess/ Hudson watches with visible pleasure and satisfaction. Their gratitude is ultimately expressed in the film's last scene when all the children, having exchanged their Korean rags for Western clothing, line up and sing "Battle Hymn of the Republic" (Hess's favorite song) in English, showing their will to assimilate American cultures and values. The war orphans' intense desire to please and be liked by an American GI-father is also elaborated in *The Steel Helmet*, in which the Korean boy Short Round writes a prayer to Buddha asking for the brusque American Sergeant Zack's love.

As much as the ROK is an "American creation," so is Chu. Played by a real orphan, Jung Kyoo Pyo, Chu epitomizes genuine Koreanness, something even American-born Philip Ahn could only partially impart. He is much more authentic than *The Steel Helmet*'s orphan Short Round, who is played by William Chun, a Korean American boy who struggles to pronounce Korean words correctly. Ironically, the reason Chu is singled out as the focus of attention is that he, of the twenty-five orphans, is most "American" (in a stereotypical sense): he is active, gregarious, funny, confident, and ever smiling. The other children seem shy, reserved, serious, and stoic—attributes that are characteristic of a neo-Confucian culture valuing self-effacement and modesty.

In the aforementioned *Life* magazine article, there is a picture that features Jung Kyoo Pyo laughing in the arms of the real Hess during the film's rehearsal. Behind them, on the right side, a little Korean girl is shown glancing askew at Kyoo Pyo and Hess with an envious yet timid look.[105] The three children who appear on the Universal pamphlet cover with Anna Kashfi (against a close-up of Rock Hudson's face in the background) have strikingly sad and wizened looks—their faces heartbreakingly conveying the actual hardship and misery the nonactors underwent during the war. The boy in the center (held by Kashfi) is likely the same orphan on whom the actress doted during the film's shooting. According to Kashfi's memoir, she fell in love with a seven-year old orphan called Kwan Yung, "a sad-faced, introverted boy...[who] was slow to respond, never smiled, and remained aloof from the other children."[106] As soon as Kwan Yung began to lower his shield and open his heart to Kashfi, the filming was completed, and he was sent back to the orphanage (from which the boy escaped for three days in a bold attempt to fly back to the United States where he thought his "movie star mother" was waiting for him). Although the sorrowful expressions of Kwan Yung and/or those like him were spotlighted in the publicity literature to induce audience compassion, the producers selected little "clown" Jung Kyoo Pyo over his more somber peers as the central orphan figure in the film—the one lucky child to receive a name credit and be given exclusive attention from Rock Hudson's Hess. After the film's production, only Kyoo Pyo—adopted by the Friars—remained in the United States, whereas his twenty-four mates had to return to their impoverished reality with a bittersweet aftertaste of tinseltown and Disneyland (where Universal took them as a treat). Regardless of their sympathy for the plight of war orphans, the Americans ultimately chose the most outwardly cheerful child as their beneficiary, the one who least bore traces of grief and pain.

Chu's constructedness as an amiable Oriental orphan is observed by famed journalist and writer Ahn Junghyo (An Chŏng-hyo), author of the Korean War novel, *Silver Stallion* (*Ŭnma nŭn oji annŭnda*, 1987). In the *Korean Herald*, Ahn recollects his first viewing of the film:

> I was a boy as young as the Korean orphans the American Colonel evacuated to safety in the movie. Naturally, I identified myself with the orphans. The boys, however, were cardboard stereotypes, without individual identities. The only boy with a name in the movie was called "Chu." In my sixty years of life, I have never met a boy with such a strange name as Chu in this country. But almost all Orientals in Hollywood movies carry stupid monosyllabic names, anyway, and Chu is a much better name for a Korean child than "Kim C" (Mr. Kim), by which a Korean mother, wearing a Chinese conical hat, addressed her young son in one of the earlier episodes of the TV series *M*A*S*H*.[107]

As cynically pointed out by the Korean novelist, Chu (a humorous homonym of "chew," an act Chu struggles to learn in the film after being handed a stick of American gum) is a fictional Korean name as unlikely as Lu Wan.

The film is in fact sprinkled with these kinds of mistakes or misrepresentations, which can provoke derisive laughter as well as spectatorial pleasure. For example, Kashfi's En Soon Yang calls Lu Wan (who hails her politely as "Miss Yang") by his name, an act of insolence in the eyes of most Koreans. According to Korean decorum, a young woman should address an old man as *halabŏji* or *halabŏnim* ("dear grandfather"). Lu Wan, however, has authority to call the young woman by her first name instead of using the honorific "Miss." A similar gaffe occurs in a scene when Hess asks Sergeant Hermann to buy candy for the orphans. After the Sergeant grumbles that Yongsan probably has no candy store, Hess advises him to try Seoul—apparently ignorant of the fact that the district is in fact located *inside* the South Korean capital. Ahn Junghyo's article summons the subversive pleasure this hilarious error offered to postwar South Korean theatergoers: "The whole theater laughed at this obvious mistake made by the almighty American; the poor little Koreans were delighted that day to learn that they knew something better than Americans."[108] This differentiated viewing position demonstrates that cultural competency and spectatorial "double consciousness" can provide the potential for a detached, resistant reading of what might be construed as a hegemonic text.

For many mainstream American audiences, however, Chu might mean something other than a "cardboard stereotype" with a ludicrous name. He is a living emblem that exhibits the benefits American aid has brought to an infantile, Third World country threatened by communist aggression. He is, after all, *our* Sam who likes us, wants us, and calls us father. His existence proves that the American way of life—democracy, freedom, and Judeo-Christian utopianism—will prevail in South Korea and other Asian countries under the U.S. defense umbrella. Unlike many grim Korean War films including *The Steel Helmet*, *One Minute to Zero*, *The Bridges at Toko-Ri*, *The Manchurian Candidate*, and *War Hunt*, *Battle Hymn* ends on an overwhelmingly upbeat note. The film reaches a self-affirming conclusion in the same vein of General Van Fleet's remark that "Korea has been a blessing"— a blessing that enabled troubled American masculinity to overcome its psychological crises and to restore its moral integrity. *Battle Hymn* closes with a euphoric moment in which the genuflectory encounter between East and West is frozen against an overhead shot of the aforementioned symbol of eternity—pine trees—assuring the American benefactors that they will be remembered forever in the hearts of Koreans whose appreciative demeanor echoes the grateful words spoken earlier by Miss Yang: "Ours is the thanks that you are with us."

CONCLUSION

Becoming "Father," Becoming Asian American

I N FEBRUARY OF 1926, Tosan An Ch'ang-ho bid farewell to his wife
and children before leaving Los Angeles for Shanghai after a one-
year visit to the United States. This was the last time that Philip
Ahn, his mother, and siblings would see him. Although Tosan spent
a total of thirteen years in America (1902–1906, 1911–1919, 1925), he
had to leave his Californian home frequently, touring American cities, as
well as Hawaii, Cuba, and Mexico, to organize the Korean community
and to raise funds for the independence movement. In his final days with
the family, Tosan had one last serious discussion with his eldest son, going
over the details of familial obligations. Handing over his role as head of
the family to Philip, the father expressed a sense of guilt, saying, "In the
eyes of God I am a grave sinner, abandoning my family and leaving them
in your charge."[1]

Fast forward nine years. In 1935, the year Philip Ahn made his
Hollywood debut, Tosan was living reclusively in a small mountain villa
(Songt'ae Villa) on the outskirts of P'yŏnyang, after serving four years in
prison on charges of violating the "Peace Preservation Law"—a piece of
colonial legislation enacted in 1925 to suppress the independence movement and anti-Japanese activities. Even after Tosan's release from prison,
the Japanese police not only banned his public speeches and gatherings
but also closely watched his daily activities and interactions with visitors.

Some time before June 1937, when he was arrested and sent back to jail, Tosan saw his eldest son once again, only this time as a member of a movie audience. Philip's sister Susan received a letter from Alice Lee, her mother's cousin in Seoul, two months after Tosan's death in March 1938. Lee's letter, dated May 9, 1938, states,

> Your father saw Philip in *The General Died at Dawn* and was mighty pleased. *The Good Earth* was being shown when he was ill in the hospital and how I wished he could have seen the picture... also the picture *Stowaway*. He asked me to tell him the story so [I]...did my very best and your dad was satisfied, although I had to practically act the scene out.[2]

Although historical and political circumstances permanently separated the anticolonial leader from his family in Los Angeles in 1926, the father and the son (or rather, flickering celluloid images of the son) could be reunited in spirit one last time in a movie theater in colonial Korea, thanks to Hollywood's global distribution network.

Coincidentally, Philip Ahn himself played the role of a father-spectator in an episode of the tellingly titled ABC series *The Time Tunnel* (1966–1967) that was originally broadcast on January 6, 1967. The premise of this science fiction series is that two scientists—Dr. Tony Newman (James Darren) and Dr. Doug Phillips (Robert Colbert)—in charge of developing the titular temporal tunnel, a $7.5 billion secret government project, are sent through time toward an unknown destination in the past or future in each episode. The episode in question, "Kill Two by Two," begins with the arrival of the two time travelers on a South Pacific island in February 1945. They are captured by a sadistic, American-educated Japanese officer (Mako) and his sidekick sergeant (Kam Tong)—two remaining members of the retreating Japanese troops. Proposing a "two-by-two" war game, the young officer gives Newman and Phillips, unarmed civilians, one hour to prepare their defense against the Japanese duo's assault. Back in the present at Tic Toc Base, a concealed underground lab for the Time Tunnel project, General Heywood Kirk (Whit Bissell) brings in Nakamura (Philip Ahn), a Japanese doctor who fought in the Japanese Army during World War II; he seeks his help in identifying the island's landmarks so that engineers can locate the whereabouts of the two scientists and arrange their transfer. So shocked is Nakamura when he witnesses the image of the Japanese officer on the Time Tunnel screen that he faints.

In the next scene, the restored doctor explains that the man is his son, a disgraced kamikaze pilot who abandoned his mission. During the retreat from the island, Nakamura left his son behind so that he could commit *harikari*. Seeing a second chance to rewrite this fatal decision, Nakamura demands that his son be brought back to the present in exchange for his cooperation. This puts the Time Tunnel team in an untenable position because their technology allows only double transfer, which means that they will have to sacrifice one of their scientists to bring back his son. Only toward the end of the episode, when the father witnesses his son's resolution to accept honorable death, does he retract his demand and reconciles to this painful past.

A USO publicity pamphlet promoting Ahn's July 1968 tour in Vietnam quotes the actor's thoughts on this episode:

> I played a doctor in the U.S. who was called to the tunnel.... I looked at a Pacific island 20 years ago. I supposedly see my son, a Japanese soldier, still fighting. And I had the weird feeling that was me 20 years before. I was playing father and son![3]

Although Ahn's character embodies the image of a model minority (a debonair, intelligent professional), he mediates the "yellow peril" stereotype (a belligerent Japanese enemy) represented by his son. The veteran actor had his own uncanny "time travel" experience upon seeing Mako, a younger Asian American performer, reenact his old routine in 1940s anti-Japanese propaganda films. As a temporal portal capable of imagistically projecting the past and future, the widescreen Time Tunnel monitor serves as a mirroring device to reflect the intersubjective reciprocity between father/Philip Ahn and son/Mako. This scene of a father gazing at his son's images (on a screen within the screen) also carries the palimpsestic trace of Tosan's spectatorship of *The General Died at Dawn*. In the television episode, Dr. Nakamura sees his (dead) son for the first time in twenty-three years through the Time Tunnel apparatus that bridges the temporal and spatial gap between the Pacific island of 1945 and Arizona of 1968.

In real life, Tosan was able to see his separated son after a ten-year stretch through the medium of a Hollywood picture imported to the Japanese colony of the 1930s. At a time predating camcorder and videotape technology, seeing moving images of a member of one's divided family living abroad must have been an exhilarating and perhaps melancholic experience, one that approximates the time travel experience. Reinforcing this bizarre parallel, both Nakamura's son in the aforementioned episode and Ahn's character Oxford in the 1936 Paramount film commit suicide in the dénouement.

"FATHERING" WHITE STARS, FROM SHIRLEY TEMPLE TO DAVID CARRADINE

As discussed in earlier chapters, Philip Ahn's on- and offscreen identities were deeply influenced by the magnitude of his father's legacy. Although American audiences might recall him as the Number One Japanese villain or David Carradine's kung fu master, South Koreans identify him as the national hero's son first and the Hollywood actor second. In various media interviews that Ahn gave in both the United States and South Korea, the most frequently mentioned subject was his father. As John Ringo Graham of *San Fernando Valley Magazine* observes in his January 1970 article, "When the subject of his father comes up, Ahn can hold the interest of friends for hours as he recites the exploits and achievements of the famous revolutionary."[4] The dutiful son was extremely hands-on regarding the preservation of his father's legacy. On December 18, 1972, when Tosan Memorial Park was being constructed in Seoul, he sent a long letter to President Park Chung Hee to remind him of the details of their earlier discussion about the project. Quoting Park's own remark that "Tosan [should] belong to all the peoples of Korea," Philip Ahn emphasized that "the area should be built in such a manner that the generations to come will be able to pay their respects at the tomb and recall the teachings and philosophies that he held for the betterment of our people."[5]

Ahn was a true disciple of the "teachings and philosophies" of his father, whom he had to share with "all the peoples of Korea." He was well aware that, as one of the many biographers of his father puts it, "Tosan was [a father], not just for his family...but for the entire Korean people."[6] Because Philip Ahn was the son of a symbolic figure who guided the nation-less people during the dark colonial period—an uncompromising patriot and inspiring teacher whose martyrdom immortalized his fame—it is impossible to divorce the father from the homeland in the diasporic actor's identity formation. The memory of the revered father incited his nostalgia for the (imagined) homeland, parts of which were off limits to him. Although Ahn made more than a dozen visits to South Korea beginning in 1959, he was never able to return to his father's hometown Torong Island nor his last haven Songt'ae Villa, both located near North Korea's capital P'yŏngyang.

Tosan An Ch'ang-ho once declined the Japanese prosecutor's plea bargain with the emphatic statement: "When I eat I eat for Korea. When I sleep I sleep for Korea. To the last breath of my life I will work for an independent Korea." Tosan's lifelong dream was to see an independent, united, democratic Korea. His death seven years before its liberation was perhaps a blessing

FIGURE 6.1 *Old Son and Young Father: Philip Ahn holding his father's portrait.* Courtesy of the Ahn Family.

in disguise, preventing the patriot from witnessing the tragedy of national division and the Korean War.

As Tosan's dream remained incomplete, so did Philip Ahn's. Both as an actor and as a person, Ahn's ideal role was his father. The biopic of Tosan An Ch'ang-ho proposed by famous Korean screenwriter Ch'oe Kŭm-dong in the early 1960s regretfully never materialized. Nevertheless, to the very last days of his life, the actor did not forsake plans of producing and starring in a film about his father. Although Ahn never had a chance to play *his* father, he played (surrogate) fathers in several film and television productions.

The earliest paternal role he was given was Sun Lo, the Chinese magistrate of Sanchow who protects Shirley Temple's orphan girl Barbara (a.k.a Ching-ching) in *Stowaway* (1936). As a good friend of the child's dead parents, Sun Lo clandestinely arranges Ching-ching's escape to his brother's house in Shanghai when notorious bandits invade the village. Before their parting, the Chinese benefactor asks the American orphan to "always remember the sayings of one wise man" that he has taught her. Unfortunately, the boatman to whom Sun Lo has entrusted the little girl steals her money and abandons her. Stranded in the streets of Shanghai, the curly-haired moppet in distress encounters American tourist Tommy Randall (Robert Young) and befriends him after translating Chinese on his behalf. After a series of mix-ups, Ching-ching inadvertently becomes a stowaway on a cruise ship where Randall is aboard. Charmed by the parentless yet jovial child, the playboy millionaire is willing to adopt her to prevent her from being sent to an institution. Randall persuades Susan Parker (Alice Faye), an unhappily engaged woman whom he has been pursuing onboard, to marry him temporarily so he can be eligible to adopt the child. The film ends with the image of an ideal Christmas that Ching-ching shares with her new parents, who realize their genuine love for each other and remain married.

Although Ahn's Sun Lo prematurely disappears from the screen after the opening sequence, his spectral presence carries on through Ching-ching's habitual quoting of his aphorisms, such as "One cannot eat gold but one cannot eat without it"; "If wishes were keys, there would be no prisoners"; and "A child without parents is like a ship without a rudder." Each time, the little ventriloquist prefaces her borrowed wisdom with the phrase, "as Sun Lo says." Despite his abiding spiritual influence, the Chinese father—a sort of male version of Stella Dallas—is quickly replaced by the white father who, by contrast, is capable of providing wealth and status, as well as a new American name (Barbara Randall) to the adorable orphan.

Shirley Temple is not the only Caucasian actress with whom Philip Ahn formed a cinematic kinship. He also played the father of Gene Tierney's character in *China Girl* (1942). Miss Young, a Chinese scholar's daughter, was the fourth Oriental role that Tierney tackled for 20th Century-Fox—the other three being an Arab in *Sundown* (1941), a Eurasian in *The Shanghai Gesture* (1941), and a Polynesian in *Son of Fury* (1942). The studio pressbook celebrates the fact that the brunette star impersonated a full-blooded "China girl" without racial makeup or eye-tape. Director Henry Hathaway is quoted as having said, "Gene photographs more like a Chinese than most natives—you can't tell a camera that it's not logical!"[7]

This publicity angle directly contradicts the film narrative. Protagonist Johnny Williams (George Montgomery), an American newsreel photographer who has escaped a Japanese prisoner-of-war camp in China, spots Tierney's character in a hotel lobby in Mandalay, Burma, and immediately becomes attracted to her. Because of her Western look, fashionable Fifth Avenue-style suit, and impeccable command of English, he mistakes her as an all-American girl. Miss Young reinforces her racial passing by informing Williams that she is a graduate of Vassar College. Her ethnic identity is exposed only when the American photographer visits her house and is introduced to her father, Dr. Kai Young (Philip Ahn). Despite Tierney's physical suggestion of whiteness, Ahn's Asian visage serves as indisputable evidence of her Chineseness by blood association.

Ahn's Dr. Young is an altruistic teacher who sells his precious art treasures to fund an educational mission for war orphans in Kunming. When his school opens, Miss Young faces the classic dilemma of a cinematic Oriental woman—a choice between her white lover and her familial duty. She chooses the latter and follows her father to Kunming. Philip Ahn takes center stage in a prolonged scene set in the school in which he gives patriotic lessons to orphaned children during a particularly nasty Japanese air raid. Having identified the nation as a worthy cause for sacrificing one's life, the patriotic teacher tries to calm the fear-ridden children with these inspiring words: "The bombs that are falling down are destroying many things we love, but there is a larger thing that they cannot kill. It is a knowledge of good in your hearts." While reciting a poem eulogizing the spirit of freedom fighters, Ahn's Dr. Young is killed by a bomb that drops upon the podium where he is standing. Although grieved by the death of her father, Miss Young takes his place and finishes the lesson. Williams arrives on the scene just in time to console his lover only to witness her death in a subsequent bombing. The initially isolationist American finally takes up an anti-aircraft machine gun to join China's fight for freedom.

At the time of the film's theatrical release, this school scene generated diametrically opposed reactions. The Office of War Information (OWI) review dated November 25, 1942, states,

> The scenes in the Chinese school at the end of the picture are particularly forceful. When Dr. Young is killed by Japanese bombs his daughter calmly organizes the children and continues to read them his message of courage. It is evident that the Chinese are in no way

defeated after nine years of fighting our common enemy. Examples of allied fortitude such as this are extremely important in motion pictures at the present time. Americans admire courage. Through the medium of motion pictures they will come to increasingly admire their Chinese ally.[8]

John T. McManus of *PM*, a New York daily newspaper, interpreted the scene otherwise. Borrowing the words of "a tested American friend and interpreter of China," he claimed that "if any Chinese teacher acted as those two [Dr. Young and his daughter] did in the film, he would be court-martialed and shot. Chinese take their children to dugouts.... They are not blithering idiots."[9] Whether or not it is realistic to portray a Chinese teacher continuing his lesson amidst raining Japanese bombs, the scene is undoubtedly loaded with pro-Chinese propaganda.

For Philip Ahn, however, Dr. Young's fortitude and martyrdom must have represented something more personal. For anyone who is familiar with Ahn's familial heritage, it is difficult to miss the resemblance between Dr. Young and Tosan An Ch'ang-ho, who established three schools (two in P'yo˘ngyang and one in Nanjing) and wrote many patriotic verses. The actor's eloquent oratory skills demonstrated in the scene remind one of his father's extraordinary gifts as a public speaker. Between 1907 and 1910 alone, Tosan gave seventeen "enlightenment" speeches urging social and educational reform of his homeland. These legendary speeches, which lasted two or three hours and captivated the hearts of thousands gathered to hear him, were reported to be "beyond oral and written descriptions," to borrow one journalist's sycophantic expression.[10] Dr. Young's tenacity in continuing to teach despite the threat to his life reflects Tosan's unbending dedication to Korean independence at the expense of his safety and well-being. Perhaps the scene is all the more powerful because Ahn could invoke the psychological and physiological trademarks that would be associated with Method acting years later, totally immersing himself in a role that symbolizes his own father.

Ahn's paternal aura permeates such disparate motion pictures as *The Miracle of the Bells* (1948), *Japanese War Bride* (1952), *Love Is a Many-Splendored Thing* (1955), *Battle Hymn* (1957), *Never So Few* (1959), *Shock Corridor* (1963), *Thoroughly Modern Millie* (1967), and *Portrait of a Hitman* (1977). In each of these films, the actor assumes the role of a sagacious, fatherly figure offering words of wisdom and advice to a young white protagonist. His patriarchal persona came to the fore in the most celebrated role of his career, Master Kan in the ABC television series *Kung Fu* (1972–1975).

Hailed by one critic as an "unlikely combination of Eastern mysticism and Western action,"[11] *Kung Fu* was a groundbreaking series produced by Warner Bros. that intermixed the martial arts genre with Wild West iconography, expanding the syntax of the television western to accommodate "foreign" elements at the scenographic and narrative levels. One can also identify *Kung Fu* as a nostalgic and parodic recasting of Hollywood's sinophilic period, which roughly coincides with the duration of the popular B movie series, Charlie Chan (1931–1949). It is significant that the Charlie Chan cycle ended the same year in which Mao Zedong's Chinese Communist Party came into power and that *Kung Fu* was first broadcast the year Richard Nixon visited China, thawing decades of Cold War antagonism between the two world powers. This obvious historical bridge is buttressed additionally by the reunion of five veteran alumni of the Charlie Chan series—Philip Ahn, James Hong, Benson Fong, Keye Luke, and Victor Sen Yung—in *Kung Fu*. Pioneering Asian American actors who began their career playing supporting roles of sons and suspects to Warner Oland's and Sidney Toler's yellowfaced Charlie Chans, these aging alumni gathered again to mentor the hybridized western hero, Kwai Chang Caine. This coveted Chinese starring role was snatched by white actor David Carradine from legendary kung fu artist-turned-star Bruce Lee, attesting to the ironic circle of racist casting politics that encompassed 1930s film and 1970s television.

Originally broadcast on February 22, 1972 under the title *Kung Fu: The Way of the Tiger, the Sign of the Dragon*, the pilot episode includes the famous scene in which Philip Ahn's Kan, the Senior Reverend and Grand Master of Martial Arts at the Shaolin Temple, interviews a young Eurasian orphan named Kwai Chang Caine (Radames Pera). Upon learning of the boy's biracial identity, the stern priest intones, "In the Shaolin Temple, we have never accepted anyone of other than full Chinese birth." Disappointed, Caine lowers his head. However, Kan quickly lifts the boy's spirits by adding, "There is a first for everything." Instead of formally announcing Caine's acceptance to the temple, the aging sage stretches out his open palm, on which a pebble rests, and tells him, "As quickly as you can, snatch the pebble from my hand." When the boy fails, Kan informs him, "When you can take the pebble from my hand it will be time for you to leave."

Throughout the series, the Shaolin Temple scenes unfold as flashbacks containing the memories of grown-up Caine (David Carradine), who wanders the American Southwest as a fugitive from China where he has killed a royal nephew in an act of revenge against the murder of his favorite teacher Master Po (Keye Luke). The peace-loving kung fu hero with no gun is forced not only to defend himself against bounty hunters and predators but also to

FIGURE 6.2. *Philip Ahn's best remembered role as Master Kan of the Shaolin Temple in the popular television series* Kung Fu *(Warner Bros., 1972–1975).* Courtesy of the Ahn Family.

confront the anti-Chinese violence and racism of the 1870s frontier. Perpetually dogged by daunting challenges and dilemmas, our hero turns to the tutelage of Masters Po and Kan. Luke's Po, a blind priest with egg-white eyes, is a loving mother figure who nicknames Caine "grasshopper" and openly dotes on him. In contrast, Ahn's Kan, whose name is notably similar to "Caine," is a disciplined surrogate father who conducts the apprenticeship with rigor and vision. Even when Master Kan does not physically appear onscreen, his disembodied voice—imparting philosophical knowledge and spiritual wisdom—often haunts Caine's psyche in aural flashbacks. As John Stanley puts it, Ahn's character is "the epitome of omniscience: There is no human situation to which he cannot respond with a pansophic metaphor or a pearl of sagacity."[12]

In a 1974 interview with Irvin Paik, the series' producers Alex Beaton and Herman Miller identify a hodgepodge of religious texts as the sources of the philosophical knowledge and wisdom imparted by Masters Kan and Po: Arthur Waley's *The Analects of Confucius* (1938), Reiho Masunaga's *A Primer of Soto Zen* (1971), Christmas Humphreys's *The Wisdom of Buddhism* (1960), and Walpola Rahula's *What the Buddha Taught* (1967).[13] As a Presbyterian in real life, Philip Ahn once commented on the series as follows:

> I'm an actor, who is said to do a job, and I read the lines as they have been written. Have I ever questioned their authenticity? I prefer to think the philosophies Kan expresses are genuine; that they are taken from the Taos religion, which teaches one to do good and which preaches non-violence until you are backed up a tree and must defend yourself. That is where kung fu becomes justified in our stories.[14]

In a 1973 interview with Jon Shirota, however, the actor admits that his father, who had been educated in Confucian classics, was an inspiration behind his projection of "the essence of oriental philosophy" in the series. Ahn goes on to say, "For me it has been a pleasure to portray a highly intelligent master of the Shaolin Temple. It reflects my own personal attitude and background."[15]

In the pilot episode, Master Kan effectively sums up his pacifist philosophy this way:

> Learn more ways to preserve rather than destroy. Avoid rather than check. Check rather than hurt. Hurt rather than maim. Maim rather than kill. For all life is precious nor can any be replaced.

Not unlike Kan, Tosan An Ch'ang-ho was a pacifist leader who strove to empower the nation through educational, cultural, and mental reforms, rather than by resisting colonial powers through the militant means of terrorist activities. The three principles of his teachings were *musil yŏkhaeng* (practicing truth), *chŏngŭi donsu* (cultivating mutual love), and *tongmaeng suryŏn* (cultivating an alliance of virtue, body, and knowledge). Although Tosan's teachings borrow more from the West (Christianity and American Pragmatism) than the East (Buddhism and Taoism), his humanist ideals and

Confucian inklings are not far removed from those of Master Kan. Set in the Shanghai of 1924, the action movie *The Anarchists* (*Anak'isŏtŭ*; 1999), the first Korean-Chinese co-production, briefly features the Tosan character as a delegate from the Korean Provisional Government who attempts to dissuade the titular radicals from using violence in the Japanese quarter. He urges the unresponsive revolutionaries to heed the following words: "Terrorism is a barbarian act that the international community criticizes. We should change our society through enlightenment." Although the modern, dandified image of Tosan is a far cry from that of the reclusive feudal monk in *Kung Fu*, Ahn's internalized identification with his father while playing the role of Kan is not difficult to understand, considering that both figures—real and televisual— were intelligent and philosophical leaders.

Through the voice of Master Kan, Philip Ahn paid tribute to his patrilineal heritage in an episode of *Kung Fu* entitled "Dark Angel" (November 11, 1972), which not coincidentally features David Carradine's real father (John Carradine) as a blind preacher. In the opening aural flashback, Caine and Kan exchange one of their usual conversations about the meaning of life:

CAINE: Master, of man's roots, which is stronger?
KAN: It is the Shaolin belief that the paternal line controls.
CAINE: What is a man without roots?
KAN: What is a tree without roots? The deeper into the earth the roots reach, the stronger the tree.

In the eyes of Korean Confucian patriarchy, Philip Ahn, as the eldest son, failed to carry on his paternal roots by producing a male heir. However, he served as a surrogate father to many young Korean immigrants in need of connection and guidance as they assimilated into American society. As his father did in the early part of the twentieth century, Ahn spared no efforts in catering to the needs of post-Korean War immigrants from the homeland, whether it was by introducing them to jobs or providing them with temporary lodging. Despite the fact he was a lifelong bachelor, he even attempted to adopt one young Korean man, Peter Lee (later Peter Ahn), who immigrated to the United States in 1964 and found a job as a bartender in Moongate Restaurant, the Ahn family-owned business. Philip Ahn accepted the young immigrant from the homeland as part of the family and invited him to live in his house. Although legal complications prolonged the procedures of adoption, which remained incomplete at the time of Ahn's death, Peter was treated as his de facto son during the final decade of the actor's life and became an official member of the Ahn family in 1982 when Ralph Ahn adopted him out of respect for his late brother's wishes. According to Peter Ahn, Philip had an intense desire to have a child until the late 1960s, when the actor had his cancerous prostate removed. Before the operation, Peter consoled the childless actor, assuring him that he would become his son.[16] After Peter got married and moved out of the Ahn residence in 1969, Philip continued to open his house to new immigrants from South Korea and sponsored their applications for permanent residency in the United States.

Yet, perhaps Philip Ahn was more than a surrogate father for the new generation of post-1965 Korean immigrants: he was also a spiritual father to many young American viewers in the 1970s who were disillusioned by their own fathers' generation. Quite opposite to *Stowaway*, in which Ahn's Chinese father figure is quickly replaced by that of Robert Young, the white father figure, the television series *Kung Fu* never shows the protagonist's dead American father; instead, his symbolic role is filled by Ahn's Master Kan from the pilot episode. Throughout the series, David Carradine's adult Caine constantly recalls Kan's paternal lessons as he grapples with moral, spiritual, and philosophical questions in recurrent Shaolin flashbacks. In a documentary interview, Tom Kuhn, former vice president of Warner Bros. Television, states that "audiences loved [Philip Ahn]. They couldn't get enough of [him]."[17] American audiences accepted and welcomed Ahn as a fatherly figure not because he was typically Oriental or foreign but because he was "whiter than white." Indeed, he is frequently presented before the camera as the epitome of intelligence, reason, maturity, and fortitude whose spiritual enlightenment is visually connoted through hazy, soft focus photography and the glow of flickering candles, which together transform his body into a site of literal as well as figurative luminosity. As Richard Dyer points out in his discussion of the aesthetic technology of photographic media, "The apparatus and practice...of a light culture, not only assumes and privileges whiteness but also constructs it."[18] In accordance with this notion, Ahn's eloquent and articulate voice sounds "whiter" than that of Carradine, who emulates a "yellow voice" by injecting artificial inflections and pauses.

Despite his appropriation of symbolic whiteness, Ahn's Master Kan is a paradoxical figure who is at once patriarchal and emasculated. In the "King of the Mountain" episode (originally aired October 14, 1972), Carradine's Caine, physically attracted to a widowed ranch woman named Amy Allender (Lara Parker), recalls his "question and answer session" with Ahn's Kan. Young disciple Caine (Radames Pera) asks, "Master, our bodies are prey to many needs. Hunger, thirst, the need for love.... Shall we then seek to satisfy these needs?" His aged master answers, "Only acknowledge them, and satisfaction will follow. To suppress a truth is to give it force beyond endurance."

Although the adult Caine suppresses his sexual desire for the white woman and leaves her ranch after killing a bounty hunter, the promised "satisfaction" follows in a subsequent episode, entitled "The Tide" (February 1, 1973). In that episode the former Shaolin priest makes love to Su Yen (Tina Chen), a Chinese ranch woman who saves his life and takes him to a hideout, a seaside cave, away from his pursuers. Before their lovemaking, Caine recalls Master Kan's teaching again, this time in a flashback set in a makeshift theater in which a young girl in a colorful costume performs an acrobatic dance in front of a male audience, including two monks (young and old) from Shaolin. Kan and Caine exchange an open conversation about the latter's sexual awakening:

> KAN: What do you feel?
> CAINE: Uncomfortable.
> KAN: The mind, the body, and the spirit are one. When the body
>   expresses the desires of the mind and the spirit, then the body is
>   in tune with nature. The act is pure. And there is no shame.
> CAINE: And what is love?
> KAN: Love is harmony, even in discord.

The memory of Kan's paternal, if not priestly, affirmation of carnal desire leads to the consummation of Caine's passion with Su Yen, who later betrays him in hopes of using him as a bargaining chip to free her father imprisoned in China as a political prisoner.

Although Kan's positioning as father in the course of Caine's rite of passage into heterosexual manhood is self-evident, the old priest is nevertheless a neutered figure whose patriarchal mastery is confined to the realm of language, not the body. To render this reading more complex and complete, at the time of the series' first-season production, Philip Ahn was no longer able to procreate (due to prostate cancer) and had to resort to a cane because of an automobile accident in January 1970, which severely injured his left leg and incapacitated him for two years. The producers of *Kung Fu* hired him regardless and rewrote the part to accommodate his crippled condition, limiting the movement of his character. In an episode from the third season entitled "The Demon God" (November 22, 1974), a restored Ahn was given a rare opportunity to display his physical skills in a scene where he knocks a couple of guards to the side and rescues a delirious Caine, who has been poisoned by the malicious son of a dying mandarin. It was the first episode directed by David Carradine, who expressed enthusiasm for remasculinizing

Master Kan in his statement: "Suddenly you see why he is a master...instead of them just talking about it all the time."[19]

Ahn's last screen role in *Portrait of a Hitman*, a low-budget potboiler, is likewise imbued with the aura of surrogate paternalism. In this cross-breeding of blaxploitation and *Dirty Harry*-style vigilantism, the male protagonist, Jim Buck (Jack Palance), is a painter who leads a double life as a contract hitman. When Buck gets an order from his Mafia boss Max (Rod Steiger) to kill a surgeon friend who has saved his life, he seeks advice from Mr. Wong (Philip Ahn), who apparently acts as the white protagonist's father-substitute. Although Wong is identified as a Chinatown resident by exterior shots of exotic architecture and a neon sign reading "Hong Kong," the interior of the room where the two men converse is not explicitly associated with Orientalist iconography. Compared with Master Kan of *Kung Fu*, Wong is an Americanized modern guru in Western attire who is nevertheless affiliated with otherness—sonically signified by the banging of a gong and visually suggested by the traditional Chinese vase that Buck buys him as a gift. Palance's character represents a troubled white masculinity torn not only between personal and professional loyalty but also between "feminine" (artist) and "masculine" (assassin) vocations. The presence of a supermasculine Jamaican gang boss, played by the blaxploitation icon Richard Roundtree (of *Shaft* fame), further tests his potency as a white action hero in the Eastwood or Bronson mold. Alienated in both the ruthless Mafia world and a crumbling domestic space (where he returns one evening to find his girlfriend in bed with his best friend and racing partner), Buck's only source of solace seems to lie in his spiritual bond with Wong. In the film's final scene, set in an art gallery, Jack Palance gently pats Philip Ahn's hand in appreciation of the latter's paternal love and care. This close-up image of the two men's joined hands is symbolic of those onscreen surrogate father-son relationships that Ahn had with a variety of white stars (including Rock Hudson, Frank Sinatra, and David Carradine) in the latter part of his career. Moreover, the unconventional New Hollywood star Palance pays respect to the exiting veteran actor, an equally unconventional emblem of Old Hollywood who provided numerous entryways into multicultural lifestyles and pacifist forms of masculinity for 1970s American male protagonists/audiences.

Philip Ahn and Asian American Identity

In a 1970 interview with Frank Chin, Philip Ahn was asked whether or not racial discrimination had affected him in any tangible way. After acknowledging the U.S. history of anti-Asian sentiments and exclusionary acts, the

Korean American actor concluded that he was not the victim of discrimination. He went on to explain that he was voted one of the twenty-four most popular students in his college years and was once told by a USC dean: "When you arrived on campus, there was this tremendous, big wall of prejudice, and...you just flew over that with the greatest ease."[20] Susan Ahn Cuddy also recalls her brother's charismatic personality: "When people recognized him, Philip thrilled them with his gracious...voice, signing autographs for them and encouraging them to buy war bonds. [I] marveled at the way Philip handled people."[21] These two accounts together paint a typical picture of the model minority member who has assimilated into and been accepted by white America on the merits of competence and confidence.

According to Robert G. Lee, the myth of Asian America as an ethnically assimilable model minority was constructed to contain "[t]hree specters [that] haunted Cold War America in the 1950s: the red menace of communism, the black menace of race mixing, and the white menace of homosexuality."[22] Although Ahn played a model minority prototype (a romancing federal agent) in *Daughter of Shanghai* as early as 1937, he embodied the icon of ethnic assimilation in several color-blind roles of the Cold War era, such as Dr. Lee, a surgeon, in *The Big Hangover* (1950); Mr. Ding, a small-town diner owner, in *The Way to the Gold* (1957); Dr. Fong, a psychiatrist, in *Shock Corridor* (1963); Mr. Emekona, a public prosecutor, in *Diamond Head* (1963); and an unnamed attorney general in the *Hawaii Five-O* pilot movie (September 20, 1968). Except for *The Big Hangover*, in which Ahn's character is unjustly evicted from his subleased apartment on racial grounds, there is no narrative imperative to cast an Asian/minority actor in these parts. Each role features Ahn as either a debonair professional of high social standing or an ordinary next-door neighbor/family man who effortlessly fits in the predominantly white environment and carries no external markers of foreignness. In these films, the Asian American actor could simply be himself without donning an Oriental mask to hide his Americanness.

From the perspective of Asian America, Philip Ahn's political positioning is contradictory and precarious. In the aforementioned 1970 interview, the Korean American actor denies the effect of institutional racism on his life, thus reinforcing the myth of the model minority—a political imperative of Cold War America. Although not a partisan member of either the Democrat or Republican Party,[23] Ahn was a patriotic American who consistently supported U.S. wars and national policies. At the age of fourteen, he received a Boy Scout Award for selling Liberty Bonds from the U.S. Treasury. During World War II, Ahn eagerly participated in anti-Japanese propaganda efforts and volunteered for the U.S. Army at the age of forty. At the Fort Benning

Infantry School in Georgia, he received training as an officer's candidate, as well as directed radio shows and amateur theatrical productions for military personnel. In 1968, he became the first Asian American USO performer to entertain the troops (both American and Korean) in Vietnam.

However, the Korean American's affirmation of conservative values cannot be fully grasped within the U.S. domestic context alone. As David L. Eng points out, diasporas can be both "sites of resistance to the nation-state" and "unusually conservative sites of nationalism."[24] As a descendant of a colonial diaspora, his allegiance to America during World War II was inversely an expression of support for Korean independence and resistance to the Japanese colonial state. Like fellow Korean American Christians, Philip Ahn readily accepted American ideals and values as a means to liberate his parental homeland from brutal colonial oppression. Ironically, he, like many other Koreans at home and overseas, was blind to the subtle transition of hegemony from Japanese colonialism to American neocolonialism in the process of national division (1945), U.S. military occupation (1945–1948), civil war (1950–1953), rehabilitation (1953–1960), and compressed modernization under military regimes (1961–1987). Disconnected from the communist northern half of Korea (where his family came from), the diasporic actor maintained political ties to the successive dictatorial southern regimes of Syngman Rhee (1948–1960) and Park Chung Hee (1961–1979) backed by the U.S. military and government. Ahn passed away before the advent of dramatic shifts in South Korean politics—Park Chung Hee's assassination in 1979, the Kwangju Massacre of 1980, the subsequent surge of anti-Americanism,[25] the massive prodemocratic movements of the 1980s, the restoration of a civil government in 1993, and the historic summit meeting of the two Koreas in 2000.

Occupying an interstitial space between two nations and cultures, Philip Ahn was an unstable and malleable subject whose on- and offscreen identities were constantly reshaped by both U.S. domestic and international politics. He was born in 1905, the same year his familial homeland lost its diplomatic sovereignty and came under the protectorate rule of Japan with the acquiescence of the United States, which had forfeited its interests in Korea in exchange for a monopoly in the Philippines. The first big wave of Korean immigration to the United States had just begun two years before he was born, with 7,226 Korean laborers being admitted to Hawaii until 1905. In the wake of Japan's annexation of Korea in 1910, Koreans were counted as Japanese nationals and subject to the Gentlemen's Agreement of 1907 whereby the Japanese government ceased issuing passports to laborers whose destinations were the United States, Canada, Mexico, and the territory of

Hawaii. However, the agreement benefited Koreans who were already in America by protecting their privilege to bring in their wives and fiancées from the homeland.[26] Accordingly, the entry of approximately 1,100 Korean "picture brides" was permitted between 1910 and 1924. The Immigration Act of 1924 eventually halted both Japanese and Korean immigration.

Despite this shared fate of exclusion, the relationship between Japanese and Korean immigrants was antagonistic because of Japanese colonial rule in Korea. In 1922, the Japanese Government-General of Korea reported, "Since 1910, all the Koreans in the United States were against the Japanese and they were united with the Chinese for business and labor contracts. This economic motive also undoubtedly played an important role in accelerating mutual dislike."[27] The increasingly strong economic and political alliances between Korean and Chinese immigrants during the 1930s (as Japanese military aggression in Chinese territories began) formed a backdrop for the friendship between Philip Ahn and Anna May Wong, who shared a passion for acting and a hatred for Japanese imperial domination in Asia. Under the influence of his Chinese American friend, Ahn successfully launched his Hollywood career in the mid-1930s and played a series of sympathetic Chinese heroes or sidekicks in Oriental detective films and China epics. During World War II, his screen persona dramatically shifted in response to the exploding demands for cross-ethnic performers to play Japanese "heavies" or collaborators in place of interned Japanese American actors. Only five years after the Japanese surrender ending World War II, the Korean War (1950–1953) occurred and modified the identity of "yellow peril" enemies to include Chinese and North Korean communists.

As a descendant of the pre-division Korean diaspora and as a northern dialect speaker, Ahn embodied an ambivalent identity (neither/both ally nor/and enemy), shuttling between two extreme poles—villainous foes and tragic victims—in the Korean War genre. In the last two decades of his career, Ahn played a composite of contradictory roles on the big and small screens— a model minority member, a psychotic murderer, an Oriental servant, a kung fu guru, a coolie Chinaman, a Chinese merchant, a *tong* warrior, a "gook" peasant, a Burmese freedom fighter, a South Korean diplomat, etc. The actor's schizophrenic oscillation between Oriental and Asian American parts is symptomatic of the "contradiction between the continuing reproduction of racial difference and the process of ethnic assimilation" in Cold War-era U.S. race formation.[28] Despite the legal incorporation of Asians into U.S. citizenry, achieved in principle once the racial bar to immigration and naturalization was lifted with the passage of the 1952 McCarran-Walter Act, the culturally embedded imagery of exotic Orientals continued to permeate

American films and television programs, such as *Sayonara* (1957), *The World of Suzie Wong* (1960), *My Geisha* (1962), *Adventures in Paradise* (1959–1962), *I Spy* (1965–1968), *Kung Fu*, and *M*A*S*H* (1972–1983).

Lisa Lowe points out an underlying heterogeneity in "the genealogy of the racialization of Asian Americans. the Chinese as alien noncitizen, the American citizen of Japanese descent as racial enemy, and the American citizen of Filipino descent as simultaneously immigrant and colonized national."[29] It is notable that the American citizen of Korean descent (Philip Ahn's position) is missing in Lowe's list, although she includes Korean as one of four major groups of pre-1965 Asian Americans in the prior paragraph.[30] During World War II, the U.S. government officially classified Koreans—who were then Japanese colonial subjects—as "enemy aliens," and correspondingly the American public seemed unsure about their loyalty, as reflected in *China Sky* (1945), in which Ahn's collaborationist Dr. Kim sabotages the efforts of his American superiors. During the Cold War, the Korean identity was split between racial enemy (North Korean) and neocolonized ally (South Korean). During and after the 1992 Los Angeles Riots, Koreans were perceived as both honorary whites possessing wealth and property (by black America) and immigrant aliens ineligible for equal state protection (by white America). Korean identity within the American mainstream has persistently fluctuated, becoming ever more fractured and indefinable. This explains why Koreans have been notably underrepresented in Hollywood cinema despite its ongoing fascination for the Orient and why Philip Ahn was destined to a career of cross-ethnic performances.

In retrospect, Ahn's life comprised a series of incompletes: his stardom, his alleged romance with Anna May Wong, his many ambitions to become involved in the Korean film industry, his on- and offscreen paternalism, and his dream to make a film about his father. It was a life in process, in a perpetual status of becoming. Having been labeled Korean (or mislabeled Chinese) for the better part of his life, Ahn acquired the Asian American identity in old age. As Sheng-mei Ma notes, "The term *Asian American*, inspired by the civil rights movement, was forged in the 1960s to empower heretofore disparate Asian American communities."[31] The Asian American movement gained momentum in the 1970s with the publication of such seminal texts as *Aiiieeeee! An Anthology of Asian American Writers* (1974) and Maxine Hong Kingston's *The Woman Warrior* (1976), not to mention the creation of media collectives and activist groups like Visual Communications (Los Angeles) and Asian CineVision (New York City).

In a 1973 interview, Philip Ahn expressed concern about the future of Asian Americans in Hollywood:

What worries me most is the acute shortage of young Oriental actors in Hollywood. We've been through the black cycle, but not the Oriental cycle. Except for *Kung Fu* there's little opportunity right now. No training ground. We're starting to get old.... Where are the young people to replace us?[32]

He translated his concern about the next generation of Asian American actors into action by participating in protests against the industry's discriminatory casting of minorities. In a collective statement entitled "We Are Not All Alike" and printed in *Daily Variety* on October 29, 1976, Philip Ahn and ninety other actors of Asian ancestry (including Rosalind Chao, Benson Fong, James Hong, Mako, Pat Morita, Soon-Tek Oh, Beulah Quo, George Takei, and Victor Sen Yung) proclaimed:

> The motion picture and television industry must catch up with times in the portrayal of Asian/Pacific Americans on the screen. Since our people participate in aspects of the mainstream of American life, we should also be considered and cast in such roles as lawyers, doctors, and next-door neighbors. In addition to the above limitation of our opportunities, we protest the current discriminatory casting practice of separating Asian/Pacific American actors into our particular ancestral origins and confining us to roles of such origins, i.e. Japanese for Japanese, Chinese for Chinese, etc.

It is intriguing that Ahn and his company not only demanded better roles but also protested "correct casting" in which Asian American actors were confined to playing roles corresponding to their own ethnicity. According to Lee Grant's report in *Los Angeles Times* on November 1, 1976, the Asian American protest group singled out Universal Studios as an unfair employer:

> *Midway* and the current shooting of *MacArthur*, both Universal productions, were cited as instances where a studio hires only Japanese actors to play the roles of Japanese. This leaves out, the group contends, the large number of Chinese, Korean, Filipino and other Asian actors who could assume such roles. "There are no actual physical differences in our appearance," said Philip Ahn.... The studio, they charge, is under pressure from distributors in the large and lucrative Japanese market to use only Japanese-surnamed actors.[33]

Here, Ahn was speaking for younger Asian American actors whose opportunities for diverse roles had ironically become more limited than those of his generation because of New Hollywood's ever-increasing dependency on the global market. As a seasoned cross-ethnic performer who had portrayed Japanese, Chinese, Korean, East Indian, Vietnamese, Burmese, Eskimo, and Hawaiian characters, the veteran actor lent his voice to advance the causes of the new generation.

Like Philip Ahn's life, this book is an incomplete project or, more accurately, the mere beginning of a long road that I hope will be explored by future scholars. Ahn's career could and should be located in the broader legacy of a group of actors whom I term the "Asian American Rat Pack." Like their more famous counterparts (Joey Bishop, Sammy Davis, Jr., Peter Lawford, Dean Martin, and Frank Sinatra), Philip Ahn, Benson Fong, Richard Loo, Keye Luke, and Victor Sen Yung performed together in numerous film and television productions from the classical studio system era to the rise of New Hollywood. Ahn's identity could also be framed in comparison with other actors of the Korean diaspora—in particular, Kim Yŏm, the "Emperor of Shanghai Movies" and the son of Kim P'il-sun, who was involved in the Korean independence movement and who regarded An Ch'ang-ho as a brother. As one of only nine Asian American stars on the Hollywood Walk of Fame (along with Sessue Hayakawa, Bruce Lee, Keye Luke, Mako, Pat Morita, Sabu, George Takei, and Anna May Wong), Ahn also deserves to be recognized as a pioneer who paved the path for the next generation of Asian American actors. Sixty-seven years after Philip Ahn's FBI agent proposed to Anna May Wong's quasi-detective in *Daughter of Shanghai*, John Cho's love-struck banker planted a passionate kiss on Paula Garcés's next-door dream girl in *Harold and Kumar Go to White Castle* (2004), a recent, potentially paradigm-shifting buddy flick starring two racial minorities. The cross-generational, ethnic linkage between the two Korean American romantic leads (Ahn and Cho) should not be missed by critics and scholars specializing in Asian images in Hollywood cinema. If I might invoke the words of Master Kan in *Kung Fu*, "There is a first for everything." In fulfilling that path-breaking role, Ahn and his "Asian American Rat Pack" cohorts were the progenitors of such contemporary screen icons as Joan Chen, Daniel Dae Kim, Jacqueline Kim, Lucy Liu, John Lone, Sandra Oh, and Grace Park.

Philip Ahn was a minor character actor who made major contributions to the construction of Asian images in Hollywood and American television from the 1930s to the 1970s. Although Ahn never achieved the status of stardom in a conventional sense, many American cult fans and critics still fondly remember him as Charlie Chan's son-in-law, Anna May Wong's romantic lead, and the head of the Shaolin Temple. In South Korea, Ahn (as the first Korean in Hollywood) is a hazily remembered legend whose name and familial affiliation (if not the specifics of his career) are known to many people. His case demonstrates the need to expand and revise traditional conceptions of stardom to properly address the rich tradition of ethnic performers who were barred from leading roles and top billings, not because they lacked talent but because of the historically specific racial attitudes of the industry and society.

At the time of this writing, the centennial of Philip Ahn's birth (on March 29, 1905) is six months past. In celebrating the 100th birthday of an outstanding Hollywood Asian, I would like to invoke Rudolf Arnheim's manifesto in praise of character actors: "Let us dethrone the studios' values and take a look around outside, and we will be astonished to see that in this, our real world, there aren't any leading men to be seen, only characters!"[34]

NOTES

INTRODUCTION

1. It is difficult to pinpoint the exact number of films and television programs in which Ahn appeared because many of his bit parts are uncredited. Most newspaper articles report the number of roles as between 200 and 300. The statistics can also vary depending on whether individual episodes of *Kung Fu* (three seasons) are counted separately. My filmography and television credits list 113 films (including TV movies) and 82 television programs (counting *Kung Fu* just as one entry).

2. Richard R. Lingeman, *Don't You Know There's a War On? The American Home Front, 1941–1945* (New York: Nation Books, 2003), 181.

3. Peter C. Rollins, ed., *The Columbia Companion to American History on Film* (New York: Columbia University Press, 2003), 226.

4. Robert G. Lee, *Orientals: Asian Americans in Popular Culture* (Philadelphia: Temple University Press, 1999), 8–14.

5. Philip Ahn was instrumental in procuring employment for a handful of Korean American "waivers" (nonunion actors) in studio-era films. He used his friendship with director Lewis Milestone in getting Keye Chang, a pastor in the L.A. Korean Methodist Church where Ahn's mother was a member, hired as a supporting cast member in *The Purple Heart* (1944). In 1945, he helped Alfred Song, then a USC law student, land a bit part as a Japanese "heavy" in *Betrayal from the East*. Ahn's two younger brothers, Philson and Ralph, enjoyed occasional acting jobs in Hollywood thanks to their family connection. Philip also assisted Bessie Loo, the Chinese American casting agent and former wife of actor Richard Loo, in recruiting Korean American bit actors in World War II films.

6. See Darrell Y. Hamamoto, *Monitored Peril: Asian Americans and the Politics of TV Representation* (Minneapolis: University of Minnesota Press, 1994), 23–26.

7. See Lee, *Orientals*, 215–22.

8. Helen Lee, "A Peculiar Sensation: A Personal Genealogy of Korean American Women's Cinema," in *Screening Asian Americans*, ed. Peter X. Feng, 133–55 (New Brunswick, NJ: Rutgers University Press, 2002).

9. Shilpa Davé, LeiLani Nishime, and Tasha G. Oren, eds., *East Main Street: Asian American Popular Culture* (New York: New York University Press, 2005), 3.

10. Feng, *Screening Asian Americans*, 10.

11. Eugene Franklin Wong, *On Visual Media Racism: Asians in American Motion Pictures* (New York: Arno Press, 1978), 11–14.

12. Lisa Lowe, *Immigrant Acts: On Asian American Cultural Politics* (Durham, NC: Duke University Press, 1996), 9. Author's emphasis.

13. Ella Shohat and Robert Stam, *Unthinking Eurocentrism: Multiculturalism and the Media* (London: Routledge, 1994), 182.

14. Jacqueline Stewart, "Negroes Laughing at Themselves? Black Spectatorship and the Performance of Urban Modernity," *Critical Inquiry* 29, no. 4 (Summer 2003) 674.

15. Ibid., 653.

16. Darrell Y. Hamamoto and Sandra Liu, eds., *Countervisions: Asian American Film Criticism* (Philadelphia: Temple University Press, 2000), 23–24.

17. Feng, *Screening Asian Americans*, 5.

18. John Flaus, "Thanks for Your Heart, Bart," *Continuum* 5, no. 2 (1992): 207.

19. As an admirer of Philip Ahn, director Robert Florey cast the actor in a number of productions calling for dynamic Asian roles—from a Chinese American FBI agent in *Daughter of Shanghai* (1937) and a Vietnamese revolutionary in *Rogues' Regiment* (1948) to later appearances in such television series as *Four Star Playhouse* ("Stuffed Shirt," January 13, 1955; "Wall of Bamboo," April 19, 1959), *Checkmate* ("Face in the Window," October 22, 1960), *Adventures in Paradise* ("One Little Pearl," November 28, 1960), and *Hong Kong* ("Lady Godiva," February 8, 1961).

20. *The Life and Death of the Hollywood Kid* was adapted into a film of the same title in 1994 by Korean New Wave director Chŏng Chi-yŏng.

21. Neil Okrent, "Right Place, Wong Time," *Los Angeles Magazine* (May 1990): 84+.

22. James S. Moy, *Marginal Sights: Staging the Chinese in America* (Iowa City: University of Iowa Press, 1993), 91.

CHAPTER 1

1. Throughout this chapter (as well as the rest of the book), Korean names and words are romanized using the transliteration system known as McCune-Reischauer, which has widely been adopted in English-language academic writings related to Korea. Exceptions are such names as Ahn Junghyo, Syngman Rhee, and Park Chung Hee, whose romanization has frequently appeared in the English-language media. Also note that, with few exceptions (such as Syngman Rhee), the surname (for example, Pak) precedes the two-syllable first name (Chung-hun) according to the order in the original language.

2. *Die Another Day* generated fierce protests in South Korea where hundreds of picketers crowded theaters and thousands of netizens inundated cyberspace discussion boards with critical invectives against the film as well as Rick Yune and Will Yun Lee who played North Korean villains. Korean boycotters voiced criticisms against the film's representation of North Korea as a high-tech rogue state and its portrayal of South Korea as a provincial backdrop under U.S. military control. Anti-007 boycotts intensified as part of a general anti-American movement triggered by the acquittal of two U.S. soldiers whose armored vehicle accidentally ran over and killed two Korean schoolgirls in June 2002.

3. Undated Paramount press kit (presumed to have been written in 1943), Philip Ahn clippings file, Margaret Herrick Library (MHL), Academy of Motion Picture Arts and Sciences (AMPAS), Beverly Hills, CA.

4. I consulted the following English-language sources on the life of Tosan An Ch'ang-ho: John Cha, *Willow Tree Shade: The Susan Ahn Cuddy Story* (Seoul: Korean American Heritage Foundation, 2002); Moon Hyung June, "The Korean Immigrants in America: The Quest for Identity in the Formative Years, 1903–1918" (PhD diss., University of Nevada, 1976); Jacqueline Pak, "Korea's Moses: An Ch'angho and the Colonial Diaspora," (lecture, UCLA, November 9, 2000); "*Dosan: Past, Present and Future*," Symposium catalogue (Los Angeles: Patriot Ahn Chang-ho Memorial Foundation/Hung Sa Dahn North America, 2001).

5. The State Department recognized the Korean National Association as the representative of overseas Koreans in 1913, discrediting Japan's claim that Koreans in America were Japanese imperial subjects. Cha, *Willow Tree Shade*, 50.

6. Hŭngsadan was conceived as a model for Korean democracy, as well as a revolutionary training organization that would be responsible for developing future leadership for postliberation Korea.

7. According to the 1920 U.S. Census, six Korean Americans born on the U.S. mainland (Peter Lee, Marie Cho, Wm H. Lee, Howard Oh, Sunda Hur, and Law Sun Paik) were of Philip Ahn's age, and six others (Frank Lee, Helen Cho, Muriel Jaisohn, Lilly Lee, Katherine Young, and Theodore Mrenkim) were one to seven years older than he was. The first Hawaii-born Korean American is Alice Hyun, daughter of Reverend Soon Hyun and Maria Lee Hyun, who was born on May 8, 1903 in the Koolau district of Oahu. I am grateful to Kenneth Klein and Duk Hee Lee Murabayashi for sharing this information with me.

8. Philip gave club members ballroom dancing lessons and arranged many coeducational activities in accordance with his father's educational philosophy. He continued to be active in community affairs after becoming a Hollywood actor. In 1940, Philip Ahn organized a group of middle-school aged Korean American boys and supervised their athletic and social activities. In 1941, he helped the KNA in organizing a rally in support of Korean independence and invited the Chinese Counsel General of Los Angeles as a speaker. In 1942, he led the Korean group in a multiethnic war bond drive held at the L.A. Shrine Auditorium and gave a speech about Korean struggles against the Japanese Empire. From 1948 to 1951, Ahn directed annual variety shows for the Korean community on behalf of the Korean Christian Youth Fellowship. Thanks to Ralph Ahn for providing this information through personal correspondence.

9. Susan Ahn Cuddy, personal interview, July 15, 2001, Northridge, CA.

10. Okrent, "Right Place, Wong Time," 84+.

11. Personal interview, March 31, 2005, Chicago. Ironically, except for Philson, who married a Korean American pharmacist, the remaining Ahn siblings (Susan, Soorah, and Ralph) intermarried. Yi Hae-ryŏn did not speak to the eldest daughter Susan for five years after her 1947 marriage to an Irish American naval officer, Francis X. Cuddy.

12. Personal correspondence, August 22, 2005.

13. The Ahn family does not confirm nor refute Philip's alleged homosexuality, simply commenting that "there is no way of knowing now." However, Ralph recalls that his older brother wanted to get married and met several Korean women through matchmakers during their visit to South Korea in 1963. Personal interview, August 18, 2003, Los Angeles.

14. "Philip Ahn News," *NewsCenter 4*, March 6, 1978. Susan Ahn Cuddy kindly provided the news tape for my research.

15. Philip Ahn Cuddy, "Philip Ahn: Born in America," Philip Ahn Admiration Society Web site, 1996. http://www.philipahn.com.

16. For example, historian Bruce Cumings writes, "Koreans in Los Angeles were particularly proud of Philip Ahn, the son of An Chang-ho, who (in a nice turn of the screw) became a millionaire playing evil Japanese officers in Hollywood movies." Bruce Cumings, *Korea's Place in the Sun: A Modern History* (New York: W.W. Norton & Co., 1997), 440.

17. Thomas Doherty, *Projections of War: Hollywood, American Culture, and World War II* (New York: Columbia University Press, 1993), 144.

18. Interview with Chinese American author Frank Chin in 1970, in K. W. Lee, "Man of The House: The Many Roles of Philip Ahn, the Path-Breaking Hollywood Actor and Son of the Famed Korean Independence Fighter," *KoreAm* 15, no. 4 (April 2004): 50.

19. Among these producers was Cecil B. DeMille, who wrote a letter to the Los Angeles Local Draft Board on January 5, 1943:

> We are producing a navy motion picture entitled *The Story of Dr. Wassell*. . . .
> We have selected Mr. Ahn for an important role . . . which . . . has been definitely fitted to Mr. Ahn's abilities and any substitution . . . might well be detrimental to the production.
>
>   Philip Ahn correspondence file, Ahn
>   Family Collection (AFC), Northridge, CA.

20. Kim Hak-su, *Sŭkrin pakkŭi han'guk yŏnghwasa* [Offscreen Korean Film History] (Seoul: Inmul kwa sasang, 2002), 164.

21. Philip Ahn clippings file, MHL, AMPAS.

22. Ahn Junghyo, *Hŏlliudŭ k'idŭ ŭi saengae* [*The Life and Death of the Hollywood Kid*] (Seoul: Minjok kwa munhwasa, 1992), 62–63. Translation is mine. Note that this passage contains incorrect information: Philip Ahn did not appear in *The Teahouse of the August Moon*.

23. "Robi aesŏ [In the Lobby]", *Chosŏn Ilbo* [Chosun Daily], March 14, 1959.

24. Yi Pyŏng-il, "A Talk between Mr. Philip Ahn and Mr. Lee Byong Il," *Kukje yŏnghwa* [International Film] (June 1959): 30.

25. Personal interview, August 18, 2003.

26. Richard Loo clippings file, MHL, AMPAS.

27. Philip Ahn correspondence file, Ahn Family Collection (AFC).

28. Ibid.

29. Cha, *Willow Tree Shade*, 264–65.

30. Personal interview, August 18, 2003.

31. Philip Ahn correspondence file, AFC.

32. Yi Pyŏng-il, "A Talk between Mr. Philip Ahn," 30.

33. Walter Briggs, "Actor Is a Villain at Home, a Hero in Korea," *New York Herald Tribune*, April 26, 1959: Sec. 4: 2.

34. Paul M. Edwards, *A Guide to Films on the Korean War* (Westport, CT: Greenwood Press, 1997), 35.

35. Philip Ahn correspondence file, AFC.

36. Ibid.

37. Ibid.

38. Cuddy, "Philip Ahn: Born in America."

39. Philip Ahn correspondence file, AFC.

40. John Ringo Graham, "Phil Ahn: Frustrated Success," *San Fernando Valley and Que Magazine* (January 1970): 6A.

41. Hyangjin Lee, *Contemporary Korean Cinema: Identity, Culture, Politics* (Manchester: Manchester University Press, 2000), 23.

42. Ronald Takaki, *Strangers from a Different Shore: A History of Asian Americans* (New York: Penguin, 1989), 363–64.

43. The Korean Independence Army (KIA) was established in September 1940 as a military arm of the KPG, then located in Chunking. With the Japanese attack of Pearl Harbor, the KIA declared war against Japan and cooperated with the Office of Strategic Services (OSS) in drafting secret guerrilla plans. They actively helped drafted Korean soldiers escape the Japanese Army on Chinese fronts. They also fought with the Allies on the Burma and India fronts.

44. John Shirota, "Authentic Wisdom in a Shaolin Temple," *Fighting Stars* (December 1973). 25, 27.

45. Judy Chu, "Anna May Wong," in *Counterpoint: Perspectives on Asian America*, ed. Emma Gee, 288 (Los Angeles: University of California Press, 1976).

46. Philip Ahn correspondence file, AFC.

47. Frank Chin, "Kung Fu Is Unfair to Chinese," *New York Times* (March 24, 1974): 137.

48. Quoted in the Philip Ahn Admiration Society Web site.

49. Shohat and Stam, *Unthinking Eurocentrism*, 182.

CHAPTER 2

1. See Anne Anlin Cheng, *The Melancholy of Race* (Oxford: Oxford University Press, 2000), 25–26.

2. David L. Eng, *Racial Castration: Managing Masculinity in Asian America* (Durham, NC: Duke University Press, 2001), 19.

3. Hamamoto and Liu, eds., *Countervisions*, 45–49.

4. Stuart Hall, "Encoding/Decoding," in *Culture, Media, Language*, eds. Stuart Hall, Dorothy Hobson, Andy Lowe, and Paul Wills, 128–38 (London: Hutchinson, 1980).

5. Manthia Diawara, "Black Spectatorship: Problems of Identification and Resistance," *Screen* 29, no. 4 (1988): 75–76.

6. bell hooks, "The Oppositional Gaze: Black Female Spectators," in *Black American Cinema*, ed. Manthia Diawara, 300 (New York: Routledge, 1993).

7. Peter X. Feng, "In Search of Asian American Cinema," *Cineaste* 21, nos. 1–2 (Winter–Spring 1995): 32.

8. Here I do not mean to lump together African American performers from different familial, religious, and social backgrounds. Sidney Poitier (although born in Miami) grew up on Cat Island in the Bahamas before coming to the United States as a teenager. Whoopi Goldberg (born Caryn Johnson in New York City) was reared as Catholic and took her last name from the Jewish side of her family.

9. Lowe, *Immigrant Acts*, 7.

10. Joan Riviere, "Womanliness as a Masquerade," in *Formations of Fantasy*, eds. Victor Burgin, James Donald, and Cora Kaplan, 38 (New York: Methuen, 1986).

11. Ibid., 41.

12. Mary Ann Doane, "Film and the Masquerade: Theorizing the Female Spectator," in *Femmes Fatales: Feminism, Film Theory, Psychoanalysis, ed. Mary Ann Doane*, 28 (New York: Routledge, 1991).

13. Ibid., 31–32.

14. Ibid., 32.

15. Judith Butler, *Gender Trouble: Feminism and the Subversion of Identity* (New York: Routledge, 1990), 33.

16. Ibid.,137. Author's emphasis.

17. Valerie Smith, "Reading the Intersection of Race and Gender in Narratives of Passing," *Diacritics* (Summer–Fall 1994): 53.

18. Michael Rogin, *Blackface, White Noise: Jewish Immigrants in the Hollywood Melting Pot* (Berkeley: University of California Press, 1996), 35.

19. Interview with Frank Chin, *KoreAm*, 44.

20. Although *A Scream in the Night* was produced in 1935, it was not released until 1943. In press interviews, Philip Ahn always identified Paramount's *Anything Goes* (1936), not *A Scream in the Night*, as his debut film.

21. Along with his brother Philip, Ralph played bit parts in several films including *Battle Circus* (1953) and *Confessions of an Opium Eater* (1962). His more recent television appearances include *E.R.* ("Rites of Spring"; April 29, 1999) and *The Shield* ("Carnivores"; May 21, 2002).

22. Personal interview, August 18, 2003, Los Angeles.

23. Amy Robinson, "It Takes One to Know One: Passing and Communities of Common Interests," *Critical Inquiry* 20, no. 4 (Summer 1994): 716, 736.

24. "International Incidents," *New York Times*, October 5, 1941: X5.

25. Although the network had doubts about casting an untested standup comedian in a dramatic lead role, Bill Cosby proved his talent by receiving three consecutive Emmys as Best Male Actor in a Dramatic Television series between 1965 and 1968. J. Fred MacDonald praises Cosby's role as a "real, mature human character—able to feel and express emotions historically forbidden black characters in mainstream entertainment media. In an early episode, Cosby actually kissed a Japanese woman, a revolutionary act that was well beyond the perimeters established for blacks in television." J. Fred MacDonald, *Blacks and White TV: Afro-Americans in Television since 1948* (Chicago: Nelson-Hall Publishers, 1983), 110–11.

26. As a term coined by French Marxist philosopher Louis Althusser, *interpellation* or hailing refers to the process by which ideology addresses the individual. Althusser uses an example of the policeman hailing, "Hey, you there!" When at least one individual turns around and answers that call, he or she becomes a subject in relation to ideology. For an elaboration on this concept, see Louis Althusser, "Ideology and Ideological Status Apparatuses" (1969), in *Lenin and Philosophy and Other Essays by Louis Althusser*, trans. Ben Brewster, 173–77 (New York: Monthly Review Press, 1971).

27. Mary Beth Haralovich, "I Spy's 'Living Postcards': The Geo-Politics of Civil Rights," in *Television, History, and American Culture: Feminist Critical Essays*, eds. Mary Beth Haralovich and Lauren Rabinovitz, 102 (Durham, NC: Duke University Press, 1999).

28. Herman Gray, "Remembering Civil Rights: Television, Memory, and the 1960s," in *The Revolution Wasn't Televised: Sixties Television and Social Conflict*, eds. Lynn Spigel and Michael Curtin, 353 (New York: Routledge, 1997).

29. In the "Warlord" episode (February 1, 1967) of *I Spy's* third season, the anachronistic Chinese warlord, a rip-off of General Yen in Frank Capra's *The Bitter Tea*

of General Yen (1932), was played by Robert Culp in yellowface, thus excluding Orientals in both representation and performance.

30. Rogin, *Blackface, White Noise*, 8.

31. In addition to the already mentioned *Dr. No* (1962) reference, there is a jibe at the bowler hat-wielding Oddjob of *Goldfinger* (1964).

CHAPTER 3

1. Gina Marchetti, Sumiko Higashi, and Robert G. Lee are among the commentators on Cecil B. DeMille's *The Cheat*. Both Marchetti and Lee have also written on *Broken Blossoms*. Nick Browne and Marchetti separately investigate *Madame Butterfly*, starring Mary Pickford. See Browne, "The Undoing of the Other Woman: Madame Butterfly in the Discourse of American Orientalism," in *The Birth of Whiteness: Race and the Emergence of U.S. Cinema*, ed. Daniel Bernardi, 226–56 (New Brunswick, NJ: Rutgers University Press, 1996); Sumiko Higashi, "Ethnicity, Class, and Gender in Film: DeMille's *The Cheat*," in *Unspeakable Images: Ethnicity and the American Cinema*, ed. Lester D Friedman, 112–39 (Urbana: University of Illinois Press, 1991); Lee, *Orientals*; and Gina Marchetti, *Romance and the "Yellow Peril": Race, Sex, and Discursive Strategies in Hollywood Fiction* (Berkeley: University of California Press, 1993).

2. See Garnett Weston, *The Honor Bright* (story), April 17, 1937. *Daughter of Shanghai*, Paramount script files, MHL, AMPAS.

3. Paramount pressbook, 1937, MHL, AMPAS.

4. *Daughter of Shanghai*, Paramount script files.

5. While Kim Lee is an official representative of law enforcement, Quan Lin is a voluntary investigator whose intention is to hand over his collection of evidence to immigration authorities.

6. Joseph I. Breen, head of the Production Code Administration (PCA) at the time of the release of the film, repeatedly urged Paramount to acquire Chinese government officials' approval of the script to confirm its presentability to Chinese audiences. His note to John Hammell of Paramount, dated September 16, 1937, states, "It is our understanding that you have assured yourselves that there will be no objection to this picture by the Chinese government or people." *Daughter of Shanghai*, PCA files, MHL, AMPAS.

7. Wong, *On Visual Media Racism*, 107–8.

8. Originally valid for ten years, the Chinese Exclusion Act was extended twice, in 1892 and 1902, and made permanent in 1904. Admission of the exempt class (teachers, students, merchants, diplomats, and travelers) was permitted despite the exclusion of Chinese laborers. The Gentlemen's Agreement of 1907 limited Japanese immigration to nonlaborers and families of those who had been already admitted to the United States. The 1917 Asiatic Barred Zone Act denied entry to people from India, Southeast Asia, and the Pacific islands. The 1934 Tydings-McDuffie Act reduced immigration from the Philippines—the only exempt Asian nation—to fifty persons per year. For additional information on anti-Asiatic exclusion acts, see Bill Ong Hing, *Making and Remaking Asian America through Immigration Policy, 1850–1990* (Stanford, CA: Stanford University Press, 1993) and Hyung-chan Kim, ed., *Asian Americans and Congress: A Documentary History* (Westport, CT: Greenwood Press, 1996).

9. Norman K Denzin, *The Cinematic Society: The Voyeur's Gaze* (London: SAGE, 1995), 89.

10. Wong, *On Visual Media Racism*, 136–37.

11. Ibid., 136.

12. Warren I. Cohen, "American Perception of China," in *Dragon and Eagle: United States-China Relations: Past and Future*, eds. Michel Oksenberg and Robert B. Oxnam, 55 (New York: Basic Books, 1978).

13. *Daughter of Shanghai* was produced between September 20 and October 14, 1937 and released on December 17. A full-scale war between China and Japan began in July of that year. On December 13, 1937, Japanese forces entered Republic-era China's capital Nanking (Nanjing) and raped at least 20,000 women and massacred some 140,000 Chinese civilians and soldiers during a seven-week period. See John S. Bowman, *Columbia Chronologies of Asian History and Culture* (New York: Columbia University Press, 2000), 66.

14. This character was based on the real-life San Francisco surgeon, Dr. Margaret Jessie Chung. For more information on Dr. Chung, see Judy Tzu-Chun Wu, *Doctor Mom Chung of the Fair-Haired Bastards: The Life of a Wartime Celebrity* (Berkeley: University of California Press, 2005).

15. The United States offered a similar credit package of $20 million to China in April 1940. In the months following Japan's signing of the Tripartite Pact with Germany and Italy in September 1940, America's credit aid to China totaled $95 million. In May 1941, China became eligible for lend-lease. See Warren I. Cohen, *America's Response to China: A History of Sino-American Relations* (New York: Columbia University Press. 1990), 124.

16. *King of Chinatown*, Paramount script files.

17. The studio additionally confirmed the suitability of the script with its sales manager in Japan. *Island of Lost Men*, Paramount production files, MHL, AMPAS.

18. Brian Taves, "The B Film: Hollywood's Other Half," in *Grand Design: Hollywood as a Modern Business Enterprise 1930–1939*, ed. Tino Balio, 313 (New York: Charles Scribner's Sons and MacMillan Library Reference, 1993).

19. Admissions dropped precipitously from ninety million a week in 1930 to sixty million in 1932. See David A. Cook, *A History of Narrative Film*, 3rd ed. (New York: W.W. Norton & Co., 1996), 300.

20. Ibid., 301.

21. Taves, "The B Film," 314.

22. The Department of Justice filed *U.S. vs. Paramount Pictures, Inc., et al.* in 1938, accusing the eight major Hollywood studios of violating the Sherman Antitrust Act with illegal exhibition practices, such as block booking, blind bidding, forced sales of short subjects and newsreels, protection of studio theaters with clearance and zoning, and discriminatory film rental rates for independent exhibitors. Despite the studios' signing of the Consent Decree in 1940, which partially mended the aforementioned practices, the Department of Justice reopened the case in 1942, demanding the studios' complete divestiture of their theater chains. In 1948, the Supreme Court ordered the studio divestiture through the Paramount Decree, contributing to the demise of the studio system.

23. Taves, "The B Film," 314.

24. James Naremore, *More Than Night: Film Noir in Its Contexts* (Berkeley: University of California Press, 1998), 140.

25. Taves, "The B Film," 313.

26. In addition to his brief yet much-ballyhooed early avant-garde career consisting of four experimental shorts—*A Hollywood Extra, The Loves of Zero, Johann the Coffin*

Maker, and *Skyscraper Symphony*—between 1927 and 1929, Florey directed and/or co-wrote 65 feature films between 1926 and 1950, as well as 225 television films and episodes between 1951 to 1963. He also penned twelve French-language books on the history of Hollywood cinema and silent stars. See Brian Taves, *Robert Florey, The French Expressionist* (Metuchen, NJ: Scarecrow Press, 1987), 8, Appendix A, B, C.

27. After directing Wong in *Daughter of Shanghai* and *Dangerous to Know,* Florey was originally assigned to direct her next film *King of Chinatown,* which eventually went to Nick Grinde.

28. For a detailed discussion of the director's visual style, refer to Taves, *Robert Florey,* 30–49.

29. Ibid., 55.

30. Ken Hanke, *Charlie Chan at the Movies: History, Filmography, and Criticism* (Jefferson, NC: McFarland & Company, 1989), xii–xiii; and Charles P. Mitchell, *A Guide to Charlie Chan Films* (Westport, CT: Greenwood Press, 1999), xviii.

31. Mitchell, *A Guide to Charlie Chan Films,* 74.

32. Hanke, *Charlie Chan at the Movies,* 223.

33. Denzin, *The Cinematic Society,* 100.

34. Wong, *On Visual Media Racism,* 40.

35. In Charlie Chan films, Asian actors were often cast in supporting roles, such as Charlie Chan's sidekick sons (Number One Son Keye Luke, Number Two Son Victor Sen Yung, and Number Three Son Benson Fong, etc) or murder suspects.

36. Robert McIlwaine, "Third Beginning," *Modern Screen* (December 1937): 41.

37. Anna May Wong appeared in three German films directed by Richard Eichberg: *Schmutziges Geld* (a.k.a. *Song;* 1928), *Grosstadtschmetterling* (a.k.a. *City Butterfly;* 1929), and *Hai-Tang* (1930), the last of which was made into British and French versions (*The Road to Dishonour* and *L'amour maitre des choses*), both starring Wong. She starred in these British films: *Piccadilly* (1929), *Tiger Bay* (1934), *Chu Chin Chow* (1934), and *Java Head* (1934). In addition, she performed opposite Lawrence Olivier in the London stage production of *Circle of Chalk* (1929).

38. Okrent, "Right Place, Wong Time," 84+.

39. McIlwaine, "Third Beginning," 41.

40. Blaud Johaneson, "Movie to Star Her as Girl 'Chan'"; and Regina Crew "'Frosted Willow' Never Having Seen Homeland Before, Actress Has Many Varied Experience," undated, unidentified clippings, Anna May Wong clippings file, Billy Rose Collection (BRC), New York Public Library for the Performing Arts (NYPLPA).

41. McIlwaine, "Third Beginning," 41.

42. Taves, *Robert Florey,* 174.

43. Ibid., 205–6. I am grateful to Brian Taves for elaborating on this and other information about Robert Florey through personal correspondences.

44. Interview with Frank Chin, *KoreAm,* 44.

45. Ibid., 46.

46. Producer Harold Hurley and director Robert Florey were paid $10,000 and $7,500, respectively. The film's total production cost was $203,064. *Daughter of Shanghai,* Paramount production files.

47. James Robert Parish, *The Paramount Pretties* (Secaucus, NJ: Castle Book, 1972), 109.

48. Critic Carlos Clarens makes the convincing claim that *Daughter of Shanghai* was the only classical Hollywood film in which an Asian played an FBI agent. See Taves, *Robert Florey,* 206–207.

49. Hayakawa's love or desire for white women is either betrayed or remains unrequited in *The Typhoon* (1914), *The Cheat*, *The Temple of Dusk* (1918), *Forbidden Paths* (1917), *His Debt* (1919), and *Li Ting Lang* (1920). Hayakawa also marries Amerasian women played by white actresses (Florence Vidor and Vola Vale) in *The Bravest Way* (1918) and *A Heart in Pawn* (1919). Shigeta wins the love of Victoria Shaw and marries Carroll Baker in *The Crimson Kimono* (1959) and *Bridge to the Sun* (1961), respectively. He was also paired with Asian romantic interests in *Walk like a Dragon* (1961), *Flower Drum Song* (1961), and *Cry for Happy* (1961). For more information on Hayakawa's stardom, see Donald Kirihara, "The Accepted Idea Displaced: Stereotypes and Sessue Hayakawa," in *The Birth of Whiteness: Race and the Emergence of U.S. Cinema*, ed. Bernardi, 81–99; and Daisuke Miyao, *Sessue Hayakawa: Silent Cinema and Transnational Stardom* (Durham, NC: Duke University Press, forthcoming).

50. See Ella Shohat, "Gender and Culture of Empire: Toward a Feminist Ethnography of the Cinema," in *Visions of the East: Orientalism in Film*, eds. Matthew Bernstein and Gaylyn Studlar, 45 (New Brunswick, NJ: Rutgers University Press, 1997).

51. *Daughter of Shanghai*, Paramount script files.

52. Personal interview, August 18, 2003, Los Angeles.

53. Quoted in Richard Dyer, *Stars* (London: BFI, 1979), 13.

54. Paramount pressbook, 1937.

55. Paramount pressbook, 1939.

56. "Anna May Wong and Old School Chum in Budding Romance," unidentified newspaper clipping (October 20, 1937), Philip Ahn clippings file, AFC.

57. "Don Forbes' Hollywood Scrapbook" script, ibid.

58. Anthony B. Chan, *Perpetually Cool: The Many Lives of Anna May Wong (1905–1961)* (Lanham, MD: Scarecrow Press, 2003), 273.

59. Graham Russell Gao Hodges, *Anna May Wong: From Laundryman's Daughter to Hollywood Legend* (New York: Palgrave, 2004), 127.

60. Cynthia W. Liu, "When Dragon Ladies Die, Do They Come Back as Butterflies?: Re-Imagining Anna May Wong," in *Countervisions*, eds. Hamamoto and Liu, 31.

61. Hodges, *Anna May Wong*, 185.

62. *Miju sosik* [American News], March 1, 1978; *Miju Video*, undated clipping (presumed to have been published in 1991), Philip Ahn clippings file, AFC.

63. *Daughter of Shanghai*, PCA files.

64. *Daughter of Shanghai*, Paramount production files.

65. In Paramount's synopsis of *Anna May Wong Story*, dated July 26, 1937, the names of the major characters are Mei-mei and Duncan Lee (later changed to Lan Ying and Kim Lee). In this version, Mei-mei travels to New York, instead of Central America, to investigate the smuggling ring. *Daughter of Shanghai*, Paramount script files.

66. E. Ann Kaplan, *Looking for the Other: Feminism, Film, and the Imperial Gaze* (New York: Routledge, 1997), 67.

67. For a more elaborate discussion of the privileged male looking positions in classical Hollywood cinema, see Laura Mulvey's seminal 1975 essay, "Visual Pleasure and Narrative Cinema," in *Feminism and Film Theory*, ed. Constance Penley, 57–68 (New York: Routledge, 1988), and Mary Ann Doane's 1982 essay, "Film and Masquerade: Theorizing the Female Spectator," in *Femmes Fatales: Feminism, Film Theory, Psychoanalysis, ed.* Mary Ann Doane, 17–32 (New York: Routledge, 1991).

68. On November 4, 1939, Joseph Breen's office sent a memo to Paramount, suggesting that the dialogue be changed or deleted. Breen expressed his concern that this

comment on the lack of efficiency of the police might provoke local censors. *Daughter of Shanghai*, PCA files.

69. Although Lan Ying's self-sufficient action can be defined as progressive from a Western feminist viewpoint, her behavior nevertheless coincides with Confucian conceptions of filial duty, insofar as sons or daughters are expected to avenge the death of their parents—a recurrent theme of kung fu cinema.

70. Anna May Wong clippings file, MHL, AMPAS. Attending various fundraising events that Anna May Wong hosted, Philip Ahn actively supported her China Relief efforts. In return, the Chinese American actress also supported Korean American community events.

71. In an earlier script, *Anna May Wong Story*, dated on September 8, 1937, the last two lines were in English:

Duncan (Kim Lee): What do you think?

Mei-mei (Lan Ying): I wanted to be sure.

Daughter of Shanghai, Paramount script files.

72. For more information on the Chinese-Irish relationship during the latter half of the nineteenth century, see Lee, *Orientals*, 51–82.

73. Although the Chinese Exclusion Act was repealed in 1943, six years after the release of *Daughter of Shanghai*, as a token of America's friendship for its wartime ally, the immigration quota for the Chinese remained nominal (105 per year) until the 1965 Immigration and Nationality Act abolished discriminations based on national origins altogether.

CHAPTER 4

1. Ruth Vasey, *The World According to Hollywood, 1918–1939* (Madison: University of Wisconsin Press, 1997), 19.

2. Dorothy B. Jones, *The Portrayal of China and India on the American Screen, 1896–1955* (Cambridge: Center for International Studies, Massachusetts Institute of Technology, 1955), 5.

3. Ibid., 37. Author's emphasis.

4. A letter from Willys R. Peck, Counselor of Legation, Nanking, to the Secretary of State, Washington D.C., April 23, 1934, Record Group 59, State Department files on China, 893.4061 Motion Pictures, National Archives and Records Administration (NARA) at College Park, MD.

5. Zhiwei Xiao, "Constructing a New National Culture: Film Censorship and the Issues of Cantonese Dialect, Superstition, and Sex in the Nanjing Decade," in *Cinema and Urban Culture in Shanghai, 1922–1943*, ed. Yingjin Zhang, 193 (Stanford, CA: Stanford University Press, 1999). Xiao's article uses different English names for the NBFC and the CMPCC—respectively, the National Film Censorship Committee (NFCC) and the Central Film Censorship Committee (CFCC). I honor the English names used in the diplomatic correspondences between the Chinese authorities and the State Department.

6. Ibid., 183–199.

7. Jubin Hu, *Projecting a Nation: Chinese National Cinema before 1949* (Hong Kong: Hong Kong University Press, 2003), 88.

8. Letter from William Phillips, Acting Secretary of State, to Nelson T. Johnson, American Ambassador, Peiping, dated August 3, 1933, State Department files on China, 893.4061 Motion Pictures.

9. Letter from Willys Peck to Nelson Johnson, dated November 21, 1933, State Department files.

10. Letter from Bessie A. Ochs at MGM Studios to Willys Peck, dated January 31, 1934, State Department files.

11. Memorandum of conversation dated on March 9, 1934, State Department files.

12. Memorandum of conversation dated January 31, 1934, State Department files.

13. Letter from Edwin S. Cunningham, American Consul General, to Willys Peck, dated January 17, 1934, State Department files.

14. Letter from Frederick L. Herron, Foreign Manager, Motion Picture Producers and Distributors of America, to Willys Peck, dated November 9, 1936, State Department files.

15. The *Good Earth* Program, "When a Little Child Fell Ill: An Epic Was Born," *The Good Earth* clippings file, MHL, AMPAS.

16. Vasey, *The World According to Hollywood*, 188–89.

17. Memorandum of conversation dated February 15, 1934, State Department files.

18. Memorandum of conversation dated March 3, 1934, State Department files.

19. Letter from the MGM representatives to the Chinese authorities, dated March 26, 1934, State Department files.

20. Jones, *The Portrayal of China and India on the American Screen*, 44.

21. See "*The Good Earth* Is Passed by Central Board of Censors," *Central News Agency*, April 24, 1937, *The Good Earth*, PCA files.

22. "General Tu Will Discuss Orient Before Group," unidentified newspaper (presumed to be the USC campus paper) clipping (March 13, n.d.), Philip Ahn clippings file, AFC.

23. "Chinese Actress Arrives Here," *Los Angeles Times*, August 10, 1941: 2.

24. One might conjecture that Hollywood's stereotypical representations of warlords might have appealed to Chinese communists and revolutionaries who opposed corrupt regimes and leaders.

25. During the makeup session for *The General Died at Dawn*, Akim Tamiroff did not look Chinese, so director Milestone ordered Wally Westmore to take an eye-mold from a Chinese actor. Westmore made a mold from Philip Ahn's eyes with a jelly-like substance, eventually transferring that mold to clay and then rubber. The rubber mask was fitted onto Tamiroff's face. See Frank Westmore and Muriel Davidson, *The Westmores of Hollywood* (Philadelphia: Lippincott, 1976), 100.

26. Central Motion Picture Censorship Committee Notification No. 71, dated November 23, 1936, State Department files.

27. A letter from T. K. Chang, the Chinese Consul at Los Angeles, to Liu Chieh, the Counselor of the Chinese Embassy at Washington, D.C., dated September 29, 1942, the "General Died at Dawn" file, Box 1433 D, General Records of the Chief, Lowell Mellett, Records of the Bureau of Motion Pictures, Record Group 208, Office of War Information (OWI) files, NARA.

28. This memo is referenced in a letter from Henry Herzbrun, Paramount vice president, to Joseph Breen, dated May 6, 1937, *The Good Earth*, PCA files.

29. In his appointment letter to Lowell Mellett (director of Office of Government Reports and later chief of the OWI Bureau of Motion Pictures), dated December 18, 1941, Roosevelt states, "The American motion picture is one of our most effective media in informing and entertaining our citizens. The motion picture must remain free insofar as national security will permit. I want no censorship of the motion picture; I

want no restrictions placed thereon which will impair the usefulness of the film other than those very necessary restrictions which the dictates of safety make imperative." See the War Activities Committee press kit released on December 24, 1941, General Records of the Chief, Lowell Mellett, OWI files.

30. An example of trade papers' criticism of OWI script censorship is W. R. Wilkerson's editorial in *Hollywood Reporter*, December 9, 1942: "The groups working in Washington AND Hollywood, in an effort to effect a control of the screen...mostly through control of the story material...[has] been trying to agree on an approach that would make it mandatory on the part of the majors to submit scripts on EVERY picture before they are okayed for production.... [O]ur producers and their company heads should know that a control of our screens, first through a control of scripts, is being talked of and planned. So watch out!"

31. Clayton R. Koppes, "Regulating the Screen: The Office of War Information and the Production Code Administration," in *Boom and Bust: American Cinema in the 1940s*, ed. Thomas Schatz, 269 (Berkeley: University of California Press, 1999).

32. "Activities of Hollywood Office, Bureau of Motion Pictures, OWI (May 1942 to April 1943)," Box 1442, General Records of the Chief, Lowell Mellett, OWI files.

33. Koppes, "Regulating the Screen," 277–78.

34. *The Good Earth*, Motion Picture Reviews and Analyses files, Box 3517, Records of the Overseas Branch, OWI files.

35. *The General Died at Dawn*, Motion Picture Reviews and Analyses files, Box 3516, OWI files.

36. *China*, Motion Picture Reviews and Analyses files, Box 3513, OWI files.

37. Lewis S. Van Gelder, "A Long Ago War Sudden Comes Alive Again," *Los Angeles Times*, September 10, 1979: D5.

38. Cumings, *Korea's Place in the Sun*, 440–41.

39. Philip Ahn, "Oriental Actors in Hollywood," undated draft, AFC.

40. Interview with Frank Chin, *KoreAm*, 50.

41. David Hanna, "Philip Ahn in the Spotlight," *Los Angeles Daily News*, December 14, 1944: 21.

42. Pearl S. Buck, *China Sky* (New York: Triangle Books, 1942), 83, 85.

43. *China Sky*, RKO script files, UCLA Arts Library Special Collections, CA.

44. Ibid.

45. "Korean Curbs Lifted by Ruling," *Los Angeles Times*, January 25, 1942: 10.

46. Ronald Takaki, *Strangers from a Different Shore: A History of Asian Americans* (New York: Penguin, 1989), 365–67.

47. President Roosevelt's radio address quoted in "The Enemy: Whom We Fight—the Nature of Adversary," Nelson Poytner files, Box 1444, General Records of the Chief, Lowell Mellett, OWI files.

48. "Proposed List of Films to Interpret the Issues of This War," Nelson Poytner files, Box 1443, OWI files.

49. This speech remarkably resembles the master plan for the Japanese conquest of Asia outlined in the so-called Tanaka Memorandum, allegedly drafted by the Japanese Prime Minister Tanaka Giichi in 1927. Although its authenticity remains disputed, American and Chinese propaganda often cited the Tanaka Memorandum as proof of the Japanese intent to achieve world domination during the Sino-Japanese War and World War II. The document was used as a key narrative component in *Blood on the Sun* and referenced in the OWI propaganda documentary *Know Your Enemy: Japan* (1945) directed by Frank Capra. Notably, in *Jack London* the name of the Japanese

officer who makes the propaganda speech is Tanaka. Real-life Tanaka Giichi was indeed a military officer in the Russo-Japanese War.

50. Buck, *China Sky*, 69.

51. *China Sky*, RKO script files, UCLA Arts Library Special Collections.

52. *China Sky*, PCA files.

53. Fred Stanley, "Hollywood Memoranda," *New York Times*, September 24, 1944: X1.

54. *China Sky*, Motion Picture Reviews and Analyses files, Box 3513, OWI files.

55. Ibid.

56. Philip Ahn clippings file, AFC.

57. The Korean character Haan can seem to have been loosely based on the real-life espionage agent Kilsoo K. Haan of the Sino-Korean Peoples' League (an anti-Japanese underground society) who warned American intelligence officials and Senator Guy M. Gillette of the Pearl Harbor attack months in advance. He also translated Kinoaki Matsuo's *The Three-Power Alliance and a United States-Japanese War*—a Japanese version of *Mein Kampf* published in Tokyo in 1940—into English, making it available to the American public under the title, *How Japan Plans to Win* (Boston: Little, Brown, and Company, 1942).

58. "Proposed List of Films to Interpret the Issues of This War," OWI files.

59. Armed Korean resistance against Japanese imperialists and their collaborators began in the 1890s and became fiercer after Japan's annexation of Korea in 1910. Therefore, this dialogue in *First Yank into Tokyo* underestimates the duration of the period of Korean underground fighting with Japan (thirty-five years would be a closer estimate considering that the film is presumably set during the final year of World War II).

60. I thank Nancy Abelmann for sharing this idea about the racial politics in *China Sky* through personal correspondence.

61. *China Sky* pressbook, MHL, AMPAS.

62. Feg Murray, "Seein' Stars," *Miami Herald*, January 7, 1945.

63. Cha, *Willow Tree Shade*, 171.

64. Takaki, *Strangers from a Different Shore*, 367.

65. The U.S. Army Military Government in Korea (USAMGIK) under the command of Lt. General John Reed Hodge supported the Korean Democratic Party (dominated by a group of right-winged landowners who benefited from the Japanese colonial rule) and suppressed the peasant-based Korean People's Republic. Concentrating its energy on the anticommunist crusade, Hodge's government failed to respond to popular expectations for land reform, the purge of former collaborators, and the radical reform of Japanese systems. The colonial legacy lingered in the southern occupation zone where Japanese officials were simply replaced by Americans and conservative Koreans who had served the Japanese government. For more information on the American military occupation of Korea, see Cumings, *Korea's Place in the Sun*, 185–236.

CHAPTER 5

1. For more information on these topics, see Bruce Cumings, *The Origins of the Korean War*, vol. 1, *Liberation and the Emergence of Separate Regimes* (Princeton, NJ: Princeton University Press, 1981), and vol. 2, *The Roaring of the Cataract* (Princeton, NJ: Princeton University Press, 1990); Charles M. Dobbs, *The Unwanted Symbol: American Foreign Policy, the Cold War, and Korea, 1945–1950* (Kent, OH: Kent State University Press, 1981); James Irving Matray, *The Reluctant Crusade: American Foreign*

Policy in Korea, 1941–1950 (Honolulu: University of Hawaii Press, 1985); and Martin Hart-Landsberg, *Korea: Division, Reunification, and U.S. Foreign Policy* (New York: Monthly Review Press, 1998).

2. This phrase was used by both Kathryn Weathersby and Park Myung Lim (Pak Myŏng-nim). See Lester H. Brune, "The Soviet Union and the Korean War," in *The Korean War: Handbook of the Literature and Research*, ed. Lester Brune, 212 (Westport, CT: Greenwood Press, 1996); Kathryn Weathersby, "The Soviet Role in the Korean War: The State of Historical Knowledge," in *The Korean War in World History*, ed. William Stueck, 66 (Lexington: University Press of Kentucky, 2004).

3. The post-*glasnost* opening of Russian archive documents related to the Korean War began in 1991 with the release of the Ministry of Foreign Affairs records. In 1994, on his visit to Seoul, Russian President Boris Yeltsin presented ROK President Kim Young Sam with a collection of approximately 200 documents on the war culled from the Presidential Archive in Moscow. In 1995, a larger collection of declassified documents from the Presidential Archive became available to researchers through an agreement between the Russian Foreign ministry and the Cold War International History Project (CWIHP) of the Woodrow Wilson International Center for Scholars. See Weathersby, "The Soviet Role." Many of these documents are available in English translation on the CWIHP Web site. http://cwihp.si.edu/default.htm.

4. See Weathersby's introduction to "New Russian Documents on the Korean War," CWIHP *Bulletin*, no. 6–7 (Winter 1995–1996). http://cwihp.si.edu/ default.htm.

5. Kim Il Sung visited Moscow and Beijing in April and May 1950, respectively, to confirm Stalin's approval and obtain Mao's consent.

6. Weathersby, "New Findings on the Korean War, Translation and Commentary," CWIHP *Bulletin*, no. 3 (Fall 1993).

7. The sixteen other U.N nations that participated in the Korean War were Great Britain, Belgium, Australia, New Zealand, Canada, France, Italy, Luxembourg, the Netherlands, Greece, Turkey, Ethiopia, the Philippines, Thailand, South Africa, and Columbia.

8. For detailed information on the Soviet role in the Korean War, see Weathersby, "New Findings," "New Russian Documents," and "The Soviet Role." For information on Chinese involvement, see Chen Jian, "In the Name of Revolution: China's Road to the Korean War Revisited," in *The Korean War in World History*, ed. Stueck, 93–125.

9. William Stueck, *The Korean War: An International History* (Princeton, NJ: Princeton University Press, 1995), 3.

10. Cumings, *Korea's Place in the Sun*, 298.

11. Undated clipping, *Variety*, Korean War clippings file, MHL, AMPAS.

12. "Let Us Make No Mistake about It," *Hollywood Reporter*, August 30, 1950: 4–5.

13. Edwards, *A Guide to Films on the Korean War*, Preface.

14. Cook, *A History of Narrative Film*, 457.

15. Ibid., 458.

16. *The Steel Helmet*, PCA files.

17. Victor Riesel, *Los Angeles Daily News*, January 16, 1951.

18. Ibid., *Los Angeles Daily News*, January 17, 1951.

19. Letter from Joseph Breen to Joyce O'Hara, Motion Picture Association of America (MPAA), dated January 17, 1951, *The Steel Helmet*, PCA files.

20. Letter from Lt. Col. Clair E. Towne, Pictorial Branch, the Department of Defense Office of Public Information, to Manning Clagett, MPAA, dated February 1, 1951, *The Steel Helmet*, PCA files.

21. "*Helmet* Racks Up Its First Million," *Hollywood Reporter*, July 11, 1951: 1.

22. Out of Lacan's tripartite schema, the *real* has resided the longest in a neglected corner of film studies because cinema is considered as the *imaginary* that presupposes the *symbolic*. Slavoj Zizek stresses the role of the Lacanian real: "it erupts in the form of a traumatic return, derailing the balance of our daily lives, but it serves at the same time as a support of this very balance." See Slavoj Zizek, *Looking Awry: An Introduction to Jacques Lacan through Popular Culture* (Cambridge, MA: Massachusetts Institute of Technology Press, 1991), 29.

23. Edwards, *A Guide to Films on the Korean War*, 45.

24. In a January 1954 press conference sponsored by the Chinese, the leader of the twenty-one American defectors, Richard G. Corden, called for "real democracy and racial equality" rather than "witch-hunts and McCarthyism." Except for James Veneris (whose parents had been communists in Greece before immigrating to the United States), defecting POWs returned to the United States by 1966. Racism in the United States was a determining factor in the defection of three African Americans in the group (Clarence Adams, William White, and Larance Sullivan). For more information, see Lewis H. Carlson, *Remembered Prisoners of a Forgotten War: An Oral History of Korean War POWs* (New York: St. Martin's Griffin, 2002), 202–12.

25. Other sources estimate the actual POW death rate was considerably higher than the 38 percent official figure. Ibid., 2–3.

26. For statistics of alleged misconduct, investigation, and prosecution, see Albert D. Biderman, *March to Calumny: The Story of American POWs in the Korean War* (New York: Macmillan, 1963), 27–37. For the testimonies of Korean War POWs on their post-repatriation experience, see Carlson, *Remembered Prisoners of a Forgotten War*, 213–24.

27. Ibid., 9.

28. Eugene Kinkead, *In Every War But One* (New York: W.W. Norton & Co., 1959), 16, 34. In his revisionist study of Korean War POWs, sociologist Albert D. Biderman criticized Kinkead's erroneous equation of collaboration and misconduct and emphasized that "by strictly *legal criteria*, only 10 of 4,000 have been proved guilty of 'collaboration.'" Biderman, *March to Calumny*, 37.

29. "Momism" is a neologism that was sprung on the American public in Philip Wylie's *Generation of Vipers* (1942), which blames overprotective American mothers for producing weak, inadequate men. The idea strongly influenced Richard Condon's 1959 novel *The Manchurian Candidate* and its 1962 film adaptation. First coined by journalist/CIA operative Edward Hunter in 1950, the term brainwashing originally referred to "reeducational" practices in Red China and was subsequently applied to describe the status of Korean War POWs exposed to intense indoctrination programs by communist captors.

30. For an excellent overview of Korean War POW films, see Charles S. Young, "Missing Action: POW Films, Brainwashing and the Korean War, 1954–1968," *Historical Journal of Film, Radio and Television* 18, no. 1 (March 1998): 49–74. For a detailed discussion of *The Manchurian Candidate*, see Susan L. Carruthers, "*The Manchurian Candidate* (1962) and the Cold War Brainwashing Scare," ibid: 75–94.

31. Gary L. Huey, "Public Opinion and the Korean War," in *The Korean War*, ed., Brune, 409.

32. Rick Worland, "The Korean War Film as Family Melodrama: *The Bridges at Toko-Ri* (1954)," *Historical Journal of Film, Radio and Television* 19, no. 3 (August 1999): 363.

33. As a vacation policy to restore troop morale during the Korean War, the R&R program offered individual soldiers a five-day paid leave in Japan during their combat

service in Korea. Some servicemen arranged to meet their families and girlfriends during R&R; others indulged in debauchery (R&R was also known as I&I [intercourse & intoxication]) or took advantage of entertainment and sightseeing opportunities. From January 1951 to June 1953, approximately 800,000 R&R participants visited Japan, significantly contributing to the nation's economic rehabilitation. In *Sayonara*, Major Gruver's R&R is prearranged by a three-star general, his prospective father-in-law, and lasts considerably longer than five days. R&R is a recurrent theme in the television series *M*A*S*H* (1972–1983) in which Hawkeye Pierce and his cohorts crave "I&I" leaves in Japan.

34. Marchetti, *Romance and the "Yellow Peril,"* 129.

35. Linda Williams, "When the Woman Looks," in *Film Theory and Criticism*, 4th ed., eds. Gerald Mast, Marshall Cohen, and Leo Braudy, 564 (New York: Oxford University Press, 1992).

36. See K. W. Lee, "Truth in His Blood: Philip Ahn Cuddy Reflects on his Patriot-Grandfather Ahn Chang Ho's Overlooked Moral Legacy," *KoreAm* 15, no. 5 (May 2004): 37–39.

37. For an elaboration on such theoretical concepts as *sous rature*, trace, and différance, see Jacques Derrida, *Of Grammatology*, trans. Gayatri Chakravorty Spivak (Baltimore: The Johns Hopkins University Press, 1976), 60–65; Derrida, "Freud and the Scene of Writing," in *Writing and Difference*, trans. Alan Bass, 196–231 (Chicago: The University of Chicago Press, 1978).

38. Soon-Tek Oh is the most prolific and distinguished Korean actor in Hollywood and television besides Philip Ahn. Although UCLA graduate Oh's career successfully flourished with such significant roles as James Bond's partner in *The Man with the Golden Gun* (1974) and an Emmy-nominated performance in the television miniseries *East of Eden* (1981), he faced a number of roadblocks in the industry as an Asian American actor and was typecast in supporting and minor roles despite his obvious talent. However, Oh channeled his creativity into establishing the East West Players and the Korean American Theater Ensemble (later reborn as Lodestone Theater Ensemble) as well as, most recently, producing and starring in an independent film shot in high-definition video, *Last Mountain* (2000). He appeared as a conservative Korean immigrant father in Chris Chan Lee's independent film *Yellow* (1998) and was the voice of Mulan's domineering father, Fa Zhou, in the popular Disney film *Mulan* (1998). Fore more information on Oh's career, see Ed Yoon, "Soon-Tek Oh: Pioneering Korean American Actor," *Korean Culture* 22, no. 1 (Spring 2001): 5–11.

39. Philip W. Chung, "The Dream Team: Honoring Korean American All Stars: Soon-Tek Oh," *KoreAm* 12, no. 1 (January 2000): 14.

40. Jon Halliday, *Sirk on Sirk: Conversations with Jon Halliday*, rev. ed. (Boston: Faber and Faber, 1997), 122.

41. Barbara Klinger, *Melodrama and Meaning: History, Culture, and the Films of Douglas Sirk* (Bloomington: Indiana University Press, 1994), 98.

42. Halliday, *Sirk on Sirk*, 120.

43. Having grossed nearly $4 million, *Battle Hymn* made the list of top twenty moneymakers of 1957. See Robert J. Lentz, *Korean War Filmography* (Jefferson, NC: McFarland & Co., 2003), 51.

44. In his comprehensive study of biopic films made between 1927 and 1960, George F. Custen fails to mention *Battle Hymn* in both his analysis of sample films and his lists of 291 biopics by studio and profession. See George F. Custen, *Bio/Pics: How Hollywood Constructed Public History* (New Brunswick, NJ: Rutgers University Press, 1992).

45. Although *Battle Hymn* and *Love Is a Many-Splendored Thing* are nostalgic classics of both the Korean War generation and that of their children, canonical Korean War films in the United States, such as *The Steel Helmet*, *Men in War*, and *Pork Chop Hill*, are little known in South Korea. For a discussion of unique South Korean canons of classical Hollywood cinema, see Hye Seung Chung, "Towards a Strategic Korean Cinephilia: A Transnational *Détournement* of Hollywood Melodrama," in *South Korean Golden Age Melodrama: Gender, Genre, and National Cinema*, eds. Kathleen McHugh and Nancy Abelmann, 117–50 (Detroit: Wayne State University Press, 2005).

46. For an overview of South Korean war films of the 1960s, see David Scott Diffrient's articles: "'Military Enlightenment' for the Masses: Generic and Cultural Intermixing in South Korea's Golden Age War Films," *Cinema Journal* 45, no. 1 (Fall 2005): 21–49, and "*Han'guk* Heroism: Cinematic Spectacle and the Postwar Cultural Politics of *Red Muffler*," in McHugh and Abelmann, *South Korean Golden Age Melodrama*, 151–83.

47. Edwards, *A Guide to Films on the Korean War*, 31.

48. Dean E. Hess, *Battle Hymn*, rev. ed. (Reynoldsburg, OH: Buckeye Aviation, 1987), 147.

49. Universal's *Battle Hymn* pamphlet, BRC, NYPLPA.

50. The number 18 and five Sino-Korean letters (translated as "Birdman of Faith") were two markers of the authentic Mustang flown by Hess in Korea. In the film, another F-51 borrowed from the Texas Air National Guard was used as a stand-in for Hess's plane (which belonged to the ROK Air Force).

51. Custen, *Bio/Pics*, 37.

52. Edwards, *A Guide to Films on the Korean War*, 35.

53. Halliday, *Sirk on Sirk*, 125.

54. Hess, *Battle Hymn*, 2.

55. Ibid., 131.

56. Ibid., 234.

57. Hess describes Craigwell as "a self-educated Negro, with a fine knowledge of mechanics…an ex-crew chief in his late twenties with whom I was to fly many missions and whom I came to love like a brother." Ibid.,124.

58. Ibid., 175.

59. James Edwards's filmography includes *The Steel Helmet*, *Men in War*, *Pork Chop Hill*, and *The Manchurian Candidate*.

60. Halliday, *Sirk on Sirk*, 127. Sirk argued that the propagandistic prologue sequence with General Partridge was shot by the studio without his knowledge, after he had moved on to his next project *Interlude* (also released in 1957) as soon as he had finished cutting *Battle Hymn*.

61. Darragh O'Donoghue's review of *Battle Hymn*, http://www.amazon.com.

62. Paul Connors' review of *Battle Hymn*, ibid.

63. Universal's *Battle Hymn* pamphlet, BRC, NYPLPA.

64. Quoted in Joseph C. Goulden, *Korea: The Untold Story of the War* (New York: Times Books, 1982), Introduction XV. Although Omar Bradley originally used the phrase in the spring of 1951 to express his opposition to Douglas MacArthur's proposal to expand the war into China, the catchy line has been widely (mis)quoted to describe the Korean War itself.

65. Quoted in I. F. Stone, *The Hidden History of the Korean War* (London: Monthly Review Press, 1952), 348.

66. Cumings, *The Origins of the Korean War*, vol. 2, 768, 770.

67. Hayden White, *Tropics of Discourse: Essays in Cultural Criticism* (Baltimore: Johns Hopkins University Press, 1978), 122.

68. Hayden White defines tropes as "deviations from literal, conventional, or 'proper' language use, swerves in locution sanctioned neither by custom nor logic... [a trope] is always not only a deviation *from* one possible, proper meaning, but also a deviation *toward* another meaning, conception, or idea of what is right and proper *and true* 'in reality'" (ibid., 2; his emphasis). He borrows Kenneth Burke's taxonomy of the four "master tropes" to map out the movement from metaphorical, through metonymic and synecdochic, to ironic in the nineteenth-century historical interpretations.

69. Robert C. Allen and Douglas Gomery, *Film History: Theory and Practice* (New York: Alfred A. Knopf, 1985), 8. Authors' emphasis.

70. Sirk complained about Hess's snooping over his shoulders and restraining his artistic freedom during the film's shooting. The director originally wanted to insert a scene of Hess drinking to express the character's psychological conflict, but had to give up the idea because "[Hess] was there on the set the whole time saying 'I didn't drink' and all that, trying to make me stick to 'truth'" (Halliday, *Sirk on Sirk*, 125). Producer Ross Hunter, however, appreciated Hess's contribution to his project, saying "no technical adviser in picture history has ever been so closely associated with or had so much direct influence on a motion picture as Colonel Hess, who lived the story to begin with." Universal's *Battle Hymn* Production Notes, BRC, NYPLPA.

71. As of early 2001, the survivors had compiled and reported the names of 181 killed, 20 missing, and 50 wounded during the three-day American attack (air strafes as well as machine-gun fire). 83 percent of the dead were men over age forty, women, and children. Survivors estimated that the death toll reached as high as 400 (taking into account unclaimed deaths). The AP's Nogun-ri report fueled further claims of the large-scale civilian killings by U.S. troops at other towns throughout South Korea, including Masan, Tanyang, and Iksan. By early 2001, sixty-one cases of American wartime atrocities had been reported to the Defense Ministry of Korea. See Charles J. Hanley, Sang-Hun Choe, and Martha Mendoza, *The Bridge at No Gun Ri: A Hidden Nightmare from the Korean War* (New York: Henry Holt & Co., 2001), 276, 291–95.

72. In a remarkable resemblance to the Nogun-ri incident, *One Minute to Zero's* climatic scene shows American soldiers slaughtering a South Korean refugee column that was infiltrated by North Korean guerrillas. The U.S. Department of Defense as well as the Army and the Air Force withdrew their official cooperation for the film after their request to excise the civilian massacre scene was rejected by the RKO producer Howard Hughes. In *Battle Hymn*, a Korean nanny who brought the orphans to Hess's camp turns out to be a North Korean agent and is killed by a ROK major when she tries to destroy the ammunition storage with a grenade. Hess's memoir records similar instances in which communist guerrillas and agents infiltrated refugee columns, often using orphaned children as their cover and/or dressing as women (*Battle Hymn*, 182).

73. The political censorship under successive, authoritarian regimes (1961–1993) in close military alliance with the United States discouraged the survivors from speaking out. In 1994, they filed repeated petitions to American leaders (including Bill Clinton and Al Gore) as well as the new South Korean civil government to no avail. In 1997, the claimants filed a request for compensation for damages to the U.S. military (under the State of Forces Agreement between the U.S. and South Korean governments), which was denied on the grounds that there was no evidence and a three-year statute of limitations had long expired. See Hanley, Choe, and Mendoza, *The Bridge at No Gun Ri*, 260–62.

74. Neither Clinton's statement nor the Pentagon report (Statement of Mutual Understanding between the United States and the Republic of Korea on the No Gun Ri Investigations) mentioned the fact that the South Korean officials had compiled a list of 251 names of dead, wounded, or missing.

75. See Bill Clinton, "Statement on No Gun Ri," *PBS NewsHour*. http://www.pbs.org/newshour/media/media_watch/jan-june01/clinton_1-11.html; and Joohee Cho and Doug Struck, "South Koreans Disappointed at No Gun Ri Findings," *Washington Post*, January 11, 2001: A18.

76. For example, in a memo dated July 25, 1950, Colonel Turner C. Rogers wrote, "The Army has requested that we strafe all civilian refugee parties that are noted approaching our positions. To date, we have complied [with] the Army request in this respect." The 8th Cavalry log (dated July 24, 1950) notes receipt of the following instructions from the headquarters: "No refugees to cross the front line. Fire everyone try to cross lines. Use discretion in case of women and children." The crucial July 1950 communications log of the 7th Cavalry—responsible for the Nogun-ri killings—is missing from the National Archives. See Hanley, Choe, and Mendoza, *The Bridge at No Gun Ri*, 75, 81, 272.

77. Hess, *Battle Hymn*, 191.

78. See *Kim, Kwan-myŏng, "Mi konggun, minganin op'an sagŭk ch'oech'o chŭngŏn [U.S. Airman Testifies to the Shooting of Civilians]," Han'guk Ilbo* [Hankook Daily], June 21, 2000.

79. Examples include Chang Kil-su's *Silver Stallion* (*Ŭnma nŭn oji annŭnda*; 1990) and Yi Kwang-mo's *Spring in My Hometown* (*Arŭmdaun sijŏl*; 1998). For a comparison between *Battle Hymn* and these films, see Hye Seung Chung, "From Saviors to Rapists: GIs, Women, and Children in Korean War Films," *Asian Cinema* 12, no. 1 (Spring/Summer 2001): 103–16.

80. In a later scene, Hess says goodbye to Miss Yang, adding "until a better day," a line she sadly repeats after his departure. The better day (apparently denoting the postwar period) seems to connote an ideal future time when racial prejudices no longer deter their presently impossible romantic union.

81. In his memoir, Hess twice makes an analogy between Korea and the American West (Hess, *Battle Hymn*, 88, 133).

82. There has been only one Korean War film—the low-budget *No Man's Land* (1964)—to feature a romantic union between an American GI and a Korean woman.

83. Universal's *Battle Hymn* Production Notes, BRC, NYPLPA. There has been a claim that Anna Kashfi was born Joanne O'Callaghan in Cardiff, Wales. In her memoir, Kashfi argued that she was born in Calcutta, India (to Devi Kashfi and Selma Ghose), and that William Patrick O'Callaghan was her stepfather whose surname she later adopted to circumvent the admission quotas on Indians into the United States. See Anna Kashfi Brando and E. P. Stein, *Brando for Breakfast* (New York: Crown, 1979), 15, 110. Kashfi's career prematurely ended after appearing in a handful of movies and television programs in the late 1950s because of her drug and alcohol abuses, as well as the prolonged custody battle with Marlon Brando following a disastrous two-year marriage.

84. Hess, *Battle Hymn*, 188–89.

85. *Battle Hymn* was awarded a Golden Globe for Best Film Promoting International Understanding in 1957.

86. Ella Shohat, "Gender and Culture of Empire: Toward a Feminist Ethnography of the Cinema," in *Visions of the East: Orientalism in Film*, eds. Matthew Bernstein and Gaylyn Studlar, 20 (New Brunswick, NJ: Rutgers University Press, 1997).

87. Hess, *Battle Hymn*, 237–38.

88. Ibid., 188.

89. Ibid., 103, 105. Ironically, Hess's prediction of Rhee's historical honors proved wrong, since Syngman Rhee is now remembered as an authoritarian dictator in his homeland. After a twelve-year rule, Rhee's corrupt regime was toppled by a student-led revolution in April 1960, which forced the President to resign and spend the rest of his life in exile in Hawaii.

90. Philip Ahn correspondence file, AFC.

91. Examples include *China Girl* (1942), *China* (1943), *Dragon Seed* (1944), and *China Sky* (1945).

92. Hess, *Battle Hymn*, 4.

93. Ibid., 100.

94. Universal's *Battle Hymn* pamphlet, BRC, NYPLPA.

95. See Hess, *Battle Hymn*, 111, 155, 176.

96. After the shocking revelation of his affliction with AIDS in 1985, Hudson's homosexuality generated widespread media coverage, increasing the public's AIDS consciousness and complicating his earlier screen image. Ahn has also been rumored to be gay, although there is no evidence to prove his sexual preference.

97. "A Saga of Sam and A Colonel," *Life*, February 25, 1957: 137.

98. Won Moo Hurh, *The Korean Americans* (Westport, CT: Greenwood Press, 1988), 33.

99. Hamamoto, *Monitored Peril*, 100.

100. Hess, *Battle Hymn*, 113.

101. Cumings, *The Origins of the Korean War*, vol. 1, Preface xxvi, xxix.

102. Robert T. Oliver, *Syngman Rhee and American Involvement in Korea, 1942–1960* (Seoul: Panmun, 1978), 297.

103. For example, see the Letters to the Editor section in *Chosŏn Ilbo's* (Chosun Daily) Web site. http://www.english.chosun.com.

104. "A Saga of Sam and A Colonel," *Life*, 143.

105. Ibid., 140.

106. Brando and Stein, *Brando for Breakfast*, 57.

107. Ahn Junghyo, "Of Confusion and *Battle Hymn*," *The Korea Herald*, October 28, 1999.

108. Ibid.

CONCLUSION

1. Cha, *Willow Three Shade*, 99–100.

2. Ahn family correspondence file, AFC. Although the letter does not specify exactly when Tosan saw *The General Died at Dawn*, one can infer that it was sometime between late 1936 and early 1937 because the film was released in Japan in October 1936 (and probably in colonial Korea around the same time).

3. "USO Shows in Association with the Hollywood Overseas Committee Presents Philip Ahn," June 21, 1968, Philip Ahn clippings file, AFC.

4. Graham, "Phil Ahn...Frustrated Success," 7A.

5. Philip Ahn correspondence file, AFC.

6. Im Chung-bin, *Tosan An Ch'ang-ho: Kŭ saengae wa chŏngsin* [*Tosan An Ch'ang-ho: His Life and Mind*] (Seoul: Myŏngjisa, 2000), 187.

7. *China Sky* pressbook, MHL, AMPAS.

8. *China Girl*, Motion Picture Reviews and Analyses files, Box 3513, Records of the Overseas Branch, OWI files.

9. John T. McManus, "Communiqué on *China Girl*," *PM*, February 8, 1943: 20.

10. Yun Kyŏng-ro, "Tosan ŭi Kungnae aesŏ ŭi haengjŏk kwa kuguk kaemong hwaldong (1907–1910) [Tosan's Exploits and Nationalist Enlightenment Movement in Korea]," in *Tosan An Ch'ang-ho ŭi sasang kwa minjok undong [Tosan An Ch'ang-ho's Thoughts and Nationalist Movement]* (Seoul: Hakmunsa, 1995), 56.

11. Leslie Raddatz, "'No.1 Son' Is Now 'Master Po,'" *TV Guide*, June 23, 1973: 27.

12. John Stanley, "Master Kan of *Kung Fu*—Wisdom in a Shaolin Temple," *San Francisco Examiner and Chronicle*, undated clipping (presumed to have been printed in 1973), Philip Ahn clippings file, AFC

13. Irvin Paik, "Kung Fu Fan Klub," in *Counterpoint, ed. Gee*, 290, 294.

14. John Stanley, "Master Kan of *Kung Fu*," Philip Ahn clippings file, AFC.

15. Shirota, "Authentic Wisdom in a Shaolin Temple," 27.

16. Personal interview, March 31, 2005, Chicago.

17. "Documentary: From Grasshopper to Caine: Creating *Kung Fu*," in the *Kung Fu* DVD Complete First Season, Disc 1.

18. Richard Dyer, *Whiteness* (London: Routledge, 1997), 122.

19. Herbie J. Pilato, *The Kung Fu Book of Caine* (Boston: Charles E. Tuttle Company, 1993), 136.

20. Interview with Frank Chin, *KoreAm*, 52.

21. Cha, *Willow Tree Shade*, 177.

22. Lee, *Orientals*, 146.

23. Although a registered Democrat and admirer of Franklin D. Roosevelt, Harry S. Truman, and John F. Kennedy, Philip Ahn also supported Republican politicians, such as Barry Goldwater and Ronald Reagan. Ahn enjoyed the patronage of prominent politicians from both parties at his Moongate restaurant.

24. Eng, *Racial Castration*, 207.

25. On May 18, 1980, in the wake of General Chun Doo Hwan's military coup, citizens of Kwangju arose in a democratic revolt, demanding the eradication of martial law and the release from jail of their political leader, Kim Dae Jung, who would be elected President of South Korea in 1998. The Kwangju Uprising was brutally suppressed by paratroopers and an estimated 1,000 to 2,000 citizens were massacred. The Kwangju Uprising served as a guiding spirit for the 1980s *minjung* (people's) movement taken up by laborers, students, and intellectuals and contributed to the surge of anti-Americanism in Korea (due largely to accounts of the alleged authorization of Chun's military operation by the United States).

26. Note that unlike their Japanese and Korean counterparts, Chinese laborers were not able to invite their brides to America during the exclusion period (1882–1943).

27. Quoted in Moon, "*The Korean Immigrants in America*," 286.

28. Lee, *Orientals*, 145.

29. Lowe, *Immigrant Acts*, 8.

30. Ibid., 7.

31. Sheng-Mei Ma, *The Deadly Embrace: Orientalism and Asian American Identity* (Minneapolis: University of Minnesota Press, 2000), XI.

32. Shirota, "Authentic Wisdom in a Shaolin Temple," 25.

33. Lee Grant, "Film Clips," *Los Angeles Times*, November 1, 1976: F10.

34. Rudolf Arnheim, "In Praise of Character Actors," in *Movie Acting: The Film Reader, ed.* Pamela Robertson Wojcik, 206 (New York: Routledge, 2004).

PHILIP AHN FILMOGRAPHY

A Scream in the Night (Commodore Pictures; 1935 [released in 1943 by Astor Pictures])

Anything Goes (Paramount; 1936)

Counterfeit Lady (Columbia; 1936)

The General Died at Dawn (Paramount; 1936)

Klondike Annie (Paramount; 1936)

Stowaway (20th Century-Fox; 1936)

China Passage (RKO; 1937)

Daughter of Shanghai (Paramount; 1937)

The Good Earth (MGM; 1937)

I Promise to Pay (Columbia; 1937)

Roaring Timber (Columbia; 1937)

Something to Sing About (Grand National; 1937)

Tex Rides with the Boy Scouts (Grand National; 1937)

Thank You, Mr. Moto (20th Century-Fox; 1937)

Charlie Chan in Honolulu (20th Century-Fox; 1938)

Hawaii Calls (RKO; 1938)

Red Barry (Universal; 1938)

Barricade (20th Century-Fox; 1939)

Disputed Passage (Paramount; 1939)

Island of Lost Men (Paramount; 1939)

King of Chinatown (Paramount; 1939)

North of Shanghai (Columbia; 1939)

Panama Patrol (Fine Arts/Grand National; 1939)

Drums of Fu Manchu (Republic; 1940)

The Shadow (Columbia; 1940)

Passage from Hong Kong (Warner Bros.; 1941)

They Met in Bombay (MGM; 1941)

Across the Pacific (Warner Bros.; 1942)

China Girl (20th Century-Fox; 1942)

Let's Get Tough (Monogram; 1942)

Ship Ahoy (MGM; 1942)

Submarine Raider (Columbia; 1942)

The Tuttles of Tahiti (RKO; 1942)

We Were Dancing (MGM; 1942)

A Yank on the Burma Road (MGM; 1942)

Adventures of Smilin' Jack (Universal; 1943)

The Amazing Mrs. Holliday (Universal; 1943)

Around the World (RKO; 1943)

Behind the Rising Sun (RKO; 1943)

China (Paramount; 1943)

December 7th (U.S. Navy/War Dept.; 1943)

Don Winslow of the Coast Guard (Universal; 1943)

The Man from Down Under (MGM; 1943)

They Got Me Covered (RKO; 1943)

Dragon Seed (MGM; 1944)

Forever Yours (Monogram; 1944)

The Keys to the Kingdom (20th Century-Fox; 1944)

The Purple Heart (20th Century-Fox; 1944)

The Story of Dr. Wassell (Paramount; 1944)

Back to Bataan (RKO; 1945)

Betrayal from the East (RKO; 1945)

Blood on the Sun (RKO; 1945)

China Sky (RKO; 1945)

China's Little Devils (Monogram; 1945)

God Is My Co-Pilot (Warner Bros.; 1945)

They Were Expendable (MGM; 1945)

The Chinese Ring (Monogram; 1947)

Intrigue (United Artists; 1947)

Saigon (Paramount; 1947)

Singapore (Universal; 1947)

The Cobra Strikes (Eagle-Lion; 1948)

The Creeper (Universal; 1948)

The Miracle of the Bells (RKO; 1948)

Rogues' Regiment (Universal; 1948)

Women in the Night (Film Classic; 1948)

Boston Blackie's Chinese Venture (Columbia; 1949)

Impact (United Artists; 1949)

The Sickle or the Cross (Roland-Reed Productions; 1949)

State Department File 649 (Film Classics; 1949)

The Big Hangover (MGM; 1950)

The Glass Menagerie (Warner Bros., 1950)

Halls of Montezuma (20th Century-Fox; 1950)

China Corsair (Columbia; 1951)

I Was an American Spy (Allied Artists; 1951)

Secrets of Monte Carlo (Republic; 1951)

Battle Zone (Allied Artists; 1952)

Japanese War Bride (20th Century-Fox; 1952)

Macao (RKO; 1952)

Red Snow (Columbia; 1952)

Target Hong Kong (Columbia; 1952)

Battle Circus (MGM; 1953)

China Venture (Columbia; 1953)

Fair Wind to Java (Republic; 1953)

His Majesty O'Keefe (Warner Bros.; 1954)

Hell's Half Acre (Republic; 1954)

The Shanghai Story (Republic; 1954)

Jump into Hell (Warner Bros.; 1955)

The Left Hand of God (20th Century-Fox; 1955)

Love Is a Many-Splendored Thing (20th Century-Fox; 1955)

Around the World in 80 Days (United Artists; 1956)

Battle Hymn (Universal; 1957)

The Way to the Gold (20th Century-Fox; 1957)

Hong Kong Confidential (United Artists; 1958)

Never So Few (MGM; 1959)

Yesterday's Enemy (Columbia; 1959)

The Great Impostor (Universal; 1960)

Mr. Garlund (TV movie: CBS Productions; 1960)

One-Eyed Jacks (Paramount; 1961)

Confessions of an Opium Eater (Allied Artists; 1962)

A Girl Named Tamiko (Paramount; 1962)

Diamond Head (Columbia; 1963)

Shock Corridor (Allied Artists; 1963)

Paradise-Hawaiian Style (Paramount; 1966)

The Karate Killers (TV movie: MGM; 1967)

Thoroughly Modern Millie (Universal; 1967)

Hawaii Five-O: Cocoon (TV movie: CBS Productions/Paramount; 1968)

Kung Fu: The Way of Tiger, The Sign of the Dragon (TV movie: Warner Bros.; 1972)

Voodoo Heartbeat (TWI National; 1972)

The World's Greatest Athlete (Buena Vista; 1973)

Jonathan Livingston Seagull (Paramount; 1973)

Judgement: The Court Martial of the Tiger of Malaya-General Yamashita (TV movie: Stanley Kramer Productions; 1954)

The Killer Who Wouldn't Die (TV movie: Paramount; 1976)

Portrait of a Hitman (American National Enterprise; 1977)

BIBLIOGRAPHY

ARCHIVAL SOURCES

Anna May Wong clippings file. Margaret Herrick Library (MHL), Academy of Motion
    Picture Arts and Sciences (AMPAS), Beverly Hills, CA; Billy Rose Collection
    (BRC), New York Public Library for Performing Arts (NYPLPA).

Battle Hymn
Clippings file, Production notes, Universal pamphlet, BRC, NYPLPA.

China
Motion Picture Reviews and Analyses files, Box 3513, the Office of War Information
    (OWI) files, National Archives and Records Administration (NARA) at College
    Park, MD.

China Girl
Pressbook, MHL, AMPAS; Motion Picture Reviews and Analyses files, Box 3513,
    Records of the Overseas Branch, OWI files.

China Sky
Clippings file, pressbook, Production Code Administration (PCA) files. MHL, AMPAS;
    RKO script files, UCLA Arts Library Special Collections; Motion Picture Reviews
    and Analyses files, Box 3513, OWI files.

Daughter of Shanghai
Paramount production files, Paramount script files, Paramount pressbook 1937, PCA
    files. MHL, AMPAS.

General Died at Dawn, The
Box 1433 D, General Records of the Chief, Lowell Mellett, Records of the Bureau of
    Motion Pictures, OWI files; Motion Picture Reviews and Analyses files, Box 3516,
    OWI files; State Department files on China, 893.4061 Motion Pictures, NARA.

Good Earth, The
Clippings file, PCA files, MHL, AMPAS; State Department files on China, 893.4061
    Motion Pictures; Motion Picture Reviews and Analyses files, Box 3517, Records of
    the Overseas Branch, OWI files.

Island of Lost Men
Paramount production files, Paramount script files. MHL, AMPAS.
King of Chinatown
Paramount production files, Paramount script file, Paramount pressbook 1939, PCA files. MHL, AMPAS.
Philip Ahn clippings file, MHL, AMPAS; Ahn Family Collection (AFC), Northridge, CA.
Philip Ahn correspondence file, AFC.
Richard Loo clippings file, MHL, AMPAS.
Record Group 59, State Department files on China, 893.4061 Motion Pictures, NARA.
Record Group 208, Records of the Chief, Lowell Mellett, Records of the Bureau of Motion Pictures, OWI files.
Record Group 208, Motion Picture Reviews and Analyses files, Records of the Overseas Branch, OWI files.
The Steel Helmet
Clippings file, PCA files. MHL, AMPAS.

*** Note: Ahn Family Collection has been relocated to the USC Korean Heritage Library as of September 2005.

ENGLISH-LANGUAGE SOURCES

Books and Book Chapters

Ahn, Junghyo. *Silver Stallion*. New York: Soho Press, 1990.
———. *White Badge*. New York: Soho Press, 1989.
Allen, Robert C., and Douglas Gomery. *Film History: Theory and Practice*. New York: Alfred A. Knopf, 1985.
Althusser, Louis. *Lenin and Philosophy and Other Essays by Louis Althusser,* translated by Ben Brewster. New York: Monthly Review Press, 1971.
Arnheim, Rudolf. "In Praise of Character Actors." In *Movie Acting: The Film Reader,* edited by Pamela Robertson Wojcik, 205–6. New York: Routledge, 2004.
Biderman, Albert D. *March to Calumny: The Story of American POWs in the Korean War*. New York: Macmillan, 1963.
Bordwell, David, Janet Staiger, and Kristine Thompson. *The Classical Hollywood Cinema: Film Style & Mode of Production to 1960*. New York: Columbia University Press, 1985.
Bowman, John S. *Columbia Chronologies of Asian History and Culture*. New York: Columbia University Press, 2000.
Brando, Anna Kashfi, and E. P. Stein. *Brando for Breakfast*. New York: Crown, 1979.
Browne, Nick. "The Undoing of the Other Woman: Madame Butterfly in the Discourse of American Orientalism." In *The Birth of Whiteness: Race and the Emergence of U.S. Cinema,* edited by Daniel Bernardi, 226–56. New Brunswick, NJ: Rutgers University Press, 1996.
Brune, Lester H. "The Soviet Union and the Korean War." In *The Korean War: Handbook of the Literature and Research,* edited by Lester H. Brune, 206–19. Westport, CT: Greenwood Press, 1996.
Buck, Pearl S. *China Sky*. New York: Triangle Books, 1942.
———. *The Good Earth*. New York: John Day, 1931.

———. *The New Year*. New York: John Day, 1968.

Butler, Judith. *Gender Trouble: Feminism and the Subversion of Identity*. New York: Routledge, 1990.

Carlson, Lewis H. *Remembered Prisoners of a Forgotten War: An Oral History of Korean War POWs*. New York: St. Martin's Griffin, 2000.

Cha, John. *Willow Tree Shade. The Susan Ahn Cuddy Story*. Seoul. Korean American Heritage Foundation, 2002.

Chan, Anthony B. *Perpetually Cool: The Many Lives of Anna May Wong (1905–1961)*. Lanham, MD: Scarecrow Press, 2003.

Cheng, Anne Anlin. *The Melancholy of Race*. Oxford: Oxford University Press, 2000.

Chin, Frank, Jeffery Chan, and Lawson Inada, eds. *Aiiieeeee! An Anthology of Asian-American Writers*. Washington, DC: Howard University Press, 1974.

Chu, Judy. "Anna May Wong." In *Counterpoint: Perspectives on Asian America*, edited by Emma Gee, 284–88. Los Angeles: University of California Press, 1976.

Chung, Hye Seung. "Towards a Strategic Korean Cinephilia: A Transnational *Détournement* of Hollywood Melodrama." In *Gender, Genre, and National Cinema: South Korean Golden Age Melodrama*, edited by Kathleen McHugh and Nancy Abelmann, 117–50. Detroit: Wayne State University Press, 2005.

Cohen, Warren I. "American Perception of China." In *Dragon and Eagle: United States-China Relations: Past and Future*, edited by Michel Oksenberg and Robert B. Oxnam, 54–86. New York: Basic Books, 1978.

———. *America's Response to China: A History of Sino-American Relations*. New York: Columbia University Press, 1990.

Condon, Richard. *The Manchurian Candidate*. New York: McGraw-Hill, 1959.

Conn, Peter. *Pearl S. Buck: A Cultural Biography*. New York: Cambridge University Press, 1996.

Cook, David A. *A History of Narrative Film*. 3rd ed. New York: W.W. Norton & Co., 1996.

Cumings, Bruce. *Korea's Place in the Sun: A Modern History*. New York: W.W. Norton & Co., 1997.

———. *The Origins of the Korean War*. Vol. 1, *Liberation and the Emergence of Separate Regimes*. Princeton, NJ: Princeton University Press, 1981.

———. *The Origins of the Korean War*. Vol. 2, *The Roaring of the Cataract*. Princeton, NJ: Princeton University Press, 1990.

Custen, George F. *Bio/Pics: How Hollywood Constructed Public History*. New Brunswick, NJ: Rutgers University Press, 1992.

Davé, Shilpa, LeiLani Nishime, and Tasha Oren, eds. *East Main Street: Asian American Popular Culture*. New York: New York University Press, 2005.

Denzin, Norman K. *The Cinematic Society: The Voyeur's Gaze*. London: SAGE, 1995.

Derrida, Jacques. *Of Grammatology*, translated by Gayatri Chakravorty Spivak. Baltimore: Johns Hopkins University Press, 1976.

———. *Writing and Difference, translated by Alan Bass*. Chicago: University of Chicago Press, 1978.

Diffrient, David Scott. "Hanguk Heroism: Cinematic Spectacle and the Postwar Cultural Politics of *Red Muffler*." In *Gender, Genre, and National Cinema: South Korean Golden Age Melodrama*, edited by Kathleen McHugh and Nancy Abelmann, 151–83. Detroit: Wayne State University Press, 2005.

Doane, Mary Ann. "Film and the Masquerade: Theorizing the Female Spectator." In *Femmes Fatales: Feminism, Film Theory, Psychoanalysis*, edited by Mary Ann Doane, 17–32. New York: Routledge, 1991.

Dobbs, Charles M. *The Unwanted Symbol: American Foreign Policy, the Cold War, and Korea, 1945–1950*. Kent, OH: Kent State University Press, 1981.

Doherty, Thomas. *Projections of War: Hollywood, American Culture, and World War II*. New York: Columbia University Press, 1993.

Dyer, Richard. *Stars*. London: BFI, 1979.

———. *Whiteness*. London: Routledge, 1997.

Edwards, Paul M. *A Guide to Films on the Korean War*. Westport, CT: Greenwood Press, 1997.

Eng, David L. *Racial Castration: Managing Masculinity in Asia America*. Durham, NC: Duke University Press, 2001.

Feng, Peter X. *Identities in Motion: Asian American Film and Video*. Durham, NC: Duke University Press, 2002.

———. "Recuperating Suzie Wong: A Fan's Nancy Kwan-dary." In *Countervisions: Asian American Film Criticism*, edited by Darrell Y. Hamamoto and Sandra Liu, 40–56. Philadelphia: Temple University Press, 2000.

———, ed. *Screening Asian Americans*. New Brunswick, NJ: Rutgers University Press, 2002.

Gray, Herman. "Remembering Civil Rights: Television, Memory, and the 1960s." In *The Revolution Wasn't Televised: Sixties Television and Social Conflict*, edited by Lynn Spigel and Michael Curtin, 349–58. New York: Routledge, 1997.

Goulden, Joseph C. *Korea: The Untold Story of the War*. New York: Times Books, 1982.

Haan, Kilsoo K. *How Japan Plans to Win*. Boston: Little, Brown, and Company, 1942.

Hall, Stuart. "Encoding/Decoding." In *Culture, Media, Language*, edited by Stuart Hall, Dorothy Hobson, Andy Lowe, and Paul Wills, 128–38. London: Hutchinson, 1980.

Halliday, Jon. *Sirk on Sirk: Conversations with Jon Halliday*. Rev. ed. Boston: Faber and Faber, 1997.

Hamamoto, Darrell Y. *Monitored Peril: Asian Americans and the Politics of TV Representation*. Minneapolis: University of Minnesota Press, 1994.

Hanke, Ken. *Charlie Chan at the Movies: History, Filmography, and Criticism*. Jefferson, NC: McFarland & Company, 1989.

Hanley, Charles J., Sang-Hun Choe, and Martha Mendoza. *The Bridge at No Gun Ri: A Hidden Nightmare from the Korean War*. New York: Henry Holt & Co., 2001.

Haralovich, Mary Beth. "*I Spy*'s 'Living Postcards': The Geo-Politics of Civil Rights." In *Television, History, and American Culture: Feminist Critical Essays*, edited by Haralovich and Lauren Rabinovitz, 98–119. Durham, NC: Duke University Press, 1999.

Hart-Landsberg, Martin. *Korea: Division, Reunification, and U.S. Foreign Policy*. New York: Monthly Review Press, 1998.

Hess, Dean E. *Battle Hymn*. Rev. ed. Reynoldsburg, OH: Buckeye Aviation, 1987

Higashi, Sumiko. "Ethnicity, Class, and Gender in Film: DeMille's *The Cheat*." In *Unspeakable Images: Ethnicity and the American Cinema*, edited by Lester D. Friedman, 112–39. Urbana: University of Illinois Press, 1991.

Hing, Bill Ong. *Making and Remaking Asian America through Immigration Policy, 1850–1990*. Stanford, CA: Stanford University Press, 1993.

Hodge, Graham Russell Gao. *Anna May Wong: From Laundryman's Daughter to Hollywood Legend*. New York: Palgrave Macmillan, 2004.

Hong, Terry. "Asian Americans." In *The Columbia Companion to American History on Film*, edited by Peter C. Rollins, 225–33. New York: Columbia University Press, 2003.

hooks, bell. "The Oppositional Gaze: Black Female Spectators." In *Black American Cinema*, edited by Manthia Diawara, 288–302. New York: Routledge, 1993.

Hu, Jubin. *Projecting a Nation: Chinese National Cinema before 1949*. Hong Kong: Hong Kong University Press, 2003.

Huey, Gary L. "Public Opinion and the Korean War." In *The Korean War: Handbook of the Literature and Research*, edited by Lester H. Brune, 100–17. Westport, CT: Greenwood Press, 1996.

Humphreys, Christmas, ed. *The Wisdom of Buddhism*. London: M. Joseph, 1960.

Hurh, Won Moo. *The Korean Americans*. Westport, CT: Greenwood Press, 1988.

Jian, Chen. "In the Name of Revolution: China's Road to the Korean War Revisited." In *The Korean War in World History*, edited by William Stueck, 93–125. Lexington: University Press of Kentucky, 2004.

Jones, Dorothy B. *The Portrayal of China and India on the American Screen, 1896–1955*. Cambridge: Center for International Studies, Massachusetts Institute of Technology, 1955.

Kaplan, E. Ann. *Looking for the Other: Feminism, Film, and The Imperial Gaze*. New York: Routledge, 1997.

Kim, Hyung-chan. *Asian Americans and Congress: A Documentary History*. Westport, CT: Greenwood Press, 1996.

Kingston, Maxine Hong. *The Woman Warrior: Memoirs of a Girlhood among Ghosts*. New York: Knopf, 1976.

Kinkead, Eugene. *In Every War but One*. New York: W.W. Norton, 1959.

Kirihara, Donald. "The Accepted Idea Displaced: Stereotypes and Sessue Hayakawa." In *The Birth of Whiteness: Race and the Emergence of U.S. Cinema*, edited by Daniel Bernardi, 81–99. New Brunswick: Rutgers University Press, 1996.

Klinger, Barbara. *Melodrama and Meaning: History, Culture, and the Films of Douglas Sirk*. Bloomington: Indiana University Press, 1994.

Koppes, Clayton R. "Regulating the Screen: The Office of War Information and the Production Code Administration." In *Boom and Bust: American Cinema in the 1940s*, edited by Thomas Schatz, 262–81. Berkeley: University of California Press, 1999.

Lee, Helen. "A Peculiar Sensation: A Personal Genealogy of Korean American Women's Cinema." In *Screening Asian Americans*, edited by Peter X. Feng, 133–55. New Brunswick, NJ: Rutgers University Press, 2002.

Lee, Robert. *Orientals: Asian Americans in Popular Culture*. Philadelphia: Temple University Press, 1999.

Lentz, Robert J. *Korean War Filmography*. Jefferson, NC: McFarland & Co., 2003.

Lingeman, Richard R. *Don't You Know There's a War On? The American Home Front, 1941–1945*. New York: Nation Books, 2003.

Liu, Cynthia W. "When Dragon Ladies Die, Do They Come Back as Butterflies? Re-Imagining Anna May Wong." In *Countervisions: Asian American Film Criticism*, edited by Darrell Y. Hamamoto and Sandra Liu, 23–39. Philadelphia: Temple University Press, 2000.

Lowe, Lisa. *Immigrant Acts: On Asian American Cultural Politics*. Durham, NC: Duke University Press, 1996.

Ma, Sheng-Mei. *The Deadly Embrace: Orientalism and Asian American Identity* Minneapolis: University of Minnesota Press, 2000.

MacDonald, J. Fred. *Blacks and White TV: Afro-Americans in Television since 1948*. Chicago: Nelson-Hall, 1983.

Marchetti, Gina. *Romance and the "Yellow Peril": Race, Sex, and Discursive Strategies in Hollywood Fiction*. Berkeley: University of California Press, 1993.

Masunaga, Reiho. *A Primer of Soto Zen: A Translation of Dogen's Shobogenzo Zuimonki*. Honolulu: East-West Center Press, 1971.

Matray, James Irving. *The Reluctant Crusade: American Foreign Policy in Korea, 1941–1950*. Honolulu: University of Hawaii Press, 1985.

Michener, James A. *Tales of the South Pacific*. New York: Macmillan, 1947.

Mitchell, Charles P. *A Guide to Charlie Chan Films*. Westport, CT: Greenwood Press, 1999.

Miyao, Daisuke. *Sessue Hayakawa: Silent Cinema and Transnational Stardom*. Durham, NC: Duke University Press, forthcoming.

Moon, Hyung June. "The Korean Immigrants in America: The Quest for Identity in the Formative Years, 1903–1918." PhD diss., University of Nevada, 1976.

Moy, James S. *Marginal Sights: Staging the Chinese in America*. Iowa City: University of Iowa Press, 1993.

Mulvey, Laura. "Visual Pleasure and Narrative Cinema." In *Feminism and Film Theory*, edited by Constance Penley, 57–68. New York: Routledge, 1988.

Naremore, James. *More Than Night: Film Noir in Its Contexts*. Berkeley: University of California Press, 1998.

Oliver, Robert T. *Syngman Rhee and American Involvement in Korea, 1942–1960*. Seoul: Panmun, 1978.

Paik, Irvin. "Kung Fu Fan Klub." In *Counterpoint: Perspectives on Asian America*, edited by Emma Gee, 289–94. Los Angeles: Asian American Studies Center, 1976.

Parish, James Robert. *The Paramount Pretties*. Secaucus, NJ: Castle Book, 1972.

Pilato, Herbie J. *The Kung Fu Book of Caine*. Boston: Charles E. Tuttle, 1993.

Rahula, Walpola. *What the Buddha Taught*. Bedford, UK: Gordon Fraser Gallery, 1967.

Riviere, Joan. "Womanliness as a Masquerade." In *Formations of Fantasy*, edited by Victor Burgin, James Donald, and Cora Kaplan, 35–61. New York: Methuen, 1986.

Rogin, Michael. *Blackface, White Noise: Jewish Immigrants in the Hollywood Melting Pot*. Berkeley: University of California Press, 1996.

Shohat, Ella. "Gender and Culture of Empire: Toward a Feminist Ethnography of the Cinema." In *Visions of the East: Orientalism in Film*, edited by Matthew Bernstein and Gaylyn Studlar, 19–66. New Brunswick, NJ: Rutgers University Press, 1997.

Shohat, Ella, and Robert Stam. *Unthinking Eurocentrism: Multiculturalism and the Media*. New York: Routledge, 1994.

Stone, I. F. *The Hidden History of the Korean War*. London: Monthly Review Press, 1952.

Stueck, William. *The Korean War: An International History*. Princeton, NJ: Princeton University Press, 1995.

Takaki, Ronald. *Strangers from a Different Shore: A History of Asian Americans*. New York: Penguin, 1989.

Taves, Brian. "The B Film: Hollywood's Other Half." In *Grand Design: Hollywood as a Modern Business Enterprise 1930–1939*, edited by Tino Balio, 313–50. New York: Charles Scribner's Sons and MacMillan Library Reference, 1993.

———. *Robert Florey, the French Expressionist*. Metuchen, NJ: Scarecrow Press, 1987.

Thomas, Bob. *Thalberg: Life and Legend*. Los Angeles: New Millennium Press, 2000.

Vasey, Ruth. *The World According to Hollywood, 1918–1939*. Madison: University of Wisconsin Press, 1997.

Waley, Arthur. *The Analects of Confucius*. London: G. Allen & Unwin, 1938.

Weathersby, Kathryn. "The Soviet Role in the Korean War: The State of Historical Knowledge." In *The Korean War in World History*, edited by William Stueck, 61–92. Lexington: University Press of Kentucky, 2004.

Westmore, Frank, and Muriel Davidson. *The Westmores of Hollywood.* Philadelphia: Lippincott, 1976.

White, Hayden. *Tropics of Discourse: Essays in Cultural Criticism.* Baltimore: Johns Hopkins University Press, 1978.

Williams, Linda. "When the Woman Looks." In *Film Theory and Criticism*, 4th ed., edited by Gerald Mast, Marshall Cohen, and Leo Braudy, 561–77. New York: Oxford University Press, 1992.

Wong, Eugene Franklin. *On Visual Media Racism: Asians in the American Motion Pictures.* New York: Arno Press, 1978.

Wu, Judy Tzu-Chun. *Doctor Mom Chung of the Fair-Haired Bastards: The Life of a Wartime Celebrity.* Berkeley: University of California Press, 2005.

Wylie, Philip. *Generation of Vipers.* New York: Rinehart, 1942.

Xiao, Zhiwei. 1999. "Constructing a New National Culture: Film Censorship and the Issues of Cantonese Dialect, Superstition, and Sex in the Nanjing Decade." In *Cinema and Urban Culture in Shanghai, 1922–1943*, edited by Yingjin Zhang, 183–99. Stanford, CA: Stanford University Press, 1999.

Xing, Jun. *Asian America through the Lens: History, Representations and Identity.* Walnut Greek, CA: Altamira Press, 1998.

Zizek, Slavoj. *Looking Awry: An Introduction to Jacques Lacan through Popular Culture.* Cambridge: Massachusetts Institute of Technology Press, 2001.

Periodical Articles and Miscellaneous Sources

Ahn, Junghyo. "Of Confusion and *Battle Hymn*." *The Korea Herald*, October 28, 1999.

Ahn, Philip. "Oriental Actors in Hollywood." Undated draft, Ahn Family Collection.

Ahn, Philip, and ninety Asian American actors. "*We Are Not All Alike*." *Daily Variety*, October 29, 1976.

Briggs, Walter. "Actor Is a Villain at Home, a Hero in Korea." *New York Herald Tribune*, April 26, 1959: Sec. 4:2.

Carruthers, Susan L. "*The Manchurian Candidate* (1962) and the Cold War Brainwashing Scare." *Historical Journal of Film, Radio and Television* 18, no.1 (March 1998): 75–94.

Chin, Frank. "*Kung Fu* Is Unfair to Chinese." *New York Times*, March 24, 1974: 137.

———. 1970 Interview with Philip Ahn. In "Man of The House: The Many Roles of Philip Ahn, the Path-Breaking Hollywood Actor and Son of the Famed Korean Independence Fighter," prefaced by K. W. Lee. *KoreAm* 15, no. 4 (April 2004): 42–52.

"Chinese Actress Arrives Here." *Los Angeles Times*, August 10, 1941: 2.

Cho, Joohee, and Doug Struck. "South Koreans Disappointed at No Gun Ri Findings." *Washington Post*, January 11, 2001: A18.

Chung, Hye Seung. "From Saviors to Rapists: G.I.s, Women, and Children in Korean War Films." *Asian Cinema* 12, no. 1 (Spring/Summer 2001): 103–16.

Chung, Phlip W. "The Dream Team: Honoring Korean American All Stars: Soon Tek Oh." *KoreAm* 12, no. 1 (January 2000): 14–15.

Clinton, Bill. "Statement on No Gun Ri." January 11, 2001. *PBS NewsHour.* http://www.pbs.org/newshour/media_watch/jan-june01/clinton_1-11.html.

Cuddy, Philip Ahn. "Philip Ahn: Born in America." Philip Ahn Admiration Society Web site, 1996. http://www. philipahn.com.

DeMille, Cecil B., Y. Frank Freeman, Samuel Goldwyn, Louis B. Mayer, Joseph M. Schenck, et al. "Let Us Make No Mistake about It." *Hollywood Reporter*, August 30, 1950: 4–5.

Diawara, Manthia. "Black Spectatorship: Problems of Identification and Resistance." *Screen* 29, no. 4 (1998): 66–76.

Diffrient, David Scott. "'Military Enlightenment' for the Masses: Generic and Cultural Intermixing in South Korea's Golden Age War Films." *Cinema Journal* 45, no. 1 (Fall 2005): 22–49.

Dille, John. "A Day of Fun and a Colonel." *Life*, February 25, 1957: 127, 130, 133.

"*Dosan: Past, Present and Future*": Symposium catalogue. Los Angeles: Patriot Dosan Ahn Chang-Ho Memorial Foundation/Hung Sa Dahn North America, 2001.

Feng, Peter X. "In Search of Asian American Cinema." *Cineaste* 21, nos. 1–2 (Winter–Spring 1995): 32–35.

Flaus, John. "Thanks for Your Heart, Bart." *Continuum* 5, no. 2 (1992): 179–224.

Forbes, Don. "Hollywood Scrapbook." CBS radio script. November 11, 1938.

Graham, John Ringo. "Phil Ahn: Frustrated Success." *San Fernando Valley and Que Magazine* (January 1970): 6–8.

Grant, Lee. "Film Clips." *Los Angeles Times*, November 1, 1976: F10.

Hanna, David. "Philip Ahn in the Spotlight." *Los Angeles Daily News*, December 14, 1944: 21.

"*Helmet* Racks Up Its First Million." *Hollywood Reporter*, July 11, 1951: 1.

"International Incidents." *New York Times*, October 5, 1941: X5.

"Korean Curbs Lifted by Ruling." *Los Angeles Times*, January 25, 1942: 10.

Lee, K. W. "Truth in His Blood: Philip Ahn Cuddy Reflects on His Patriot-Grandfather Ahn Chang Ho's Overlooked Moral Legacy." *KoreAm* 15, no. 5 (May 2004): 34–42.

Lee, K. W., Dr. Luke, and Grace Kim. "Whispers from the Past." *KoreAm* 14, no. 1 (January 2003): 54–57.

McManus, John T. 1943. "Communiqué on *China Girl*." *PM*, February 8: 20.

McIlwaine, Robert. "Third Beginning." *Modern Screen* (December 1937): 41, 80.

Michener, James A. "The Forgotten Heroes of Korea." *Saturday Evening Post*, May 10, 1952.

Murray, Feg. "Seein' Stars." *Miami Herald*, January 7, 1945.

Okrent, Neil. "Right Place, Wong Time." *Los Angeles Magazine* (May 1990): 84+.

Pak, Jacqueline. "Korea's Moses: An Ch'angho and the Colonial Diaspora." Unpublished speech draft delivered at UCLA, November 9, 2000.

Raddatz, Leslie. "'No.1 Son' Is Now 'Master Po.'" *TV Guide* (June 23, 1973): 27–33.

Riesel, Victor, "Column on *The Steel Helmet*." *Los Angeles Daily News*, January 16–17, 1951.

Robinson, Amy. "It Takes One to Know One: Passing and Communities of Common Interests." *Critical Inquiry* 20, no. 4 (Summer 1994): 715–36.

Shirota, Jon. "Authentic Wisdom in a Shaolin Temple." *Fighting Stars* (December 1973): 22–27.

Smith,Valerie. "Reading the Intersection of Race and Gender in Narratives of Passing." *Diacritics* (Summer–Fall 1994): 100–14.

Stanley, Fred. "*Hollywood Memoranda*." *New York Times*, September 24, 1944: X1.

Stanley, John. "Master Kan of *Kung Fu*—Wisdom in a Shaolin Temple." *San Francisco Examiner and Chronicle*, undated, Philip Ahn clippings file, Ahn Family Collection.

Stewart, Jacqueline. "Negroes Laughing at Themselves? Black Spectatorship and the Performance of Urban Modernity." *Critical Inquiry* 29, no. 4 (Summer 2003), 650–77.

"USO Shows in Association with the Hollywood Overseas Committee Presents Philip Ahn." USO publicity pamphlet. June 21, 1968.

Van Gelder, Lewis S. "A Long Ago War Sudden Comes Alive Again." *Los Angeles Times*, September 10, 1979: D5.

"*War over Hollywood*." *Newsweek*, August 28, 1950: 76.

Weathersby, Kathryn. "New Findings on the Korean War, Translation and Commentary." CWIHP *Bulletin*, no. 3 (Fall 1993): 1, 14–18.

———. "New Russian Documents on the Korean War." CWIHP *Bulletin*, no. 6–7 (Winter 1995–1996): 30–84.

Wilkerson, W. R. "*Trade Views*." *Hollywood Reporter*. December 9, 1942. 1

Worland, Rick. "The Korean War Film as Family Melodrama: *The Bridges at Toko-Ri* (1954)." *Historical Journal of Film, Radio and Television* 19, no. 3 (August 1999): 359–77.

Yoon, Ed. "Soon-Tek Oh: Pioneering Korean American Actor." *Korean Culture* 22, no.1 (Spring 2001): 5–11.

Young, Charles S. "Missing Action: POW Films, Brainwashing and the Korean War, 1954–1968." *Historical Journal of Film, Radio and Television* 18, no.1 (March 1998): 49–74.

"You Surprised I Speak Your...." *The Houston Post*, November 6, 1966.

KOREAN-LANGUAGE SOURCES

Ahn, Jung-hyo (An Chŏng-hyo). *Hŏlliudŭ k'idŭ ŭi saengae* [*The Life and Death of the Hollywood Kid*]. Seoul: Minjok kwa munhaksa, 1992.

"Robi aesŏ [In the Lobby]." *Chŏsŏn Ilbo* [*Chosun Daily*]. March 14, 1959.

Im, Chung-bin. *Tosan An Ch'ang-ho: Kŭ saengae wa chŏngsin* [*Tosan An Ch'ang-ho: His Life and Mind*]. Seoul: Myŏngjisa, 2000.

Kim, Hak-su. *Sŭkrin pakkŭi hankuk yŏnghwasa* [*Offscreen Korean Film History*]. Seoul: Inmul gwa sasang, 2002.

Kim, Kwan-myŏng, "Mi konggun, minganin op'an sagŭk ch'oech'o chŭngŏn [*U.S. Airman Testifies to the Shooting of Civilians*]." *Han'guk Ilbo* [*Hankook Daily*]. June 21, 2000.

"P'il-ip An, Sŏul ŭi hyuil [Philip Ahn's Holiday in Seoul]." *Han'guk Ilbo* [*Hankook Daily*]. March 16, 1959.

"Philip Ahn obituary." *Miju sosik* [*American News*]. March 1, 1978.

Yi, Pyŏl-il. "A Talk between Mr. Philip Ahn and Mr. Lee Byong Il." *Kukje yŏngwha* [*International Film*] (June 1959): 28–31.

Yun, Kyŏng-ro. "Tosan ŭi Kungnae aesŏ ŭi haengjŏk kwa kuguk kaemong hwaldong (1907–1910) [*Tosan's Exploits and Nationalist Enlightenment Movement in Korea*]." In *Tosan An Ch'ang-ho ŭi sasang kwa minjok undong* [*Tosan An Ch'ang-ho's Thoughts and Nationalist Movement*], edited by Tosan sasang yŏnguhŏi [*The Society for Tosan Studies*], 33–91. Seoul: Hangmunsa, 1995.

INDEX

ABOUT THE AUTHOR

Hye Seung Chung is Visiting Assistant Professor in the Department of Comparative Literature at Hamilton College. Her writing has appeared in the anthologies *South Korean Golden Age Melodrama* and *New Korean Cinema*.